D1452697

WITHDRAWN
FROM
COLLECTION

FORDHAM
UNIVERSITY
LIBRARIES

# KESHUB CHUNDER SEN

# KESHUB CHUNDER SEN

## A Search for Cultural Synthesis

Meredith Borthwick

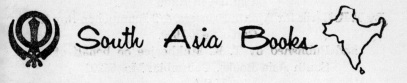

BL
1265
·S4 B6
Cg.2

SOUTH ASIA BOOKS
Columbia, Mo. 65201 : USA
in arrangement with
Minerva Associates (Publications)  Pvt. Ltd.
7-B, Lake Place, Calcutta-700 029 :  India

Fordham University
LIBRARY
AT
LINCOLN CENTER
New York, N. Y.

© Meredith Borthwick, 1978
First Published :  1978
ISBN :  0-88386-904-7

Printed in India
By T. K. Barik for Ajanta Printers, 4/2 Rammohon Roy Rd.
Calcutta-700 009.
and Published by T. K. Mukherjee on behalf of
South Asia Books, Columbia, Mo. 65201
U.S.A.

# CONTENTS

# INTRODUCTION

In writing this book I have attempted to reawaken an interest in an individual whom I consider to be one of the most outstanding but also one of the most neglected figures of the nineteenth century, Keshub Chunder Sen. I feel that there is a need for such a re-appraisal of Keshub, as very little has been written on him since his generation faded from prominence in the 1920s and 1930s. He is always mentioned in any general history of the nineteenth century, but only superficial coverage is given to him, doing very little justice to his complexity. Of the many biographies and works on the Brahmo Samaj that were written within his lifetime and in the forty years following his death, all are heavily biased in particular directions, being written either by authors from one of the two rival Brahmo Samaj congregations, the Adi Brahmo Samaj and the Sadharan Brahmo Samaj, or by one of Keshub's own disciples, by followers of Ramakrishna, or by Christian missionaries. I am, in this study, attempting to correct the imbalance by assessing material from all these different factions, as well as contemporary newspaper reports and Keshub's own works.

I have arrived at a view of Keshub that sees him in the terms of his own lecture on 'Great Men'[1]—a representative man, but one in whom the common qualities he shared with others of his generation were writ large, and so also a great man. He was undoubtedly a brilliant man and a colourful personality, but his significance went beyond this. I have argued that he is representative in that his life and career exhibited most clearly the confusion and rootlessness inherent in the background of almost every English-educated Bengali growing up under British rule. His background was Hindu, but his intellectual growth was most influenced

---

1. Keshub Chunder Sen, *Lectures in India*, fourth ed. (Calcutta, 1954), pp. 37-73.

by Christianity. After an initial reaction against Hin
duism, Keshub came to realize the validity of both the
Hindu and Christian, the Indian and English, parts o
his heritage, and spent his life trying to synthesize and
integrate the two. I found that in the end, although
his own outlook was truly universal, his attempts to
filter this through to the rest of society were a failure
I think that one of the major reasons for this failure was
his commitment to British rule in India. His religious
universality was not a neutral concept, as it was bound
up with his view of British rule as a 'Providential' agent
in promoting religious harmony and progress. His views
were also essentially alien in that despite his theoretical
appreciation of Hinduism, his way of thinking had been
influenced to a much greater degree by Christianity.
The final product of his universalist views, the doctrine
of the New Dispensation, failed because it was only a
collection of diverse symbols, superficially absorbed into one comprehensive doctrine, but on a deeper level
proving too complex to mesh so easily and thus resisting
or even severing the surface bonds that had been established. Throughout Keshub's career the forces of traditional Hinduism and nineteenth century Protestant
Christianity were continually pulling against each other,
with Keshub trying to resolve the confusion by incor-
porating all the disparate tendencies into a view of world
harmony. In fact, Keshub did not consciously recognize
any confusion, but the tensions are quite obvious to the
later observer.

I have not attempted a critical examination of the
validity or otherwise of his religious views, but have
shown how they fitted in with his views on society, and
how taken together they reflect his persistent attempts
to integrate East and West. I have also tried throughout
to relate his ideas and activities to what was going on
in the rest of society at that time. I have followed a
chronological framework because many of Keshub's
ideas changed and developed in response to outside influences, the changes taking place in society. In turn
he also gave impetus to such changes. In brief, I have

attempted to display the forces that were crucial in producing a man like Keshub, and the effect that he had on society. I feel that it is necessary therefore to have an idea of the sequence of his ideas and activities to be able to see a pattern or an overall scheme in his development. He was a man of great imagination and energy, and this can only be shown by a coverage of as much as possible of his multifarious career.

For the sake of consistency in spelling, because most of the material I have used was written in the nineteenth century, I have used the main variant of names and terms as they were spelled then, for example, Keshub Chunder Sen.

This book is based on the thesis I submitted for my Master of Arts degree at the University of Melbourne. I am indebted to my supervisor, Mr Sibnarayan Ray, head of the Indian Studies Department, University of Melbourne, for stimulating and sustaining my interest in the social history of nineteenth century Bengal. To my colleagues in the Indian Studies Department, I am grateful for the intellectual debate and critical suggestions provided during the time I was working on this book. I would also like to thank Professor A. L. Basham, Dr J. T. F. Jordens, Pauline Rule, C. J. Borthwick, Dipesh Chakrabarty and J. F. Hannoush, who were especially helpful with advice and criticism during the varying stages of writing. Finally, I would like to thank the many people in Calcutta who gave so generously of their time in assisting my research on my visits there.

# CHAPTER ONE

# FAMILY BACKGROUND AND ADOLESCENT STRUGGLES (1838-1857)

KESHUB CHUNDER SEN was born on 19 November 1838, at the family home in Colutolah, Calcutta. He came of a distinguished line, whose ancestral home was at the village of Garifa, 24 miles from Calcutta. In an unsuccessful bid to raise the caste status of the family, Keshub's renowned grandfather, Ram Komul Sen, said that they were Kshatriyas, descendants of the King Ballal Sen.[1] However, in later accounts[2] Keshub's great-grandfather, Gokul Chandra Sen, is said to be of the Vaidya caste, and that is the caste attributed to Keshub[3]. Gokul Chandra Sen was a *sheristadar* (chief clerk) at the Hugli court. He was a devout Vaishnava, and in his piety he established a pattern that was followed by his children and grandchildren, and in a less orthodox manner, by his great-grandson Keshub.

Ram Komul Sen was born on 15 March 1783. As his father had a respectable social position, he learnt Persian, Sanskrit and some English. He left the village to take up permanent residence in Calcutta in 1800[4]. Like most of the Calcutta intellectual elite at the turn of the nineteenth century, he saw that his greatest chances of success lay in co-operation with the British. He was not motivated only by a desire for material success, but had a genuine interest in working with the British Orientalists to attain their desired end of revitalizing India from within. He fully approved of their policy of 'acculturation'[5].

In December 1802 he was employed as a subordinate clerk's assistant in the office of the Calcutta Chief Magistrate[6]. He got married in December 1803, and soon after this took office under the Government Architect. The Chief Magistrate was a member of the Persian group of the Asiatic Society, and probably helped him gain acquaintance with other members of the Society. In 1804 W. W. Hunter and J. Gilchrist, directors of the Hindoostanee Press, invited him to become its compositor at a salary of eight rupees per month. In 1806 he became assistant typesetter at the Asiatic Society. In 1810 he became friendly with the famous Orientalist H. H. Wilson, who was a partner in the Press, and this connection was to be maintained throughout their lives. Wilson had a high opinion of Ram Komul's competence, and by 1814 had made him native manager of the Press.[7] He raised himself to a position commanding influence and respect from both the European and Indian communities. From being an employee of the Asiatic Society, by 1818 he was asked to be its co-ordinator as it was to be the historical and archaeological headquarters for all India. After 1821 this position entailed a salary of 70 rupees. He later became Native Secretary of the Asiatic Society, and was a member of its Council. His rise to prominence is a reflection not only of his own merits, but also of the high esteem which the British Orientalists had for their Bengali colleagues, and their readiness to recognize such merits and reward them with positions of responsibility.

The list of Ram Komul's achievements is a long one. In 1816 H. H. Wilson was assay-master of the Calcutta Mint. In 1828, three years before he left India, he appointed Ram Komul Sen as head, or *Dewan,* of the native establishment of the Mint. In November 1832 he became Treasurer of the Bank of Bengal on the princely salary of 200 rupees per month. It is not surprising then, although he does not seem to have been engaged in commerce, that on his death he left an estate of eight *lakhs* of rupees. He encouraged thrift, and was a member of the Government Savings Bank Committee in 1833. From the lead given by Ram Komul Sen, banking was to become the accepted mode of employment for most members of the Sen family.

Besides making his fortune, Ram Komul Sen was an active member of the new Calcutta elite. He supported, and was involved in, all new developments that took place owing to the immense but unaggressive stimulus from the Orientalists. He was active in the establishment of the Hindu College and the Sanskrit College, and was on the committee of the Parental Academic Institution, a school for European and Eurasian children—which also shows that the British at that time were ready to accept a Bengali in a position of authority on equal terms. He was on the Medical Education Committee, and wrote on the sanitation of Calcutta[8]. He was joint founder (with another close friend of his, the missionary William Carey) of the Agricultural and Horticultural Society. He became its native secretary in 1829, and with Radhakanta Deb he was joint Vice-President in 1844.

Ram Komul Sen's greatest tangible contribution to scholarship and intellectual growth was his two volume *Dictionary of the English and Bengalee Language*, published in 1830 and 1834, which took as its model Dr Johnson's dictionary of the English language. In the introduction to this he drew attention to Carey's part in the revitalization of Bengali, thus establishing Carey's prime place in the nineteenth century literary revival.[9] In turn Dr Marshman, in *Friend of India*, praised Ram Komul Sen's achievement:

> This dictionary is the fullest, most valuable work of its kind which we possess, and will be the most lasting monument of Ram Komul Sen's industry, zeal and erudition. It is perhaps the work by which his name will be recognized by posterity.[10]

With Carey, Ram Komul also edited the Agricultural and Horticultural Society's *Transactions*, to which he contributed an article on 'The Manufacture of Paper in India', showing how diverse his range of interests was. His importance in the community as a whole is indicated by the fact that he was the only Indian other than Rammohun Roy to be mentioned in the 1845 edition of Maunder's *Biographical Treasury; A Dictionary of Universal Biography,[11]* published in England.

It is unfortunate that he is now primarily famous as

a staunch 'conservative' and opponent of progress[12], although it is easy to see how this stereotyped view arose. He was a charter member of the Dharma Sabha[13], whose members opposed the abolition of *sati*. It was also Ram Komul who called for the dismissal of Derozio for injuring the morals of his students, and introducing "some strange system, the tendency of which is destructive to their moral character and the peace of society"[14]. These examples are not presented to illustrate his resolute opposition to progress, or modernisation, but to show that his conception of modernity was set within the stable framework of Hindu society. He wanted gradual assimilation of new ideas, adjusting them to fit in with previous thought patterns rather than overthrowing old ideas for new. He took a pragmatic view of the utility of Western knowledge, and its benefits for society. However, as he was not dissatisfied with the state of Hindu society, he took a traditional stand on matters to do with the family, caste and religion. He was, in his time, a progressive and intelligent man, a colleague of some of the greatest Orientalists, like Carey and Wilson. It is only in retrospect, and in comparison with the exceptional liberalism of Rammohun Roy, that he is harshly judged. Despite being more resistant to social change than Rammohun, Ram Komul was in practice and in his interests similarly alert and wide-ranging.

Ram Komul Sen died in 1844, having raised his family to prominence. His grandson Keshub was then only six years old, but had already impressed the old man with his originality and intelligence. Ram Komul is reputed to have said of him, "Keshub will be able to sustain the family reputation".[15] His prophecy was borne out to an extent, in that although the other family members were worthy men, none achieved fame in their chosen careers, following securely but unexceptionally in the avenue of employment created for them by Ram Komul Sen.[16] Ram Komul had four sons. The eldest, Bansidhar, was keeper of the Calcutta Mint. Hari Mohan became *Dewan* of the Bank of Bengal from the time of his father's death until 1847. Piari Mohan, Keshub's father, held the post of Bullion-keeper of the Calcutta Mint. Only one son chose a different vocation —Murali Dhar became a distinguished attorney. One of Ram Komul's nephews was connected with the Calcutta Branch of the Bank of Hindustan, another was *Khazanchi* of the Agra Bank, and yet another was *Khazanchi* of the Bank of Bengal.

Little seems to have been written about Keshub's father, Piari Mohan Sen. From available accounts[17] it is known that he was born in 1814, and was a student at the Hindu College at the time of Peary Chand Mitra and presumably the rest of Young Bengal, although he does not seem to have been affected by their enthusiasm for the West and is not mentioned as having taken part in any of the events generated by that dynamic, radical group of youths. He was in fact a pious Vaishnava, and a skilled sitar player, famous mainly for his charitable and kind disposition. He died in 1848, but the only influence he appears to have had on his young son was to foster the growth of a religious disposition in him and to introduce him to the spirit of Vaishnava devotions. Keshub was closer to his mother, Sarada Devi, who was a devout Sakta.[18] It is possible that her being a Sakta who married into a Vaishnava family set an example of religious harmony and tolerance that provided the basis for Keshub's later synthetic interpretation of religion, and for her later acceptance of the ideas and practices of her son. Keshub's early life and education was actually organized and presided over by the head of the joint household, his uncle Hari Mohan Sen, a conservative Hindu.

Piari Mohan left three sons. The eldest, Nabin Chandra, followed the usual family career in the Bank of Bengal, as Native Head Assistant of the Depositor's Department. Keshub was the second son. The youngest was Krishna Behari Sen, the first sub-editor of the daily *Indian Mirror*, associate editor of this for many years with his cousin Norendranath Sen, and then editor of the *Sunday Mirror* and rector of Albert College.

Piari Mohan also left four daughters[19], about whom no information is available.

Keshub was thus one of a very privileged group in society, being born into a prominent and wealthy family of the Vaidya caste, one of the leading castes in Bengal. The only account of his early years comes from Protap Chunder Mozoomdar[20], a distant relative of his, who came from the same village. For the first eight years of Keshub's life they saw each other only occasionally, when Keshub went back to Garifa for ceremonies and festivals. However, Protap came to Calcutta when he was nine to be educated, and lived close to Keshub in Colutolah. Their firm friendship dates from that time. With only one account of Keshub's childhood it is difficult to check its veracity, but although this biography was written by a loyal sympathizer, it did not really attempt to hide any faults and inconsistencies in Keshub's character. Protap recalled that Keshub was a very quick, intelligent boy, and one very conscious of his own gifts. He did not have particularly close friends like everyone else did, although he "descanted generally on the advantages of friendship".[21] He seldom joined in games started by anyone else—if he did consent to play with his fellows he would start an unknown game and take the lead role for himself. The picture created is that of an isolated yet dominating youth, who asserted his authority by remaining aloof and separate from his playmates. He was not very religious, but he enjoyed going through the traditional forms of religious observance.[22]

He was also very moralistic. According to Protap, "He was a noble, pure-minded boy, free from falsehood, free from vice". However, the total effect of his superior virtues contributed to the impression that "he did not seem to be a warm hearted boy".[23] Many of his young friends perceived this and accused him of being conceited. Protap gave the excuse that Keshub's behaviour was inhibited by a terrible shyness, but this could not always have been so, as at the same time he often insisted on being the centre of attention. Protap maintained that Keshub never really outgrew any of these early behavioural traits.

His interests at this stage, until the age of 12, were primarily concerned with his own advancement in the scholastic field. His first studies were with an aged *Guru Mahashay,* where he learnt Bengali.[24] In 1845 he was admitted to the Hindu College, the most prestigious scholastic institution of the time, and also his father's old school. His academic career was at first very promising, and Keshub was a regular recipient of annual school prizes. This early scholastic promise was never fulfilled. Protap attributed this to his uncle's decision to move him, in 1853, to the new Hindu Metropolitan College, which had been set up by prominent members of society (including Radhakanta Deb and Debendranath Tagore) as a protest against the admission of a prostitute's son to study at the Hindu College.[25] The new school tried to ensure its success by flattering the boys, moving them into higher classes than those from which they came, with the result that they found the higher standard of work much too difficult. The Hindu Metropolitan College did not fulfil its early promise, and collapsed not long after it was started. Keshub and many others returned to the obviously superior Hindu College, but his confidence had been undermined, and he never regained his scholastic eminence. His main interest then was in philosophy, and he spent a lot of time studying this. Although he did not leave the Hindu College till 1858, the activities he was involved in for the last two or three years of his studies were much more wide-ranging and public-spirited than those of most schoolboys.

Keshub himself left an account of his feelings as a young man in his spiritual autobiography, the *Jeevan Veda.*[26] In this he said that "the first beginning of asceticism was as early as the fourteenth year", when the voice of his conscience directed him to give up eating fish. This was not a very outstanding step, as complete vegetarianism was not unusual among Vaishnavas, but making such a decision shows a certain measure of

independent thought for one of that age. Protap qualified the magnitude of the gesture further by explaining that Keshub had initially given up fish because it
was not allowed him when he had chicken pox, and
after that he did not eat fish again.[27]  Around this time
his religious spirit began to develop more fully. Keshub
did not mention exactly when he became dissatisfied
with Hinduism, but said that under the influence of a
liberal English education his belief in idolatry died a
natural death.[28]  When he said in his *Jeevan Veda*
that the first word of the scripture of his life was
prayer[29], he was not referring to the formal prayers
which would have accompanied the traditional Hindu
rituals.  He said that the impulse to pray came to him
before he was a member of any religious community
and before he had come into the company of any pious
men—but he heard a voice in his heart saying, "Pray,
thou shalt be saved; thy character shall improve...."[30]
This is most unusual in that it describes a type of religion alien to the Hindu tradition.  Prayer which is
morally elevating and not merely an expression of devotion, which is helpful to the supplicant, who prays
for specific things, and which drives away sin—seems
to be much more akin to a Christian concept.  This
being so different from a traditional Hindu or Vaishnava concept, it is possible that Keshub, in retrospect,
tended to remember his spiritual awakening as a more
spontaneous process than it actually was, and it may in
fact have followed after his association with Christian
missionaries.  Another possible explanation is that
Keshub's experience may not have been very much
outside the familiar tradition, but his phraseology in
recapturing the experience was obviously very much
influenced by Christian concepts and terms.  He did
not show much interest in Hinduism.  He never learnt
Sanskrit,  and his knowledge of the Hindu scriptures
was very much inferior to his extremely thorough
knowledge of, and ability to quote from, the Bible. He
said that English education had unsettled his mind and
left a void.[31]  To resolve his doubts, and to satisfy his

burgeoning religious feelings, he turned away from his own religion to that religion which was so much a part of the novelty of English education, Christianity. He studied philosophy and theology, and discussed these new subjects with his missionary friends.

These missionaries were of the more liberal of their kind, as there was not much mutual sympathy or understanding between Indians and Europeans in the 1850s. Most missionaries tended to be patronizing and condescending. Three exceptions, all interesting and dynamic men, were the Reverend T.H. Burns, Reverend James Long, and Reverend C.H.A. Dall. They were not merely proselytizers, but shared a keen interest in the people and country to which they had come. Burns was domestic chaplain to Bishop Cotton, Bishop of Calcutta, and used to give Keshub Bible lessons from the New Testament. Long was a missionary of the Church of Christ. He made a thorough study of the Bengali language and its proverbs, but it probably more famous for being sent to jail for a month because of his courageous publication of *Neel Darpan,* a play depicting the injustices inflicted on the workers on indigo plantations by their British masters. He was in India from 1840 till 1872. Dall was sent out by the American Unitarian Association in 1854, and stayed in India for the rest of his life. As the Unitarian Association was the orthodox and more conservative branch of the American Unitarian movement[32], Dall was probably not considered to be a radical, but he was interested in temperance and social reform, and was in touch with the writings of Unitarian radicals like Theodore Parker[33], who provided Keshub with much of his inspiration. Although their ultimate aim may have been conversion, these men did not have the dogmatically overwhelming zeal of others such as the famous Dr Alexander Duff, who was incapable of appreciating any merit at all in India.[34]

Men like Dall, Long and Burns were a great solace to Keshub at this time because most of his friends ridiculed him for his biblical studies and accused him of

being a Christian, a formidable charge in those days
His association with missionaries would also have bee:
frowned upon, as the atmosphere was then very resis
tant to missionaries because of their conversion activi
ties, especially among young people. Reading th
memoirs of early Christian converts like Lal Behar
Dey[35] or Jogesh Chunder Gangooly[36] it is evident tha
becoming a Christian was a step which meant a tota
severance of all family and kinship ties—in fact, be
coming an outcast. This was not usually because of anti
pathy on the part of the convert, but because Hinduism
could not tolerate such an open break with the tradi
tional way of life. Keshub, however, may have given
some grounds for ridicule for reasons apart from his
interest in Christianity, as some of his activities do
seem to have been rather eccentric. His religious feel
ings went beyond an examination of his own convictions, and he felt compelled to gain the attention of
outsiders to the truths he was discovering. He composed and circulated slips with exhortations like, "Attend
ye passers by to your future concerns. There is no
peace in this transitory world. Think of death and be
wise".[37] In his fervour he also stuck these up on walls
round the neighbourhood to be seen by all.

Keshub's adolescence was marked by an extended
period of traumatic experiences. The first of these was
when he was accused of cheating in one of his Senior
Scholarship examinations in 1856, and was publicly dis-
graced. Protap admitted that the irregularity of com-
paring papers could have originated either with Keshub
or the other party, leaving open the possibility that
Keshub could have been to blame.[38] If this was the
case, to be exposed would have been extremely humilia-
ting in view of the high standards of honesty he had
always preached. On the other hand, if he was not to
blame, the affair was still as disturbing, because it
cast doubts on his integrity in the public mind, which
he had no real way of refuting. Keshub's cousin,
Norendranath Sen, gave another version, described to
him by Keshub himself, which was intended to clear

him of all blame:—

> What actually happened was this: when Keshub
> was sitting for the examination, one of the boys
> near him spoke to him. Keshub, who was natu-
> rally polite and affable, replied to his fellow student,
> with the result that both of them were sent out of
> the examination hall........[39].

Whether or not Keshub cheated at that point is not of
central importance. Even to have been suspected of
such dishonesty meant public disgrace, and produced a
state of intense depression in him.

1856 was also the year of Keshub's marriage. His
bride was a nine or ten year old village girl, Jagan-
mohini Devi. Keshub deeply resented the marriage,
which naturally had been arranged for him, and avoided his wife for many years. His marriage coincided
with a state of deep depression, a major crisis period in
his life which he recalled vividly in the *Jeevan Veda*.
His depression seems to have been compounded of
many elements. It was difficult for him, when all-
absorbed in devotion to God and the examination of
his own soul, to face an intimate sexual relationship.
He associated religiosity with asceticism, probably because of examples within the Indian tradition rather
than Christianity, and therefore felt that wife and
family were a distraction from the true pursuit of
spirituality and the intensity of religious experience.
He was at this time of a puritanical nature—Protap also
noted that he gave up playing cards, and threw away
his violin.[40] There is also the possibility that he had
imbibed an abhorrence of the Hindu custom of child
marriage from his missionary friends, and from the social reformist sector of the Bengali intelligentsia represented by Vidyasagar and Akshay Kumar Dutt.

> As I dreaded lust and anger, so did I consider wife,
> children and the world to be dangerous. Lest I
> loved these more than God, lest I regarded the
> world to be dearer,—this fear made the world look
> like a terrible demon..........[41]

His fears indicate an awareness of the strong passions
within himself. The conviction that these had to be
restrained caused great tension.

Although Keshub did not mention that he had any struggle to give up his ancestral faith, it must still have been a disturbing experience.    It alienated him from his family. He became taciturn and melancholy. He said that his chief companion in this hard time was Edward Young's *Night Thoughts,* one of the English literature texts on the school syllabus.    The poem itself can be construed as a clue to his feelings.  It was written in 1742-44, and the narrative begins with fear at the thought of death, followed by 'The Christian Triumph'—"Here is firm footing, here is solid rock!".[42] This is not yet the end however—there is a relapse, and then 'The Infidel Reclaimed'.    Keshub's melancholia obviously led him to the same goal as Young's protagonist.  Keshub, too, put his faith in God, though it took him three years, between the ages of 18 and 20, to feel at peace with the world.[43]    It was the experience of prayer that was his salvation : —

> Day after day I kept on praying, and in the course, I assure you, of a few days I found as it were a flood of light entering into the inmost recesses of my heart and dissipating the darkness of my soul, the darkness of death........[44].

Keshub was a natural leader and organizer of men, and throughout his adolescence he organized his friends and relatives into various clubs and societies of which he was the head.  In 1857 he formed the British India Society, which drew its membership mainly from the students of the Presidency College, although the missionaries Long and Dall were also members.  The purpose of the society was to discuss "the culture of literature and science".[45]  It is worth noting that it was not religious, but more in the secular cultural path of other societies of the time, like the Bethune Society or the Family Literary Club.  There is no record of how long this went on for,  but as it is not mentioned later it seems to have been supplanted in his interest by other societies that he had founded.  In 1856 he had started the Colutolah Evening School, with Protap and his cousin Norendranath, for poor and working-class boys. This institution lasted for three or four years.    The most important society of all, with regard to his later religious development, was the Goodwill Fraternity, founded in 1857. The membership was composed largely of the staff of the Evening School, but there is no numerical record of how large Keshub's following was at that stage. This was a purely religious and devotional organization. Keshub was, as usual the leader—and he addressed each gathering with readings from theologians like Theodore Parker, and with extempore sermons in English. Protap recalled the first devotional meeting, where five or six young men and Keshub met behind closed doors in a dimly lit room, "and each poured out his innermost thoughts in sincere prayer...... Keshub spoke and we all wept........".[46] Keshub got so excited that he poured forth torrents of words and was hoarse and exhausted by the end. This Fraternity lasted for two years only, until it was absorbed into the larger community of the Brahmo Samaj.

Keshub's societies were run in English, even though at that time there was a growing consciousness of the need to cultivate the use of Bengali, as is evidenced by the growth of societies for that purpose, like the Jnanachandrodaya, the Bangabhasa Prakasika Sabha, and the Bangabhasasanuvadak Samaj.[47] English came much more naturally to Keshub than Bengali, especially in the religious sphere, as his inspiration there was from the Bible and other more contemporary Western theological writings and discussions with the missionaries. As his following and audience at that stage was comprised of other English-educated middle-class people like himself, there was certainly no necessity to use Bengali in order to communicate.

Debendranath Tagore attended one of these Fraternity meetings, impressing everyone with his princely appearance. This is said to have been where Keshub first met Debendranath[48], but as Debendranath's second son, Satyendranath, was a fellow student of Keshub's at the Hindu College it is probable that they were acquainted before then.

At this stage Keshub's religious thoughts seem to

have been fairly confused and largely derivative of the current English and American theological writings he had read. He had not formulated a distinct set of beliefs to follow, but was emotionally excited at the discovery of a personal meaning in his religious observances, and of a sense of purpose in his life and a way out of his previous deep depression.

### NOTES AND REFERENCES

1. D. Kopf, *British Orientalism and the Bengal Renaissance* (Berkeley, 1969), p. 117.

2. P. K. Sen, *Biography of a New Faith* (2 vols., Calcutta, 1950), Vol. I, p. 223, and P. C. Mozoomdar, *The Life and Teachings of Keshub Chunder Sen*, third ed. (Calcutta, 1931), pp. 42-43, claim that Ballal Sen was a Vaidya king. See also F. B. Bradley-Birt, *Twelve Men of Bengal in the Nineteenth Century* (Calcutta, 1910), p. 143.

3. P. K. Sen, *Biography*, op. cit. Vol. I, p. 223 ; G. S. Leonard, *A History of the Brahma Samaj* (Calcutta, 1879), p. 107, and L. Ghose, *The Modern History of the Indian Chiefs* (2 vols., Calcutta, 1881), Vol. II, p. 127.

4. L. Ghose, ibid. p. 129, gives 1800 but D. Kopf, op. cit. p. 117 gives 1790.

5. D. Kopf, op. cit. uses this term to mean the cultural exchange resulting from the contact of two autonomous civilizations.

5. D. Kopf, op. cit. uses this term to mean the cultural exchange *Ramkamal Sen,* second ed. (Calcutta, 1955) unless otherwise cited.

7. Although for an interval from 1808-1811 he seems to have been in charge of the native hospital at Chadney, and in 1812 he was employed by Fort William college. L. Ghose, op. cit. pp. 129-130.

8. C. E. Buckland, *Dictionary of Indian Biography*, new ed. (New York, 1968), p. 383.

9. The tribute to Carey in the Preface of Ram Komul's *Dictionary* is quoted in S. K. De, *Bengali Literature in the Nineteenth Century*, second ed. (Calcutta, 1962), p. 143.

10. Quoted in D. Kopf. op. cit. p. 289.

11. S. Maunder, *The Biographical Treasury ; A Dictionary of Universal Biography*, 13th ed. (London, 1866) no longer included him. It explained that names were left out if they were 'judged unlikely to be asked for, except perhaps by half-a-dozen persons in half-a-dozen years.'

12. See N. S. Bose, *The Indian Awakening and Bengal* (Calcutta, 1969), p. 34.

13. D. Kopf, op. cit. p. 289.

14. Quoted in T. Edwards, *Henry Derozio, the Eurasian Poet, Teacher and Journalist* (Calcutta, 1884), p. 74.

15. F. B. Bradley-Birt, op. cit. p. 145 and P. C. Mozoomdar, *Life,* op. cit. p. 49.

. Details of the Sen family history are taken from L. Ghose, op. cit.

. L. Ghose, op. cit. p. 148 and P. C. Mozoomdar, *Life,* op. cit. p. 49.

. P. K. Sen, *Biography,* op. cit. Vol. I, p. 225.

. J. C. Bagal, *Keshabchandra Sen* (Calcutta, 1958), p. 8.

. P. C. Mozoomdar, *Life,* op. cit.

. Ibid. p. 56.

. Although his cousin, Norendranath Sen, said that he was of a religious and meditative disposition from childhood. N. Sen, *A Needed Disclaimer,* new ed. (Calcutta, 1909), p. 4.

. P. C. Mozoomdar, *Life,* op. cit. p. 58.

. G. S. Leonard, op. cit. p. 108.

. Keshub's uncle had taken part in a similar scheme in 1845, when he was joint Secretary, with Debendranath Tagore, of the *Hindu Hitarthi Vidayalaya,* a school founded as a protest against the conversion to Christianity of a young Hindu and his wife. S. Sastri, *History of the Brahmo Samaj,* second ed. (2 vols., Calcutta, 1919), Vol. I, pp. 97-98.

. The Jeevan Veda was a series of sermons preached by Keshub to the Calcutta congregation between July and December 1882. A good translation is printed in P. S. Basu, *Life and Works of Brahmananda Keshav* (Calcutta, 1940), pp. 442-483. This is a reliable and accurate translation of the original Bengali *Jibanbed,* 8th ed. (Calcutta, 1954) and is certainly better than the translation by V. Rai, *The Bible of Life* (Calcutta, 1928).

. P. C. Mozoomdar, *Life* op. cit. p. 62.

. Keshub Chunder Sen, *Keshub Chunder Sen in England,* third ed. (Calcutta, 1938) p. 135, from an address on 'The Book of Life'.

. P. S. Basu, op. cit. p. 442.

. ibid. p. 443.

. Keshub Chunder Sen, *In England* op. cit. p. 136.

. E. M. Wilbur, *A History of Unitarianism* (Boston, 1969), p. 464.

. Theodore Parker was a controversial figure who believed that the teachings of Christ were more important than his historical personality. He was also a social reformer, active in the anti-slavery movement.

. See A. Duff, *A Description of the Durga and Kali Festivals* (New York, 1846).

. Lal Behari Dey, *Recollections of Alexander Duff* (London, 1879).

. J. C. Gangooly, *Life and Religion of the Hindoos, with a sketch of my life and experience* (London, 1860).

. G. S. Leonard, op. cit. p. 114.

. S. Sastri, *History* op. cit., Vol. I, p. 115. The quotation given therein must be from the first edition of P. C. Mozoomdar's *Life,* op. cit. as this incident is not mentioned at all in the third edition.

. Norendranath Sen, op. cit., p. 4. This originally appeared as an article in *Unity and the Minister,* and was then reprinted and distributed as a pamphlet by the Brahmo Tract Society.

40. P. C. Mozoomdar, *Life,* op. cit. p. 62.

41. *Jeevan Veda,* in P. S. Basu, op. cit. p. 448.

42. E. Young, *The Poetical Works of Edward Young* (London, 1866) Vol. I, p. 69.

43. From the vantage point of middle-age, Keshub may have exaggerated the extent of his asceticism, as in 1856 he also started a dramatic society in which he played Hamlet.

44. Keshub Chunder Sen, *Lectures in India* (London, 1904) p. 267 The contents of this differ from the later Indian edition.

45. P. C. Mozoomdar, *Life,* op. cit. p. 65.

46. P. C. Mozoomdar, *Life,* op. cit. p. 67.

47. N. S. Bose, op. cit. pp. 220-221.

48. F. B. Bradley-Birt, op. cit., p. 149.

# CHAPTER TWO

# KESHUB CHUNDER SEN'S RISE TO PROMINENCE IN THE BRAHMO SAMAJ
## (1857-1861)

IN 1857, Keshub Chunder Sen joined the Brahmo Samaj by privately signing the membership covenant. He left an account of the process by which he came to this decision in one of his lectures in England, 'The Book of Life'.[1] He first referred to his period of spiritual doubt, and its resultant God-realization. He came to feel that not only belief in God, but also in brotherhood on earth, was necessary. He had tried to achieve this through his own Goodwill Fraternity, but as this involved only a small group it tended to encourage narrowness rather than brotherhood, and it had no influence at all on the surrounding society. He felt that what he needed was a church, but none of the existing sects and churches answered his purpose. He came across a small publication of the Calcutta Brahmo Samaj, Rajnarain Bose's lecture on 'What is Brahmoism'[2], which corresponded exactly with the inner voice of his heart, and he determined that he would join the Brahmo Samaj.

To understand this crucial decision in Keshub's life more fully it is necessary to consider the state of the Brahmo Samaj in that decade. The Brahmo Samaj, created by Rammohun Roy, continued to function only at the most minimal level after his death in 1833, with a mere handful of members. It was not revived until Debendranath Tagore, who was already loosely connected with the Brahmo Samaj as his father Dwarkanath provided the financial backing for it after Rammohun's death[3], took a renewed interest in it after having been convinced of the truth of monotheism by a series of religious experiences. The most important of these was his accidental finding of a stray page from a Sanskrit text, which when he had it translated turned out to be from the monotheistic *Isha Upanishad*.[4] In 1839

2

Debendranath also started the Tattwabodhini Sabha as
a sister organization, fulfilling a secular intellectual
purpose in conjunction with the purely religious basis
of the Brahmo Samaj. This separation enabled him to
involve a much wider section of the Calcutta intellectual elite than a purely religious organization would
have done. The *Tattwabodhini Patrika* was started in
1843 as a mouthpiece for the views and ideas of both
organizations. The Tattwabodhini Sabha started off
with ten members, but membership had reached 500 by
1841.[5]

Debendranath decided that, in order to survive and
to be worthy of survival, the Brahmo Samaj must
make some definite demands on its followers, who
must in turn be committed to keeping the organization
going. Debendranath instituted the Brahmic Covenant
for this purpose in 1843. The intending member was
henceforth required to vow to worship the Supreme
Being, through loving him and doing works he loves,
never to worship any created object, to strive for good
and to avoid evil, and "to contribute something every
year for the furtherance of the Brahmo Samaj".[6]
Debendranath himself was initiated along with 20 others
in 1843.[7] There were 500 initiated members by 1845[8],
and 767 by 1847.[9]

The Brahmo Samaj was an active and renewed presence in Calcutta society owing mainly to the efforts
of the three major leaders, a group presenting a series
of conflicts and contrasts which in themselves typified
much of the complexity and confusion of the English-
educated elite of the time.

At the centre of the organization was Debendranath Tagore. It is he who was responsible for establishing the Brahmo Samaj as a distinct alternative to
current Hinduism. He reformed all the major Hindu
life-cycle rituals to exclude the idolatrous portions, so
that members could still participate in the rituals without compromising their monotheistic faith, thus not
being entirely alienated from their background.
Debendranath was not a man of great dynamism, but

had an impressive, awe-inspiring spirituality arising from a deeply mystical sense of union with God.    He was more concerned with meditation than with prose-lytizing, but he had a strong sense of his Hindu cul-tural heritage, which was aroused in defence of Hin-duism against the attacks of the missionaries. He did not attempt to defend popular beliefs, but resented the missionaries for misrepresenting the true nature of Hinduism, which to him was monotheistic.

Akshay Kumar Dutt, a pure rationalist, was the leader of another body of opinion in the Samaj. He was the editor of the *Tattwabodhini Patrika*. Debendra-nath chose him for this because of his charming and graceful literary style[10], but his intellectual contribu-tion was just as important.    He held views far in advance of his time.    Through his writings he advo-cated a free and compulsory education in Bengal up to the age of 15,    courtship before marriage, and even divorce in cases of cruelty or adultery. He held libe-ral views on punishment and the education system, and favoured the introduction of the vernacular as the medium for both government and education.    He did not believe in God, except as constituting nature, the ruling principle of the universe.[11]    Holding these views it is clear that he was not attracted to the Brahmo Samaj by Debendranath's religious spirit but by Ram-mohun Roy's rationalism and social reform. He used the Samaj as yet another channel for trying to influence a group of essentially enlightened members of society. He tried to enrich the critical, non-conformist and purely intellectual tradition of the Brahmo Samaj.

Rajnarain Bose was Debendranath's closest asso-ciate.    Rajnarain had been educated at the Hindu College, and had passed through a series of phases in his religious development.[12]    He started out a Vedan-tist, which was unusual for the time, but as his father had been a follower of Rammohun Roy his upbringing was much less traditional than that of many of his con-temporaries. He then made himself well acquainted with Islam, though this started as a joke to shock a friend of his who was becoming a Christian. This had a serious effect in that he found himself taking a real interest in the writings of Islam. He also went through a stage of being a sceptic, in the tradition of early Young Bengal, believing in nothing beyond the hedonistic pleasures of forbidden food and alcohol. He was finally warned off these not by his father's liberal arrangement of giving him a set portion of Muslim food and sherry provided he did not drink or eat these at all elsewhere, but from the fright he got when he fell seriously ill as a consequence of excessive drinking. He was finally attracted to Brahmoism, and took the vows in 1845 because of disillusionment and dissatisfaction with all other religions, and because of the emptiness of pure scepticism. His religious feelings were devotional, and he said himself that he was the first to introduce the sentiment of the love of God into his sermons in the Brahmo Samaj.[13] As Rajnarain was much younger than both Debendranath and Akshay Kumar, and as he tended to regard himself then as a follower of Debendranath, he was not as important a leader at this stage.

These three disparate people, because of their differences, gave a greater flexibility to the outlook of the Samaj than would otherwise have been possible. This became clear over the debate on Vedic infallibility. Debendranath had accepted the infallibility of the Vedas but Akshay Kumar had doubts as to their logical coherence. As neither of them could read the original Sanskrit, Debendranath decided to send four young *pandits* to Benares in 1845 to find out what the Vedas really contained. They were recalled in 1847 because of Debendranath's financial crisis after the death of his father, but they had been there long enough to report on their findings. This resulted in continued debate between Debendranath and Akshay Kumar, the latter finally convincing Debendranath that there were errors and contradictions in the Vedas which made it impossible to regard them as infallible. Debendranath agreed, and in 1850 Akshay Kumar announced publicly

at the annual gathering of the Brahmo Samaj that the
Vedas were no longer to be regarded as infallible, and
that universal nature, or man's intuition, was henceforth to be the basis of faith and belief.    Rajnarain
was not a major party in arriving at this decision, except that he supported Debendranath and resented the
tendency of Akshay Kumar's supporters to give all credit to him alone.[14]    This episode also underlined the
rivalry and uneasy co-operation between the two broad
groups of religious, spiritual thinkers and intellectual
reformers.    Although this incident did not cause an
internal split in the Samaj, it did signify a major crisis
for the Samaj in Bengali society.

The Brahmo Samaj under Debendranath was
characterized by a strong anti-Christian feeling.
Debendranath had been instrumental in founding the
*Hindu Hitarthi Vidyalaya* to combat missionary activity, and to further the same object Rajnarain had
written *Vedantic Doctrines Vindicated* in 1845.    To be a
Christian in those days was to cross over into a completely alien social framework.    Christian converts
were treated as outcastes by their families, but were
not accepted by the European Christian community
either, apart from the missionaries.    Theirs was therefore a very narrow, rather depressing, circle.    They
were not even given full equality in the church, as
Reverend Lal Behari Dey was to find out.[15]    The missionaries further helped to alienate converts from their
backgrounds by exaggerating the evil nature of Hinduism and by forcing acceptance of their own Western
value systems.    E.B. Cowell, Principal of the Sanskrit
College from 1858 to 1863, confirms this impression quite
strongly in one of his letters home : —

A Hindu who turns Christian has in his way to
undergo a Martyrdom, though not of fire and sword,
—and this makes such numbers 'linger shivering
on the brink'.[16]

Many middle-class Christian converts in Bengal had
already tried, and rejected, Brahmoism.    Reverend Lal
Behari Dey, in one of his lectures on Brahmoism, dec-

lared that he was once a Brahmo.[17] Like them, he did not believe in book-revelation, and believed that repentance was sufficient atonement for sin. However, he was still troubled as he had no promise of a pardon for his sins, and his doubts were only resolved when he discovered the Christian doctrine of atonement, whereby although God was infinitely merciful sinners were still the objects of divine displeasure. He finally rejected Brahmoism as being only a 'half way house'.[18]

Jogesh Chunder Gangooly, who later became a Unitarian through his friendship with Reverend Dall, had become a Brahmo in the early 1850s, but was dissatisfied with the gap between faith and practice among Brahmos. He wrote,

> They do not have much faith in idols I think, but they have idols at *their houses*, which are worshipped and taken care of at their expense. How far they repudiate the caste system I am not sure, for I have not seen nor heard of high-caste deists dining with low-caste brethren publicly, nor have I known a Brahmun deist to marry the daughter of other castes...........[19]

However, Keshub joined the Samaj precisely *because* Brahmoism was a half way house. He wanted to avoid the complete alienation of becoming a Christian, and his religious convictions prevented him from the stagnation of remaining a Hindu. By joining the Brahmo Samaj he was establishing a new identity for himself which was more flexible than either of these. He also had definite ideas for improving society, which he wanted to put into practice, and the best channel for doing this was obviously the road between the two extremes of Hinduism and Christianity. The Brahmo Samaj appeared to cater adequately for both his spiritual needs and his secular aims.

When Keshub joined the Brahmo Samaj, it was at its lowest ebb since the revival of 1843. The crisis over the Vedas had broken its spirit. It had pushed the Samaj further away from Hinduism, as a belief in the infallibility of the Vedas was one of the hallmarks of an orthodox Hindu, and had laid itself open to ridicule from the missionaries at the uncertainty of its dogma after this public admission of having been wrong. Dr Duff gave an account of how he managed to wring a 'confession' of this weakness out of one of the Brahmo leaders. Duff pressed him about "the practical uselessness of his system, from its constant fluctuation and changeableness, contrasting the same with the glorious truths of Christianity, which, like the author, are the same yesterday, today and for ever...." In his reply, the Brahmo supposedly admitted,

> The plain fact is, that when we gave up the inspiration and divine authority of the Vedas, we cut our cables, got loose from our old moorings, and have since been drifting about wherever wind and tide may carry us.[20]

Few were ready to give praise to the Brahmo Samaj for its flexibility and openness to change.

Debendranath had other interests, and was no longer wholly absorbed by Samaj affairs. In 1851 he was the first Secretary of the British Indian Association, and held this post till 1853. He was also prominent in the establishment of the Bethune Society at that time. He was becoming increasingly convinced of the futility of labouring on in the Brahmo Samaj. Rajnarain Bose, Debendranath's chief supporter and good friend, had left Calcutta to become headmaster of Midnapore High School in 1851, and so could no longer be involved in the centre of Brahmo Samaj activities. In 1854, at a meeting of the Atmiya Sabha started by Akshay Kumar Dutt, the various attributes of God were, to Debendranath's utmost horror, decided by a show of hands.[21] He showed his disapproval by withdrawing his financial backing from the *Tattwabodhini Patrika* and disbanding its editorial board. He no longer felt any urge to stay and fight this onslaught of godlessness, but retired at the end of 1856 to meditate in the Himalayas. In 1855 Akshay Kumar Dutt had already retired from the Brahmo Samaj and resigned the editorship of the *Tattwabodhini Patrika* because of ill health.

Apart from the appeal of its religious principles,

Keshub may have been attracted to the Brahmo Samaj by the social reform ideas of men like Dutt and Vidyasagar.[22]   The general lack of leadership and direction provided an added inducement to join, as his leadership potential and his desire to exercise that role were already obvious from his boyhood.   The field was open to him.   Even Debendranath acknowledged this. In answer to a query on why he ended his autobiography in 1858, he said, "After that is Keshub's period."[23]

Keshub joined the Brahmo Samaj some time in 1857, but was a fairly quiet member until he became a close associate of Debendranath, after the latter's return from the hills in 1858.   Debendranath was 41, Keshub only 20.   They recognized each other's merits instantly—Debendranath seeing Keshub as a possible successor and the new hope of the flagging Brahmo Samaj, and Keshub seeing Debendranath as his spiritual guide and mentor.   Keshub was also a prestigious gain for the Samaj, coming from one of Calcutta's most prominent Hindu families.   Keshub's reliance on Debendranath's advice began almost immediately after Debendranath's return, when the question arose of whether or not Keshub should be initiated by the family *guru*.   Debendranath did not make the decision for him, but advised him of the social consequences of a refusal to be initiated.   Seeing Keshub's determination to accept these consequences, he then supported him in his decision to refuse.[24]   Keshub spent the day set for his initiation at Debendranath's house, causing great consternation to his mother, who thought he had gone to become a Christian.[25]

Again, in 1859[26], Keshub defied his family to go on a trip to Ceylon with Debendranath and his son Satyendranath, Keshub's classmate.   This was doubly frowned on because not only was he crossing the seas and losing his caste, he was also accompanying the Tagores, Brahmins who had lost their caste.   The third major domestic incident involving Debendranath marked a turning point in Keshub's relations with his family, liberating him from their influence and finally making them more tolerant to his cause. This was on the occasion of taking his wife to the festivities making his appointment as an Acharya in 1862. His family refused to let her go, because it was against the zenana tradition, and again because of the caste status of the Tagores. Sunity Devi, Keshub's daughter, gave a highly romantic account of the events, told to her by her mother. The family put pressure on Keshub's wife not to go, but on the day, Keshub sent her a note saying "I am waiting". Keshub's wife felt the call of love and went to him. He then said to her,

> I want you to realize your position fully.   If you come with me, you give up caste, rank, money and jewels.   The relations who love you will become estranged from you. The bread of bitterness will be your portion. You will lose all except me.   Am I worth the sacrifice?[27]

After such a direct emotional appeal, his wife, of course, joined him. They were prevented from leaving the house by guards, but these finally gave way when they realized the strength of Keshub's determination. The result was a formal rupture with his family. They would not receive him back home, and he even had to go to court to ensure that he retained his share of the paternal property. Keshub and his wife stayed at Debendranath's throughout most of this period. Fortuitously, in the circumstances, Keshub fell very ill, and this moved his family to readmit him into the home, on his own terms. It was a minor victory for him, and meant that from then on he could follow his career without the restraints or pressures of more conservative family members.

By 1859, Debendranath had already singled Keshub out to be his associate in Brahmo Samaj affairs. On 25 December of that year, Keshub and Debendranath were made Secretaries of the new Managing Committee of the Brahmo Samaj, of which Ramaprasad Roy, Rammohun's youngest son, was President.[28] In 1860 Keshub started another religious group within the Samaj, the Sangat Sabha. This formed the nucleus of Keshub's

missionary brotherhood, as it included most of the members of the old Goodwill Fraternity. Most of these young
men had joined the Brahmo Samaj along with Keshub,
but they obviously still felt a need for an organization
entirely their own where they could be completely open
and not have to defer to their elders. They were a group
of very earnest youths, who cultivated an evangelical
Christian style of public prayer and repentance. Keshub
used this group as a testing ground for his ideals. The
young men resolved to practice what they preached,
which involved a renunciation of caste and the sacred
thread, and idolatrous festivals. Debendranath, characteristically, did not at first interfere with the performance
of *Durga Puja* at his home, but showed his disapproval
by his annual absence from home during that period.
However, after reading Keshub's final codification of these
resolutions in *Brahma Dharmer Anusthan*,[29] Debendranath was induced to give up the sacred thread and to
banish *Durga Puja* observances from his home, convert-
ing the former Durga Puja hall into a domestic chapel.[30]
They also resolved to uphold temperance, to promote
female education among their wives and sisters, and to
be always truthful. The young Brahmos were renowned
for their absolute honesty. Rather than commit themselves
to a possible untruth, they would say to exonerate themselves, '*bodh hay*' (perhaps) and instead of saying they
would do something, they would say that they would try
to do it.[31] They were ridiculed for the extreme serious-
ness of their morality, but it did have a marked effect on
society.[32] Brahmo morality, influenced largely by mid-
Victorian Nonconformist morality, was puritanical and
strict.[34] Krishna Kumar Mitra gave up cards, smoking, and going to *jatras* when he became a Brahmo.[33]

In June 1861 Keshub resigned from his position in
the Bank of Bengal. He had been employed there, following the family tradition, from 1859, working as a clerk
at a salary of 25 rupees per month. This was raised
shortly after he joined to 50 rupees per month, because
the bank officials had been impressed by the neatness of
his handwriting.[34] This is a good illustration of the trivia-

ity of the job, and it is not surprising that the routine work of a bank clerk did not suit either Keshub's fervent eligiosity or his ambition to lead society. His decision to resign was inevitable. From then on he became a Brahmo missionary, relying only on God's providence—although he did also receive 20,000 rupees from his share of the paternal property in 1862.[35]

A year before that, in June 1860, Keshub published the first of his *Tracts for the Times*.[36] This was entitled *Young Bengal: This Is For You*.[37] In this he began by congratulating Young Bengal for beginning to abandon their "sceptical notions", which were a result of their "godless education". He launched a bitter attack on a phenomenon which he himself was associated with—the 'Improvement Societies, Friendly Meetings, Debating Clubs, Literary Associations", and the "bodies of young men unanimously pledging themselves with solemnity to momentous resolutions like these : we shall enlighten the masses—elevate the condition of the females—encourage brotherly feeling". He dismissed these as "mere prattle without practice", despite the resemblance those resolutions he enumerated bore to those of the Sangat Sabha. Keshub's remarks on the various societies of the time were sharp and perceptive, showing both a familiarity with and distaste for their function, which was to give the impression of enlightenment without having to act on it. His conclusion was closely in line with the evangelical belief in practical works for social improvement being the true service of God :—

> Alas ! the moral nature is asleep : the sense of duty is dead. There is lack of moral courage—want of an active religious principle in our pseudo-patriots. Else why is it that while there is, on the one hand, so much of intelligence and intellectual progress, there is, on the other, so little of practical work for the social advancement of the country ?......[38]

At this stage Keshub's aim was clear—to cultivate the spiritual life of the Calcutta intellectual elite, addressing his appeal to the young, and to use this religious sentiment in reforming his country.

There were 11 other tracts in this series, written

monthly over a year long period. Some were in the
form of question and answer, between an Inquirer and
a Brahmo, while others were selections from works by
European authors. The *Tracts* were Keshub's mouthpiece for his idea of Brahmoism, which already differed
in emphasis from that of Debendranath. He followed
Debendranath in saying that the basis of Brahmoism was
intuition and not revelation, but stressed at length that
Brahmoism was a catholic, anti-sectarian creed and so
laid much more emphasis on non-Hindu sources. He also
saw social reform as a major priority.

> This is the very object of Brahmoism, that sweet
> religion of universal love. Her mission is to sum-
> mon together the various sections of humanity and
> establish among them a peaceful and blessed
> brotherhood.[39]

This gave the ultimate extent of his plan, which went
beyond India to include the world, an idealistic and impressive aim, though the breadth of his vision perhaps
contained the seeds of a grandiose ambition as well.

In the *Tracts* Keshub made no reference to Hinduism,
yet used frequent biblical illustrations to make his point.
Tracts eight and nine were on 'Testimonies to the Validity of Intuitions', most of which was a collection of
extracts from various philosophers through the ages. The
list covered Aristotle, Hallam, Locke, Morell, Hamilton,
Shaftesbury, Buffier, Hume, Reid, Beattie, Jacobi, Ancil-
lon, Coleridge, Dugald Stewart, Thomas Brown, Aber-
crombie, Cousin, M'Cosh, and John Tulloch. This impressive array of names, though probably partly calculated
merely to impress, shows the extent of Keshub's familiarity with Western thought and philosophy, and his lack
of similar roots in the Indian tradition.[40] These *Tracts*
also show Keshub's lack of originality in this period.
Never again did he rely so blatantly on other people's
ideas to support his own.

However, although Keshub's ideas may not have
been very original and in fact often seem to be culled
from a variety of European sources, they did give
Brahmoism a new emphasis and orientation. It is un-

certain amongst whom or how the *Tracts* were actually circulated, but it is certain that he presupposed an educated readership.  He also stressed the humanitarian as well as the religious side of Brahmoism, so that it could accommodate both the young sceptics who were feeling lost at having rejected traditional Hinduism, and others with genuinely strong religious urges who were likewise intellectually dissatisfied with Hinduism.  Keshub realized the need to broaden the base of the Brahmo movement to include the younger generation, as it had stopped expanding at all during the 1850s.  In August 1861 the *Indian Mirror* was started as a weekly paper, giving Keshub a regular channel to give vent to his opinions.

In May 1861, Keshub went to Krishnagar.  He was supposed to be on holiday[41], but the trip turned out to be the first of many mission tours taking him all over India.  In Krishnagar Keshub took the opportunity of giving some public lectures on Brahmoism, which attracted large crowds.  Two prominent Christian missionaries, Reverend Greaves and Reverend Dyson, were moved by indignation to reply to what they heard—Greaves in written pamphlet form, Dyson in public counter-lectures. Keshub thrived on this opposition and at this opportunity for open debate, and replied with gusto, speaking till a doctor ordered him to stop lest he damage his lungs. Keshub was very well received in Krishnagar—paradoxically, not only by the young men, but also by the orthodox *pandits* who hailed him, if not as a champion of Hinduism, certainly as a vanquisher of Christianity. Though they did not embrace Brahmoism, they saw it as a much lesser threat to their way of life than Christianity.

It is interesting to see the opinion of Reverend Greaves, Keshub's adversary, on the Brahmo *Tracts*, which, though anonymous, he thought were by the Secretary, "a young man considerably in advance of the President, who is still almost a Vedantist".  He said that the *Tracts* were "mere plagiarism and imitation". He condemned Keshub most vehemently, saying.

Indeed, the Babu has so buried himself (intuitions and all) under a weight of borrowed ideas and expressions, that he is scarce to be recognized except by that peculiar inflated style of composition which sufficiently betrays its authorship........[42]

Greaves accused Keshub, not unjustly, of using Christian language and doctrines, biblical terms and phrases, without acknowledgment. This attachment to the Bible should not have seemed so odious to a missionary, but it is apparent that his rancour was because Keshub would not accept Christianity as a religion or a dogma, or the Bible as revelation, but used them freely to support his own arguments in favour of Brahmoism. The Christian missionaries saw Keshub as a serious threat, and used aggression and sarcasm, in print and in speech, to denounce him and his beliefs. His confidence was unscathed, as he was well able to give firm rebuttals to their charges[43], and he knew that public sympathy was on his side in any confrontations with them.

Keshub was beginning to give to the Brahmo Samaj that sense of purpose and direction which had been lacking since the debate on Vedic infallibility. The Indian Year Book estimated the number of Brahmos in 1861 as about 1,630.[44] This represented a large proportion of the educated population of the time.

Keshub was not content to merely prattle without practising. He was full of energy and ideas, and he had the organizational ability to carry these out. After one lecture he told his audience, "The three hours I have spent in addressing you might have been more profitably spent had we devised some means for female education, or some other work of reform".[45] He began to introduce his ideas of the social purpose of a church community by trying to make his own religious community take some responsibility for the state of their countrymen. As a part of this, he held a fund-raising service to aid victims of famine in the North-West Provinces in 1861 and a similar service was held later that year to help those suffering from epidemic fever in Lower Bengal. People gave generously to such worthy causes, and the result was very much to the credit of the Brahmo community. In fact, Keshub used this action as part of a defence of the Brahmo Samaj in an address entitled 'The First Youth Movement'—a stirring tribute to his youthful followers, who formed an earnest and efficient 'task force'. Keshub seems only to have directed their operations, not taking part in the collecting of funds himself. He provided the inspiration, they the manpower. The Samaj had been criticized for the numerical strength of its youthful component, which was argued to be a sign of its weakness and decline. Keshub claimed that the youthful membership was a sign of vigour rather than weakness, and enumerated their part in fund-raising as evidence : —

> What the young men of our Church did on the occasion of the famine a few months ago, is still fresh in my memory. It is a lasting monument to the glory of our 'Church, and in my life I shall never forget it. Did they not go about from door to door soliciting contributions, begging their friends, their fathers, mothers, sisters, brothers, their kinsmen, and neighbours to unite in that sacred work ? Did they not in noble self-denial part with many a comfort of life and even some of the necessaries of life to feed their starving brethren ? Did not even their wives and sisters in blessed sympathy readily part with their ornaments ?[46]

Keshub had already been corresponding with prominent Theists in Britain—Miss Frances Power Cobbe, and Mr F. W. Newman, author of *Theism, doctrinal and practical* and brother of J. H. Newman. Keshub's confidence seemed unbounded, as he wrote to Newman and proposed a plan for simultaneous educational agitation in India and England for more efficient schools and colleges in India. Newman complied with this scheme by printing and distributing an *Appeal to the English Public*. Keshub's side of the agitation probably attracted more attention. He held a big public meeting in 'Calcutta in October 1861. At this he indicated the three main lines of work to be followed :—a radical reformation of the education system, to cater for the needs of the heart as well as of the mind ; the education of the lower classes and the education of women.[47] Some of these principles were put into practice at the Calcutta College, founded

in 1862, which replaced the Brahmo School founded
by Keshub and Debendranath in 1859. The school cor-
rected the imbalance between secular and religious
education and stressed training in morality. It had an
alternative syllabus prepared for teaching women in
their homes, and another for more elderly women.
Keshub reiterated his idea of service in the name of
religion in this public address on education : —

> Let us then strive to make our Church what it
> ought to be—a source of real usefulness—foregoing
> all that apathy, inconsistency and compromising
> policy, which have hitherto made us Brahmas the
> butt of merited censure, derision, and contempt.
> Firmness of purpose, steadiness of resolution, con-
> sistency of character,—these constitute a genuine
> Brahma. It is the recognition of these truths that
> is bringing our Church into the arena of public
> enterprise.[48]

In this same address, 'The Promotion of Education
in India', Keshub mentioned for the first time his faith
in the Indian connection with Britain. He held to a kind
of laissez-faire policy, saying that the Government was
not bound to help the promotion of education in the
proposed scheme, though it should of course do what it
could—but instead he felt it was up to the Indian people
to carry out this task while being "bound to acknowledge with fervent gratitude the benefits it[49] has conferred on our country by bringing the light of Western
ideas to its shores". The influence that not only Western
abstract ideas, but also Western social values and
terminology had on Keshub were very apparent in this
address. He expressed the very un-Indian idea that
every child had a birth-right to education, and also
insisted that the light of education should be extended
to every cottage and mechanic's shop, appropriate English
terms, but not applicable to the Indian situation. He
said that the British did have a 'mission' in India, but
did not really clarify the nature of this, in this instance
only calling on the English people for their rather nebu-
lous support and encouragement for the Indian project.
  In the midst of this incredible confidence and energy,

Keshub is presented in a more human light in an incident recounted by Rajnarain Bose in his autobiography.[50] There was a saying at the time that the Vaidyas were cunning. Keshub naively believed this, and was always fearful that he had inherited this caste defect, feeling that he had to be especially circumspect so that none of his actions could be judged in this light. He even asked Rajnarain apprehensively whether it was true that Vaidyas had a bad name for cunning, and Rajnarain felt bound to affirm that it was. Keshub was an idealist. He wrote in a report to Debendranath on his Krishnagar campaign, that love was the main means of preaching for a missionary[51]—although that quality seemed to be singularly absent from the competitiveness of the Krishnagar proceedings.

Keshub's position as the new leader of the Brahmo Samaj was firmly established by the end of 1861. Debendranath was still the spiritual head, but he did not compete with Keshub in the field of activity. He was impressed by Keshub's energy. He was also happy to leave Keshub to carry out his plan to attract younger members, as Debendranath felt himself to be out of touch with the minds of the younger generation.[52] Debendranath's patronage was an important factor in establishing Keshub's influence initially, as other Brahmos were accustomed to respect his judgement. Keshub was thus free to mould the Samaj according to his high ideals of universal brotherhood and love of God. He was attracting a wide following, composed mainly of a younger, more impressionable and also more flexible group than the older Brahmos. Full of energy and looking for leadership, they readily supported Keshub's aims of reform. To them Keshub's bias towards European thought and tradition was not alien—it was the familiar mode of their own English education. There is little mention of the reaction of the older Brahmos at this time, but it is likely that they would not have been pleased at having the errors in their religious faith and practice pointed out to them by their junior, and that they would not have adjusted easily to a style so different from what

they had been used to. Keshub was nothing like either
Debendranath or Akshay Kumar in temperament. He
was neither a rationalist nor of a contemplative nature;
his was a fervent energetic kind of religiosity.

He was forming his own religious style—heavily
influenced by Christianity. Strangely, negative reaction
at this period came from the missionaries only, not from
the orthodox Hindus. Although Keshub leaned much
more heavily towards Christianity than Hinduism, he
was only in open conflict with the missionaries. They
resented his intrusion on their territory and interruption
of their activities. Dr Duff called Brahmoism "the
grand counter-antagonist of an aggressive Christianity".[53]
The Hindus were glad that he was not a Christian, and
the Christians were annoyed for the same reason. In
1861 there was little reaction in Hindu society against
Keshub. He was more concerned with propagating
Brahmoism than with attacking Hinduism. His activities
had been confined to establishing his own place in the
Brahmo Samaj, and reaching out mainly to others who
were already marked off from traditional Hindu society
by being part of the English-educated sector.

Keshub was an eminently practical man, and an
eloquent speaker who knew how to use words in a rous-
ing and persuasive way. Whether or not his ideas were
completely original is not of major importance in an
assessment of his position. In fact, he drew heavily on
the works of Western thinkers. However, by presenting
them to the Indian public he made them feel that these
doctrines were addressed to them, as part of a world
brotherhood, a thought which would have boosted the
morale of those educated Indians who wished to take
part equally in the intellectual life of the West. As well
as giving them a new ideological framework, Keshub
held the interest of his followers because of his constant
activity. There was always something practical for his
followers to do, some way in which they could feel that
they were helping the progress of the country. Keshub
gave the English-educated elite a sense of belonging.
Many had been cut off from their families for their

refusal to give up Western indulgences like forbidden food and drink, and so formed a small band united only by the negative quality of having rejected their tradition. There was nothing in this mode of living to sustain them. It is this group which Keshub set out to win over, to whom he addressed the *Tracts*—and it is this group who, at this period, responded.

In the course of his lecture on 'The Promotion of Education in India' Keshub had said in passing, "Brahmaism is destined to become a power in the world".[54] Dr Duff went even further than this:—

> Its regular and formally initiated membership now exceeds 1500 in this metropolis and neighbourhood; while there are hundreds and thousands who may be regarded as inquirers or partial adherents. The Samaj is therefore a Power—and a Power of no mean order—in the midst of us.[55]

### NOTES AND REFERENCES

1. Address at the Unitarian Spring Social Meeting, 28 April 1870. In Keshub Chunder Sen, *In England* op. cit., pp. 135-138.

2. Rajnarain Bose, *Atmacharit*, third ed. (Calcutta, 1952), p. 78.

3. S. Sastri, *History* op. cit. Vol. I, p. 81.

4. Debendranath Tagore, *Jiban-charit*, second ed. (Calcutta, 1911), pp. 14-15.

5. S. Sastri, *History*, op. cit. Vol. I, p. 87.

6. The 1843 Covenant is no longer extant. This is taken from the 1850 Covenant, printed as Appendix B in S. Sastri, ibid. p. xiv.

7. Debendranath Tagore, op. cit. p. 29.

8. Ibid. p. 30.

9. S. Sastri, *History* op. cit. Vol. I, p. 94.

10. Debendranath Tagore, op. cit. p. 30.

11. Accounts of Akshay Kumar Dutt are given in B. B. Majumdar, *History of Indian Social and Political Ideas* (Calcutta, 1967) and in A. Poddar, *Renaissance in Bengal* (Simla, 1970).

12. Biographical details are from his autobiography—Rajnarain Bose, op. cit.

13. Rajnarain Bose, op. cit. pp. 54-55.

14. Rajnarain Bose, op. cit. p. 68.

15. G. Macpherson, *Life of Lal Behari Dey* (Edinburgh, 1900).

16. Letter dated 5 April 1863, in G. Cowell, *Life and Letters of E. B. Cowell* (London, 1904), p. 186.

17. G. Macpherson, op. cit. p. 55.

18. G. Macpherson, op. cit. p. 56.

19. J. C. Gangooly, op. cit. p. 249.

20. From a letter from Duff to Reverend Dr. Cavendish, in J. Murdoch, *Indian Year Book,* 1861-62 (Madras, 1862), pp. 126-127.

21. Debendranath Tagore, op. cit. p. 115.

22. Vidyasagar was a member of the Tattwavodhini Sabha. Keshub was obviously influenced by his ideas, as in 1859 he staged a play about widow remarriage.

23. P. K. Sen, *Biography,* op. cit. Vol. I, p. 218.

24. G. S. Leonard, op. cit. p. 116.

25. J. C. Bagal, *Keshab* op. cit. p. 26.

26. Dates for most events in the life of Keshub Chunder sen seem to vary widely, but I have referred throughout to those given by P. S. Basu, op. cit. as this seems to contain the most thorough and detailed chronological account.

27. Sunity Devee, Maharani of Cooch Behar, *The Autobiography of an Indian Princess* (London, 1921), p. 4.

28. J. C. Bagal, *Keshab,* op. cit. p. 30.

29. The practice of Brahmoism.

30. S. Sastri, *History,* op. cit. Vol. I, pp. 136-137.

31. Ibid. p. 130.

32. In his autobiography, N. C. Chaudhuri vividly recalled the influence of Brahmoism on his moral upbringing. During his childhood in the early twentieth century Chaudhuri grew up in an atmosphere of moral awareness, where conduct was openly and rationally discussed and criticized.
    N. C. Chaudhuri, *The Autobiography of an Unknown Indian* (London, 1951), pp. 213-221.

33. Krishna Kumar Mitra, *Atmacharit* (Calcutta, 1974), pp. 7, 56.

34. L. Ghose, op. cit. p. 151.

35. P. C. Mozoomdar, *Life* op. cit. p. 95.

36. This was also the title of the controversial works published and circulated by John Henry Newman of the Oxford Movement in 1833-34. Keshub must have been aware of this, given his familiarity with British ecclesiastical history, and his choice of the same title would indicate perhaps an aspiration to occupy a similar position in the history of Brahmoism, in influence if not in ideological bias.

37. P. S. Basu, op. cit. pp. 6-8.

38. P. S. Basu, op. cit. p. 7.

39. P. S. Basu, op. cit. p. 14, Tract three, 'Religion of Love'.

40. A recent unpublished doctoral thesis by O. L. Piette, '*Responses of Brahmo Samaj to Western Cultural Advances, 1855-1880: An Episode in India's Intellectual History* (Syracuse University, 1974) gives a detailed account of Western influences on Keshub's intellectual development.

41. P. C. Mozoomdar, *Life* op. cit. p. 80.

42. J. Murdoch, op. cit. p. 124.

43. See 'The Brahmo Samaj Vindicated' in his *Lectures* 1904, op. cit. pp. 161-205. (This lecture was delivered in 1863.)

44. J. Murdoch, op. cit. p. 125.

45. Keshub Chunder Sen, *Lectures* (1904) op. cit. p. 204.

46. P. K. Sen, *Biography* op. cit. Vol. I, p. 263.

47. Ibid. p. 268.

48. P. S. Basu, op. cit. p. 46.

49. British rule.

50. Rajnarain Bose, op. cit. p. 103.

51. P. K. Sen, *Biography* op. cit. Vol. I, p. 264. Keshub's report is reprinted in G. G. Roy, Acharya Keshabchandra, Vol. I, (Calcutta, 1938) p. 141ff.

52. Rajnarain Bose, op. cit. p. 103.

53. J. Murdoch, op. cit. p. 203. From reprint of an article which originally appeared in *Christian Work*.

54. P. S. Basu, op. cit. p. 46.

55. J. Murdoch, op. cit. p. 203.

# CHAPTER THREE

# EVENTS LEADING TO THE FIRST SCHISM IN THE BRAHMO SAMAJ (1862-1865)

THE YEAR 1862 began eventfully with the celebration of the anniversary of the Brahmo Samaj on 23 January, at which the bond between Keshub and Debendranath was publicly consolidated. At a special Divine Service, Debendranath addressed a prayer of thanksgiving to the Supreme Spirit for sending such a saintly man to help him to "destroy India's darkness of ignorance and pollution of atmosphere". Debendranath said of Keshub, "Of all people I have met I never found one so pure, so steadfast, so endowed with wisdom and piety as this man of God".[1] He prayed that Keshub would always remain with him, to be a stay and a help in his old age. Keshub's prayer by comparison was much less personal, more grandiosely general. He began by referring to Debendranath and his family in intimate terms as his "father, mother and sisters", but did not go on to mention him again. Instead Keshub went on to describe his world-vision, and his hopes for the union of the world into one enormous family, which could only happen when people began to forget their worldly cares and gave themselves up to God. This did not mean that Keshub did not reciprocate Debendranath's feelings for him, but it is evident that he was more immediately concerned with carrying out God's mission in the world. Debendranath, however, seemed to have a tremendous sense of relief that this task was no longer his alone, as he found a suitable successor. All his hopes and wishes centred around Keshub, who was grateful for this patronage, but whose gladness lay in that he had found an organization suited to his needs and beliefs, an appropriate field for his energies. Evidently at that stage the most obvious differences in their temperaments—one old, contemplative and conservative, the other young, active and forward looking—did not trouble Debendranath at all, but rather impressed him.

Debendranath's feeling for Keshub was given official recognition in his installation of Keshub as *Acharya* (Minister) on Bengali New Year's Day, 13th April 1862. This was a momentous step in the history of the Brahmo Samaj, as it was the first time a non-Brahmin had been installed in a position in the Samaj hierarchy of *Acharyas* and *Upacharyas* (Assistant Ministers). It was also very rare for anyone to be appointed directly to the position of *Acharya*. At the time, Debendranath was the only one holding that title. The other office-bearers were all *Upacharyas*. These two points accentuate the exceptional nature of the appointment, and show how great Debendranath's esteem for Keshub must have been, that he was prepared to contravene the accepted rules so blatantly. It was clear that Debendranath was leaving no room for doubt as to his choice of a successor.

As Debendranath's title had been amended to *Pradhan Acharya* (Chief Minister), Keshub was now officially second in the Brahmo Samaj hierarchy. To achieve this he had been promoted over the heads of the existing *Upacharyas,* his seniors in years and length of membership, a situation which was bound to, and did, create resentment. Debendranath was not deterred, as he was convinced that he heard the voice of God telling him to appoint Keshub as *Acharya*[2], and no human voice was going to overrule that, as the elder Brahmos discovered when they pleaded in vain with Debendranath to go no further than appointing Keshub as an *Upacharya*. Even that would have been exceptional, as that title, too, was normally reserved for Brahmins. They could not but have resented Keshub's appointment as none of them seemed to share Debendranath's esteem for him, and also because the very activity and fervour that Debendranath admired in him threatened their position, because they took no part in his new schemes. Keshub's revitalization of the Brahmo

Samaj exaggerated their inactivity by contrast with his
activity. Debendranath must have reinforced their
sense of inadequacy when he said that, in seeking help
to spread the knowledge of God, before he met Keshub
he had been disappointed.[3] Thus the peak of Keshub's
recognition contained within it the potential for disruption within the Samaj.

At the ordination service Debendranath openly expressed his hopes for Keshub. He specified that Keshub
must endeavour to dispel darkness from the minds of
Brahmos, and sow the seeds of Brahmoism in their
hearts. Interestingly, he did not include the propagation of Brahmoism among non-Brahmos as a part of
Keshub's duties.[4] He showed some awareness of the
feelings of the elder Brahmos in reminding Keshub to
show them respect. He presented him with a copy of
the *Brahmadharma Granth* to help him "to keep alive
the flame of the Brahmo faith"[5], and also presented him
with a list of his duties and responsibilities as an *Acharya*. The whole ceremony focussed on and magnified the
relationship between Debendranath and Keshub.

The quality in Keshub that most appealed to
Debendranath was summed up in the title he gave him
at that same ceremony, *Brahmananda,* or 'Rejoicer in
God'. Debendranath recognized that Keshub had the
rare quality of God-vision which he himself had ex-
perienced. According to Protap, they used to sit facing
each other for hours on end, "absorbed in the ecstasy of
transcendent spiritual intercourse, drunk with mutual
sympathy and communion".[6] Debendranath was not
merely impressed by Keshub, he seemed as if infatua-
ted by him : —

> Everything he did or said carried a good omen to
> Devendra's fatherly heart ; every feature of his face
> and mind was a gleam of the Light Eternal to his
> imaginative trusting soul. Keshub's enthusiasm
> filled him with the electricity of the highest spheres,
> Keshub's sympathy intoxicated him, Keshub's intelli-
> gence deepened and confirmed his own wisdom, he
> found a marvel of religious genius in Keshub Chunder
> Sen........[7]

Understandably, as the elder Brahmos had not known Debendranath ever to respond to anyone in such a way before, they found the relationship disturbing. Keshub's followers were pleased, as they mistakenly interpreted it as an endorsement of their attitudes and activities, whereas it was really a personal commitment to Keshub. Debendranath himself acknowledged the power of Keshub's personality :

> Whatever he thought in his mind, he had the power to express in speech. Whatever he said, he had the power to do.

Whatever he did he had the power of making other men do.[8] Debendranath's regard for him must have given Keshub much confidence and encouragement, and it was for this kind of support and sustenance that Keshub looked to him, rather than as a source of inspiration. Debendranath was a father-figure to him, a refuge in times of trouble, a sure support in the face of unpopularity with the original members of the Samaj.

Keshub's major innovation during this period was the missionary system. There had been Brahmo missionaries in the past, but they had been isolated individuals rather than an organized group. Keshub's missionary system was closely modelled on that of the British missionaries in India. Following the Biblical text, "Take no thought for the morrow", Keshub and his missionaries gave up all other employment and worked solely at spreading a knowledge of Brahmoism, with an aim to convert. They went on tours, gave public lectures, and also went and lived in rural towns for months at a time. They used the methods of Christian missionaries—public preaching, divine service, welfare activities —while competing with them, and in fact had an advantage because as Indians they were less likely to offend their hearers by ignorance and tactlessness. The diary of a missionary for an average week could include, as one did[9], a service and sermon (after which one young man gave up his sacred thread), a conference with orthodox Hindus, a public lecture (which included a confrontation with a Christian clergyman), family services, religious conversation (including arguments with a "fashionable looking young man" who advocated the opinions of Herbert Spencer and Auguste Comte), a procession and *sankirtan,* and an open air meeting for the masses. It was probably in the field of missionary activity that Keshub won most support and approval from the original Brahmos, as in this he was helping combat Christianity, which was one of their main preoccupations during the 1840s and 1850s.

Keshub was the first of the young Brahmos to devote himself entirely to mission work. The second was Bijoy Krishna Goswami, who was to become one of the most controversial figures in the Brahmo Samaj. He was also from a Vaishnava family, and had been a Vaishnava *guru* for some years before coming to Calcutta to take up studies at the Medical College.[10] Even there, as a student, he stood out. He was the spokesman for a group of boys who left school in protest at remarks made by the Principal which they found offensive. He told Vidyasagar, who was acting as conciliator, that they would not return to school because they were more eager for self-respect than for their own well-being.[11] This great concern for integrity was to mark his whole career in the Brahmo Samaj. He became a missionary in 1863, and gave up his studies a year later. He was less of a central organizer than Keshub, but he was a very successful missionary. In answer to a petition from Pirali Brahmin families, he visited Baganchra village in Jessore and was able to initiate 23 of these families into Brahmoism.[12] A good social worker, he did not merely leave it at that, but made this village the centre of his mission work. He visited it regularly, along with other young Brahmos, and opened a school and a dispensary there as well as a Samaj.

Other young men, including Protap Chunder Mozoomdar, joined gradually, forming a small band of about eight men, directed by Keshub. The commitment to mission work was not easy, as it required a great deal of hard work and self-sacrifice. Often they were without funds and had to rely on 'Providence' for their maintenance, but this did not deter their zeal. 31 new Samajes were founded between Keshub's joining in 1857 and the establishment of his own Samaj in 1866.[13]

The highlight of Keshub's missionary activity during this period was his trip to Madras and Bombay, from February to April 1864.[14] The fame of the Brahmo Samaj had spread, and Keshub made the trip in response to urgent requests for missionary visits.[15] Another reason for his going may have been because he was conscious of his unpopularity with the Brahmo elders, and even some of his young followers had compared unfavourably the heaviness of his Bengali sermons and prayers with Debendranath's eloquence. Keshub, aware of his own awkwardness with Bengali, was disturbed by this criticism.[16]  He told Protap at this time that he considered English lectures to be his real sphere of work, and that he found the Brahmo Samaj pulpit uncongenial because his preaching there was ineffective.  He even hinted that he might resign.[17] The mission tour was a way of escaping from these pressures, and if successful, it could have been a way of transforming this hostility into admiration.

Keshub travelled by ship from Calcutta to Madras. Here he established a pattern which he was to follow in Bombay as well. The first week was spent making the acquaintance of public figures, in generally making himself known to them, and in sightseeing.  He knew full well the value of maintaining influential contacts— his approach here differing from the missionaries, who usually went straight to the people without a mediator, thus meeting with little success. Madras was the most conservative of the three Presidencies, and caution had to be exercised when new ideas were being presented. Keshub's main public lecture there did not deal directly with Brahmoism, but was on 'The Duties and Responsibilities of Educated Madrasis'. His address was impressive, earning him the title 'Thunderbolt of Bengal'.[18]

He went from Madras to Bombay by rail and sea, stopping off at various places along the way.  When he arrived, on 8 March, he again did not thrust himself into public view straight away. He gave his main lecture in the Town Hall on 17 March, on 'The Rise and Progress of the Brahmo Samaj'. The choice of topic was an indication of the relatively more advanced position of Bombay than Madras. There was already in existence in Bombay an association, the Paramhansa Sabha, which bore some relation to the Brahmo Samaj, at least in the area of social reform. This was a secret society, aiming at abolition of caste, renunciation of idol worship and the introduction of widow remarriage. At its meetings members had food cooked by low castes and other forbidden food and drink.[19] Members of the Sabha in Bombay and Poona were most eager to hold discussions with Keshub, and to learn from him some of the reasons for his success.

Keshub returned to Calcutta on 10 April. The tour had been a major landmark in many ways. Up till then, travel through India by leading public figures had been a rarity. At a meeting of the Bethune Society in 1867 Mutu Kumara Svamy of the Ceylon Legislative Council, in a lecture on his own travels in northern India, made specific mention of Keshub's and Debendranath's visits to South India[20], and of the visit of Dr Bhau Daji from Bombay to Calcutta.[21] That these could be singled out so easily, and commented on as extraordinary, shows what a major undertaking each was, and, being such novelties, what an impact each visitor would have made.

Keshub's visit also led to the establishment of branch associations of the Brahmo Samaj in south and western India. The Paramhansa Sabha was disbanded, and in 1867 (after Keshub's second tour) a few of its members, including the outstanding social reformer M. G. Ranade, founded an organization closely based on the Brahmo Samaj, which was known as the Prarthana Samaj.[22] In Madras the Ved Samaj[23] was founded after Keshub's visit in 1864.[24] The Prarthana Samaj was probably closer, in fact, to the Brahmoism of Debendranath than that of Keshub, even though the latter provided them with their inspiration. Heimsath calls them 'Hindu Protestants', meaning that they were reformers of Hinduism who did not set themselves totally apart from Hindu society.[25]   Ultimately the Prarthana Samaj was to have greater missionary impact in South India than the Brahmo Samaj[26]—probably because of their more moderate and conciliatory attitude towards Hinduism.

This and subsequent tours were important because they made clear the all-India basis of the Brahmo Samaj. Keshub was not attempting to unite people for any specific, concrete task, but his aim was to encourage brotherhood.   By his conviction that such brotherhood could be achieved through a common, enlightened religious faith, and by not seeing regional differences as a barrier to unity at a deeper level, Keshub was setting an immensely important precedent. Keshub can be said to have laid the basis for dialogue between the English-educated middle-classes all over India.   He was the first major all-India figure, and the Brahmo Samaj under him was the first major India-wide organization.[27]  This is often cited as Keshub's (albeit unwitting) contribution to the nationalist movement.[28] He set a precedent for action on a national scale by showing the feasibility and possibilities of a nation-wide organization. Keshub's motive was religious, but others quickly saw how his methods could be adapted for other spheres. In many ways his methods were suitable for political use—the importance of oratorical skill, the necessity and value of making the acquaintance and gaining the patronage of community leaders in an alien place—all these patterns were subsequently followed by political organizers.

On Keshub's return he gave a lecture to the Bethune Society on 'A Visit to Madras and Bombay ; with notes of the differences between their customs and those of Bengal'.[29]  In this talk he commented on the orthodoxy of Madras, but was willing to recognize the achievement of the gentlemen there with regard to female emancipation.   He felt that both Madras and

Bombay were in advance of Bengal in the fields of
female education, temperance, and (in Bombay) charity.
They were also superior in activity and enterprise,
while the Bengalis were more intelligent but less active,
a shortcoming he had stressed much already. He assigned to each Presidency a mission in keeping with its
own self-image :—Bombay's mission was the promotion
of the material prosperity of India, that of Madras was
to prevent the introduction of foreign fashions and to
guard the purity of India's national institutions and
'primitive' manners, and that of Bengal was the promotion of intellectual and political prosperity. Keshub
concluded by calling for co-operation among the educated natives of the three Presidencies "in promoting
the general welfare of their common country, India".
The concept of 'nationhood' had never before been so
clearly formulated, emphasizing the fact that Madrasis,
Parsis, Bengalis—all different races with different customs—still belonged to a single entity.

On Keshub's return from this highly successful
tour, he found the antipathy towards him in the Brahmo
Samaj not minimized but heightened. His detractors
had used the time he was away to try to convince
Debendranath of Keshub's failings and to frighten him
by stressing the radical changes Keshub had in mind
which would destroy the fabric of Hindu society.[30] They
were working on Debendranath's vulnerable points—
prior to this he had succeeded in overlooking the differences in basic outlook between himself and Keshub,
concentrating only on what they shared. The situation was aggravated by the performance, under Keshub's
auspices and without Debendranath's sanction, of an
inter-caste and widow marriage in October 1864.

Social reform was one of the most controversial
issues in the Brahmo Samaj. At the outset of 1863
Keshub outlined his commitment to social reform in a
lecture on 'Social Reformation in India'.[31] In this
Keshub emphasized the 'moderate' nature of the Brahmo
Samaj. This was a term of praise, as it represented
the highest of the four categories he had devised to

classify Young Bengal—Sceptical, Speculative, Ultra and Moderate.   The lecture contained nothing which would have offended even the most conservative Samaj members, probably because Keshub was conscious of lecturing to a branch of the Samaj.   He stressed the religious nature of reform and voiced his belief that reform of all religion would inevitably entail reform of society, recognizing the important fact that in India and in Hinduism religion and society could not be treated independently.   He scorned the 'destructives', who thought they could combat caste by promiscuously dining in public with different castes, and signing pledges to ignore caste distinctions—although his membership of the Sangat Sabha involved just such a pledge.   His proposed solution here was a very gradualist one, aiming to bring all men within the bosom of one church, when caste would "naturally perish".   In presenting this philosophy Keshub hardly deserved to be labelled as a dangerous radical.   His eventual aim was a casteless society, but he implied that he was working towards it by religious teaching rather than by flouting social norms.   He was not, however, retreating to the other extreme, of which he had accused previous generations of Brahmos, of living a life governed by such distinctions.   This lecture was not an entirely accurate index of Keshub's social reform policy though, as it aimed to avoid controversy and did so by omitting mention of any specific reforms.

It was Keshub's activities in the field, rather than his theoretical expositions of policy, that aroused opposition.   His most central concern was with the betterment of the condition of women.   Unlike Vidyasagar, Keshub's view of the condition of Indian women did not stem from a deeply personal sense of indignation. Keshub did not see the improvement of the condition of women as an end in itself, but as a necessary part of his ideal of harmony—between castes, sexes, religions—which meant that women should be given an equal chance, through education, to become enlightened Brahmos.   He also recognized that the women in Hindu

society functioned as the custodians of tradition, and
they had to be reached in order to effect any changes
in the rest of society. He never declared himself to be
in favour of the complete emancipation of women. It
was only in religion that Keshub recognized complete
egalitarianism, in that everyone had a right to know
God.

Keshub's followers enthusiastically supported his
interest in women's issues, and in fact took the lead in
initiating action to further their cause. The Bamabodhini Sabha was founded in 1863 for publishing books
and magazines for women, to run essay competitions,
and for their general welfare. It was not founded by
Keshub, although it had his full support, but by Bijoy
Krishna Goswami, Umesh Chandra Datta and Basanta
Kumar Ghose.[32] An associated journal was founded,
the Bamabodhini Patrika, with Umesh Chandra Datta
as editor. This interest in women was unprecedented
in Brahmo Samaj affairs. The Samaj had, through its association with Vidyasagar, always lent support to prog-
rammes to improve the general condition of women,
but it had never been actively involved. The older
generation may have seen Keshub's methods as a sign
of over-Anglicization, as he had been influenced by the
missionaries in his desire to bring women out into society—not on equal terms, but as a gracious civilizing
influence, in the Victorian tradition. Keshub's own
family disapproved of the way he brought his wife
out into Brahmo society, and he also came under public
criticism for taking some Brahmo ladies to the house
of a Christian missionary in October 1865.[33] The Brah-
mika Samaj, or Ladies Prayer Meeting, was also started in 1865.

The only kind of reform initiated by Brahmos previously had been directly connected with religion. For
instance, Debendranath had had his second daughter
married according to Brahmo reformed rites in 1861,
which was permissible because it was a matter of bringing the original Hindu rites into line with his monotheistic beliefs, with only minor changes to the form.

Debendranath's efforts to remain within Hinduism had disappointing results, as the Hindu orthodoxy would no more accept his minor changes than they would Keshub's major ones.   On both the occasion of his daughter's marriage and on his father's *sradh,* Debendranath was isolated from his family because of his insistence on monotheism. He did not intend to be a radical, but was unwavering in his commitment to monotheism, and he was prepared to risk alienation rather than compromise that.

Debendranath was not a reactionary in social reform matters.  He mentioned in various letters that he thought caste would eventually disappear, that Brahmos should not be guided by caste prejudices, and that Brahmins did not necessarily make good *Acharyas* in the Samaj.[34]  The letters containing this view of caste were written before he knew Keshub, but his practical gestures in the direction of reform, such as renouncing his sacred thread, were due largely to Keshub's influence.   Keshub had been excommunicated from his caste, and as he did not choose to seek re-entry by performing due penances, he was then free to live without reference to caste duties or distinctions at all. There is a chapter in his *Jeevan Veda* on "My Caste Ascertained", but the view stated therein makes it evident that he was not really writing about caste, but about the 'classes' of rich and poor : —

> Though sprung from high ancestry, though possessed of things that indicate wealth, yet in my mind are not found corresponding sentiments.   I have wealth but no desire for it ; dainty dishes are available but there is no appetite for them ; my mind is pleased with plain things.   Honour and esteem surround me, but my heart takes no notice of them. If both classes of people come, I leave the rich and seek the poor ; my mind feels contended in the company of the poor.  All these facts clearly show to which class my soul belongs........[35]

The language here may seem too melodramatic, a lengthy display of false modesty, but Keshub's claims for himself were not totally without substance.   He

4

may not have sought out the company of the lowest
castes, but differences of caste did not matter to him.
There is no record of his having ever observed caste
distinctions.

Marriage reform was another vital social reform
issue with which the Samaj was involved. Vidyasagar's
proposed legislation to enable widow marriage had been
passed in 1856, but few had taken advantage of it without being offered material inducement by him.    The
young Brahmos, however, with their insistence on integrity and their idealism and moral fervour, were fer-
tile ground for his ideas.    The first Brahmo widow
marriage took place in August 1862[36], and another,
which was also an inter-caste marriage, in August
1864.[37]    Keshub was chiefly instrumental in bringing
about these marriages, while Debendranath held aloof
from them. This underlined Debendranath's practical,
rather than theoretical, conservatism . In theory
Debendranath had supported Vidyasagar's marriage reforms, and with regard to inter-caste marriages had
written to Rajnarain Bose in 1863 that "there are no
caste distinctions among the Brahmas,—giving and
taking in marriage between Brahmanas and Sudras is
allowable........".[38]    The younger party, sensing the
hostility in society and in the Samaj, did not dare make
these marriages public. Despite their caution, the controversial nature of the marriages ensured that it soon
became widely known that they had taken place, arousing much opposition.    Debendranath did nothing to
prevent the marriages, partly because of his own am-
bivalent attitude towards them,    but also because he
felt that such things were personal and so it was not
his place to intervene.    The ultimate proof that caste
values did not matter to Keshub came after the two
wings of the Samaj had separated. This was the most
daring marriage of all, in which a Brahmin girl married
a Vaidya man. This was a courageous marriage, as the
Hindu taboos against a woman, especially a Brahmin
woman, marrying a man from a caste lower than her
own, were extremely strict.

As a centre for theoretical discussion of the above-mentioned social reform issues, and for general cultural enlightenment, Keshub founded the Brahma Bandhu Sabha in 1863, as a kind of successor to the old British India Society of 1856. This move was prompted by the suggestion of Dr Bhau Daji, a leading public figure from Bombay, who felt that the Brahmos should have their own counterpart to the Bethune Society, as without that they practised too much contemplation and too little benevolence.[39] Membership of the Sabha was drawn from many branches of the Samaj. Its list of functions covered all Keshub's major concerns—the propagation of Brahmoism through the printing and distribution of literature, the printing of reading matter especially for women, and the establishment of schools and medical dispensaries. The spread of Brahmoism was at the core of all other activities. It was impossible for Keshub to be totally secular. The meetings of the Sabha were more like church services than like the lectures and discussions of the Bethune Society.[40]

Behind this flurry of activities on Keshub's part, there was a growing tension in the Samaj between the older, original Brahmos, and Keshub and his followers. Although it was the elders who seemed previously to have been the dissatisfied party, because they disapproved of Keshub's schemes, the first overt and public expression of discontent came from the younger men. Towards the end of 1864 Bijoy Krishna Goswami wrote to Keshub protesting against the custom of allowing only Brahmins, with the exception of Keshub, to preach from the pulpit.[41] His protest had the backing of the Sangat Sabha. All underlying tensions of the past years were hence brought into the open. However, Debendranath and Keshub had a much more complex relationship than that typified by their respective followers, who could fairly easily be divided into two distinct groups under the broad categories of 'conser- part of Hindu society, the latter wanting a definite vative' and 'progressive', the former wanting to remain break with it. Debendranath and Keshub could not be

so easily categorized. It was the strength of their relationship that had kept the two opposite wings of the
Samaj together till then. However, in sending the protest to Keshub it is clear that his followers were forcing
him to take a definite stance on the issue. Both Keshub
and Debendranath seemed taken by surprise at the protest. They conferred, neither having predicted the
course of events or decided on a course of action. Given
the bond that existed between himself and Debendranath, it is not surprising that Keshub did not instigate
the chain of events leading to the schism. Nonetheless, he does seem to have been strangely unaware of
the militancy that was brewing among his followers. It
is possible that his followers felt him to be growing
away from them, and that Bijoy Krishna Goswami was
giving Keshub a gentle reminder that he had been
too concerned with his own personal advancement,
and had neglected the well-being of his followers. He
had been made an *Acharya* under special circumstances,
so it was then his turn to make this possible for his
followers, none of whom were still thread-wearing
Brahmins. The letter also reminded Keshub that he
was responsible to the younger section of the Samaj.
Having been attracted to it, they needed constant rein-
forcement of the principles that had attracted them.
Bijoy Krishna Goswami was himself a Brahmin, but
had given up all caste distinctions on becoming a Brahmo. As a logical part of this, after much personal struggle, he had renounced his sacred thread and was excommunicated from his caste. He felt that he should
be able to demand similar sacrifices from others, and
that the Brahmo Samaj should not perpetuate caste
distinctions.

Debendranath had expressed his agreement with
these principles in a letter written in 1860, in which he
wrote "We must knock the idea on the head that one
cannot be a minister unless one is a Brahmin. Is a hypocrite of a Brahmin to be preferred to a true Brahma".[42]
Thus Debendranath and Keshub were able to agree to
solve the conflict in a manner most immediately satis-

fying to the petitioners, which was to agree that caste had no place in the Samaj, and that it was possible for anyone to become an *Acharya*. As practical proof of this, Bijoy Krishna Goswami and Annada Prasad Chatterjee, both Brahmins by birth who had renounced their sacred threads, were created *Upacharyas* in place of the three Brahmins already holding the position, Anandachandra Vedantavagish, Ayodhyanath Pakrashi and Becharam Chatterjee.[43] As soon as the new appointments were made public, the elder Brahmos turned on Debendranath and demanded that he halt the progress of reform in the Samaj. Ayodhyanath Pakrashi especially had been held in high esteem, and his deposition was deemed to be a great insult.[44] Debendranath was swayed by their indignation, and agreed to their demands. This complete about-face was not a sign of weakness. As with Keshub, the indignant protests of the older Brahmos were a reminder to him of his responsibility to his followers. In the past they had stood by him, so now it was his turn to stand by them and safeguard their interests. His vacillation in decision making brought out the tension and conflict within him. On the one hand there was his affection for Keshub and a confidence in everything he did, on the other there was his own dislike of rapid changes and his responsibility to those he had drawn into the Samaj. It was impossible for him to please both, so he too was forced to take sides.

To try to clarify the issues, Keshub was at the same time involved in founding the Pratinidhi Sabha (Representative Assembly). The foundation meeting was held on 30th October 1864, with Debendranath as President and Keshub as Secretary. Debendranath was less enthusiastic than Keshub as he saw no real need for a representative assembly. Apart from endorsing liberal ideas about the desirability of some form of democracy, Keshub had a more crucial purpose in establishing the Pratinidhi Sabha. He was aware of the hostility that some members of the Samaj felt towards him because of his actions and his favoured position.

The Sabha included representatives from all the branch Samajes, and when they met Keshub had an opportunity to canvass for their commitment. He was confident of their support, as most branches had been founded either by him or by other missionaries under his auspices. At the same time Keshub had also founded a Bengali fort-nightly paper, the Dharmatattva, to circulate his views amongst a wider audience.

Debendranath made the next provocative move. On 5 October 1864 there was a violent cyclone in Calcutta which destroyed the Brahmo building, so services had to be held in Debendranath's house.[45] One Wednesday[46], before the two new Upacharyas had arrived, he rein-stated the old Brahmin Upacharyas. The service com-menced early to avoid any opportunity for protest. Al-though Keshub sat through the service, most of his followers were dissuaded from entering the house by the persuasion of Bijoy Krishna Goswami, who stood at the door.[47] Debendranath's action precipitated the secession of Keshub and his followers—the bulk of the Samaj—from the original body.

Debendranath justified his actions by saying,

> For the sake of the hesitant and the pusillanimous, let us refrain from laying down severe tests for ministry or membership. Let not the go-aheads petulantly break away from the lag-behinds, in a haughty spirit of impatience. Let them do their best to keep together, so that the conservatives, who are slow of movement, may pick up speed from the progressives. Otherwise, there is always the risk that those who are lagging behind today will lag behind forever.[48]

The 'go-aheads' were unimpressed by this appeal. They felt that Debendranath had acted autocratically in not consulting them. Consequently they began to hold their own separate services, although Keshub was still trying to bring about a reconciliation. Debendranath, how-ever, did not seem to envisage reunion as a very strong possibility. He had charge of the Samaj property and affairs, and he dismissed the Managing Committee and its Secretary, Keshub, and appointed a new one favourable to his ideas. Debendranath's son, Dwijendranath, was appointed to replace Keshub as Secretary, and Ayodhyanath Pakrashi replaced Protap Chunder Mozoomdar as Assistant Secretary.[49]    Keshub's party met in January 1865, and decided that they would relinquish the administration of the trust property to the elders, and retain for themselves only the missionary operations.

The situation in the Brahmo Samaj had suddenly developed into a serious crisis, with Keshub and Debendranath taking antagonistic and hostile positions. After giving much thought to the problems facing the Brahmo Samaj they both decided that their duty lay with their followers, and that that responsibility was more important to them than their own relationship which had, on its own, been able to accommodate different points of view.    Their friendship almost disintegrated at the height of the crisis—Debendranath told Keshub to make his own arrangements for services[50], and Keshub accused him of behaving in an autocratic fashion and violating the rules of the Samaj.

This open disagreement made it impossible to continue their former close relationship, even though they never lost the respect they had for each other.[51] Keshub expressed his esteem of Debendranath publicly in an article on 'Theism in India' in the *Indian Mirror* in 1865 :—

> They mistake and wrong him who failing to discover in him some of the characteristics which they expected, and which great reformers have prominently exhibited, refuse to accord to him the tribute of gratitude and admiration. They do him grave injustice who for some deficiencies and faults in his character refuse to recognise that latent and inherent greatness of his soul to which the whole country is immensely indebted. Of anything like the original genius of a revolutionary reformer he does not boast, to that lofty title he makes no pretensions. Yet he has excellencies which the world has yet to appreciate and admire, excellencies for which India at least will ever cherish his name with profound gratitude. Imperfection he had—and what man has not ?—but

that he is commissioned by God to fulfil an important mission in the history of his country does not in our opinion admit of the slightest doubt; and for this he has laboured with singleness of purpose and indomitable firmness truly characteristic of great minds. That mission is, so far as we can understand it, *the worship of God as a living reality, in spirit and love...*[52]

It is this which formed the strong common ground between them and was the basis for their friendship—and it was probably recognition of this that led Max Müller to claim that there was no ideological difference between Keshub and Debendranath, only a practical one.[53] His estimate overlooked the differences that did exist between them. What united them was not so much a doctrine as the intense religious and emotional force of their perception and worship of God. The differences are easily pointed out. Debendranath endorsed the values of Hindu society, with some modifications, whereas Keshub was an active champion of social reform, engaged in combatting caste, women's seclusion and ignorance, and the oppression of widows. Keshub was drawn to and heavily influenced by Christianity, yet Debendranath saw Christianity, along with idolatry and Vedantism, as the three dangers from which the Brahmo faith must be protected.[54] Within Hinduism, Keshub was attracted to Vaishnavism and the spirit of *bhakti*—which Debendranath eschewed as being sentimental. The list of differences could go much further, but the point has been made. What they actually agreed on was the intuitive perception of one God to be loved and worshipped. This was not for them merely an agreement on a factual statement, but entailed a bond at a much deeper emotional level, which was of central importance to their relationship. In addition, initially their relationship was also mutually beneficial. Debendranath had finally found a man worthy of succeeding him. Keshub, a newcomer to the Samaj, was grateful for Debendranath's patronage and kindness, which greatly facilitated his rise to positions of responsibility and power. Still, even in Keshub's tribute to Debendranath quoted above, there was a sense of Debendranath's being a historical figure, a man who had been important in the past but was no longer so vital in the present. Keshub assessed Debendranath's position in the history of the Brahmo Samaj as the leader of one phase in it, implying that his phase was past and that Keshub was the leader of the new reformist phase. Even though Debendranath had encouraged Keshub in this role earlier it is possible that he felt hurt when he realized that Keshub had become so confident of his own abilities. Therefore when Debendranath was forced into taking a position in opposition to Keshub, the many differences between them that he had overlooked in the past seemed to be highlighted, overwhelming their former shared outlook.

The conflict within the Brahmo Samaj was not primarily a struggle between two personalities, but between two opposing factions. These could be broadly divided in terms of generation, although the 'younger' group included the Derozian Shib Chunder Deb, and the 'elder' group included Debendranath's sons. Basically the division was between the followers of Keshub, who favoured social progress and reform, and the followers of Debendranath, who wanted to retain their ties with Hindu society. Most of the 'conservative' group were men who had joined the Brahmo Samaj in the 1840s, at which time taking the Brahmo covenant was a much more isolated and radical action than it later became. They were part of the educated elite of the day, and so lent their support to the cause of social reform and improvement, but few exerted much vigour or initiative in that direction themselves. Having found a faith that satisfied their advanced requirements, they were content with their mode of life. The 'progressive' Brahmos, led by Keshub, heralded a new wave of social indignation and concern. The emphasis in this was on works and activity, partly as a result of Keshub's own tremendously energetic nature, and partly from his observation of missionary concerns, which showed that social reform was an indispensable part of religious reform. The conflict and later split in the Brahmo Samaj did not reflect a similar cleavage in the rest of society at the time, as the main reform activity in Bengal, outside the Brahmo Samaj, was being carried out almost single-handedly by Vidyasagar.

One of the major implications of the reform controversy was the need to define the position of the Brahmo Samaj with regard to the rest of society. The 'conservative' Brahmos, and also Debendranath, had already made the changes that they thought necessary, and were not prepared to stray any further from the bounds of Hindu society. They must have had at least a vestige of the feeling expressed by one educated Hindu of the period about his contemporaries :—

> In his eyes it is less a dereliction of duty to conform occasionally to the absurd social customs and usages of Hindu society (for many of them are undoubtedly absurd and pernicious) than to tear asunder ties which bind him to all that is noblest, holiest, and sweetest upon earth—his parents, his wife and his children—the angels and cherubs, real, tangible, and substantial.[55]

Keshub and the younger Brahmos felt strongly that one of the functions of the Samaj was to change society, not merely to stand apart and tolerate the differences. Theirs was a missionary attitude, where they saw themselves as bringing light to the darkness, and replacing idolatry and superstition with the 'true' notion of God which was destined to change people's whole attitude to life. The Brahmo movement was a movement of dissent, and such conflicts and schisms have often appeared within dissenting movements.[56] There is always a tension between those who make the break with orthodoxy originally and those who want to go further.

Though the Brahmo Samaj is the focal point of this discussion, it would be misleading to assume that its internal conflicts were the dominant issue in society. Many other groups were also active, though not in the field of religious and social reform. The British Indian Association, various journals, and those involved in local government affairs were beginning to arouse a political consciousness among the middle-classes, and met with much less resistance to their ideas than Keshub did in the more deeply entrenched sphere of religion.   Some educated Hindus felt that by remaining within their own community, they were in a better position to bring about change.   They could drop certain obnoxious rules, their families would connive at this, until gradually such breaches of orthodoxy became widely accepted.[57]

Keshub himself felt that the conflicts within the Brahmo Samaj had some bearing on the rest of society. He gave a public lecture on 'Struggles for Religious Independence and Progress in the Brahmo Samaj' on 23rd July 1865.[58]   The lecture lasted for three hours, and in it Keshub enumerated the high-handed dealings of the Samaj authorities, and the inability of the younger party to introduce constitutional control over Samaj affairs successfully.   In the lecture Keshub appeared as a champion of freedom and liberty against the forces of reaction, and gained many adherents to the 'progressive' cause.   It was after hearing this lecture that the reformer Sasipada Banerji gave up his sacred thread.[59]

The final details of secession were settled in a very formal and civilized manner.   Keshub and his followers sent representation to Debendranath in July 1865, requesting that no Brahmo ministers wear distinguishing caste marks.[60]   If consent was not given to this, then they asked permission to hold their services on a separate day.   The reply they received refused such compromises. Debendranath said that he could not deny to the loyal supporters of the Brahmo Samaj privileges that had previously been taken for granted, and that there was one day of prayer for all.   The choice open to the protesters was thus either to rejoin the Samaj on Debendranath's terms, or to leave it altogether.

Debendranath felt that the latter solution would be acceptable, because the formation of another Samaj meant wider worship of God.[61]   Throughout this controversy, although there were many attempts at compromise and reconciliation, it was never suggested that a

split should be avoided to preserve the stature of the
Samaj in society and present a united front. Both leaders,
in deciding to part ways, must have thought that their
respective groups were strong enough to withstand the
schism. They had different personal motives, too, in
accepting a schism—Keshub wanted organizational
strength, while Debendranath looked forward to the
opportunity for a meditative life.

In a final assessment Keshub lost less in the schism
than Debendranath did. He lost a good friend, but he
gained much greater scope and freedom to go ahead
with his own plans for the Samaj. A tract published
in July 1865, 'An Appeal to Young India'[62], bears wit-
ness to this. In it he gave the clearest outline to date
of his social reform priorities, and also stressed again
the need for co-operation on a national scale. He said
that the root of all evils in Hindu society was idolatry,
then came caste, thirdly marriage customs and fourthly
the *Zenana*. The earnestness and directness of Keshub's
style was emotionally powerful:—

> I offer no new theme for discussion or criticism,
> but a few simple well-known truths for action. If
> a few earnest souls at least be ready to do their
> duty fearlessly and conscientiously, they will natu-
> rally co-operate with each other with cordial
> brotherly love, and may thus form eventually a
> powerful national reform alliance. Thus as indivi-
> duals unite, may families co-work, may communities
> be formed, may Young Bengal and Young Bombay,
> Young Madras and Young Punjab combine; and may
> the circle gradually widen itself till it brings the
> whole nation within its embrace! Then truth shall
> shine throughout the length and breadth of India
> and harmony reign among its vast population![63]

Keshub's career and ambition were not hampered by
the split, but stimulated and advanced by greater freedom. He was in no way a driving force in bringing
about the schism, but once the situation seemed inevitable, he soon took advantage of the positive side of it.
Although he made no claim on other Samaj property,
he did take over the *Indian Mirror*. He even took the

list of subscribers, thus handicapping Debendranath's
chances of starting again. He also retained control of
the Calcutta College.

After the split Debendranath virtually retired from
public life for a second time. He left the administration of the Samaj to his sons. The most commited
personality in it seemed to be his close friend Rajnarain Bose, and although Debendranath shared much
more, ideologically, with Rajnarain than with Keshub,
the relationship did not give him the same satisfaction.
Debendranath was left broken-hearted and shattered by
the loss of Keshub's friendship.[64]    The immense trust
and confidence he had had in Keshub, the hopes he had
placed in him, had all been failed and disappointed.
Debendranath never entirely reconciled himself to the
rupture of their relationship. Even as he looked back
on it in later years, the tremendous love he felt for
Keshub was not abated, as the following passages so
movingly show : —

> That handsome face is still a living reality in my
> heart. If in my mind there lives the image of any
> man, it is his image. His whole form, from the
> peculiar manner in which he dresses his hair to the
> bright nails on his feet, at this moment, even as I
> write this letter, appear in my mind like living
> realities. If for anyone I have shed the tears of
> love, it is for him...[65]
> When I had him near, I considered myself the
> master of all the wealth which the kings of the
> world could command. When I sat up with him,
> often till one or two in the morning, conversing
> with my departed friend, I never perceived how
> the time passed. The union between our souls is
> never to be destroyed.[68]

After the split, Debendranath's branch became
known as the Adi Brahmo Samaj, and Keshub's later
became the Brahmo Samaj of India. As they still
shared the Brahmo name, it is clear that they were still
looked on as two branches of the same organization, although they were administratively separate. Over the
years immediately following the schism there was some
communication between the two branches. Keshub and

his followers still sometimes went to hear Debendranath's services, and he was invited to preach at theirs.

In retrospect the schism seems inevitable. Differences
between the old and the new groups began to
show up from the time Keshub started to make his
voice heard, as his main concerns were religious and
social reform, both strongly influenced by the West.
The differences were somewhat obscured at the time by
the close friendship of Debendranath and Keshub, which
seemed to be a harmonious combination of two very
different personalities, each representing a different outlook. Despite their deeper unity, given the disparities
that did exist between them, even though they were not
voiced, it would have been unlikely that their relationship could have run entirely smoothly for an indefinite
period. This is only to say that the potential for conflict
already existed in their relationship. It was not them,
but their followers, who broke up this 'marriage of oppo-
sites'. Debendranath's followers did so because they resented his neglecting them in favour of a newcomer whose
views were anathema to them, and because they wanted
to remain a part of Hindu society ; Keshub's did so because they wanted to get on with the work he had inspired them to do and not be held back by conservative
forces. Keshub and Debendranath, on their own, just
may have been able to weather their differences, had
they not been forced into taking sides with their followers,
who were not bound by any of the ties that held the
two of them together. It was the inability of these two
groups to work harmoniously together that forced their
leaders into opposite and hostile camps, thus relinquish-
ing a deep personal relationship which had been very
dear to both of them.

### NOTES AND REFERENCES

1. This translation, from P. S. Basu, op. cit., pp. 57-58, is a good
   rendering of the original Bengali prayers, printed in J. K.
   Koar, *Maharshi Devendranath and Brahmananda Keshub
   Chandra : Two Documents Reprinted* (Calcutta, 1935). The
   translation given by Koar in this pamphlet is not very accurate.

2.  S. Sastri, *History* op. cit. Vol. I, pp. 138-139.

3.  P. S. Basu, op. cit. p. 57.

4.  P. K. Sen, *Biography* op. cit. Vol. I, p. 281.

5.  P. S. Basu, op. cit. p. 60.

6.  P. C. Mozoomdar, *Life* op. cit. p. 93.

7.  loc. cit.

8.  Quoted in P. C. Mozoomdar, *Life* op. cit. p. 88.

9.  P. C. Mozoomdar, *The Faith and Progress of the Brahmo Samaj* second ed. (Calcutta, 1934), p. 123.

0.  B. C. Pal, *Saint Bijaykrishna Goswami,* new ed. (Calcutta, 1964), pp. 17-18.

1.  S. C. Mitra, *Life of Pandit Iswar Chandra Vidyasagar* (Calcutta, 1902), p. 218.

2.  S. Sastri, *History* op. cit. Vol. I, p. 145.

3.  S. Sastri, *History* op. cit. Vol. II, (first ed. 1912) pp. 548-550.

4.  P. S. Basu, op. cit. p. 78 gives the only detailed account of this tour.

5.  S. Sastri, *History* op. cit. Vol. I, p. 150.

6.  P. C. Mozoomdar, *Life* op. cit. pp. 97-98. When Keshub joined the Samaj in 1857 the Colutolah *pandit* had to write out the declaration for him because his Bengali was not good enough to do so himself. G. G. Roy, op. cit. Vol. I, p. 61.

7.  P. C. Mozoomdar, 'A Passing Sketch of Keshub Chunder Sen', The *Liberal and New Dispensation,* 17 August 1884. Reprinted from the *Christian Register.*

8.  F. B. Bradley-Birt, op. cit. p. 155.

9.  S. Natarajan, *A Century of Social Reform in India* (Bombay, 1962) p. 53.

0.  He must have been referring to Debendranath's and Keshub's visit to Ceylon, as there is no mention elsewhere of Debendranath having visited South India.

1.  *The Proceedings and Transactions of the Bethune Society,* 1859-69 (Calcutta, 1870).

2.  C. H. Heimsath, *Indian Nationalism and Hindu Social Reform* (Princeton, 1964), p. 105.

3.  S. Sastri, *History* op. cit. Vol. II, p. 550. This was reconstituted as the Southern India Brahmo Samaj in 1871.

4.  C. H. Heimsath, op. cit. p. 109.

5.  Ibid. p. 108.

6.  Ibid. p. 109.

7.  The British Indian Association was theoretically an India-wide organization, with similar associations existing in Madras and Bombay, but in practice it was only active in Bengal.

8.  R. C. Majumdar, *British Paramountcy and the Indian Renaissance* (Bombay, 1965) part II, pp. 468-469 and A. Seal, *The Emergence of Indian Nationalism* (Cambridge, 1971) p. 249.

9.  Bethune Society, op. cit. pp. lxix-lxxi.

0.  P. C. Mozoomdar, *Faith* op. cit. pp. 99-100 and P. S. Basu, op. cit. p. 74. None of this 'elder' group is mentioned by name.

31. P. S. Basu, op. cit. p. 60. Lecture given at the Bhowanipur Brahmo Samaj.

32. N. S. Bose, op. cit. p. 226.

33. S. Sastri, *History* op. cit. Vol. I, p. 167.

34. From a collection of Debendranath's letters, *Patravali*, edited by Priyana Sastri, some of which are quoted in P. K. Sen, *Biography* op. cit. Vol. I, pp. 210-214.

35. P. S. Basu, op. cit. pp. 473-476.

36. P. C. Mozoomdar, *Life* op. cit. p. 100.

37. P. S. Basu, op. cit. p. 78.

38. P. K. Sen, *Biography* op. cit. Vol. I, p. 214.

39. S. Sastri, *History* op. cit. Vol. I, p. 143.

40. See P. S. Basu, op. cit. p. 80 for a description of the format of a Sabha meeting—although that described is perhaps atypical because conducted in English in deference to the many Europeans present.

41. S. Sastri, *History* op. cit. Vol. I, p. 152.

42. P. K. Sen, *Biography* op. cit. Vol. I, p. 212.

43. K. Mitra, op. cit. pp. 114-115.

44. S. Sastri, *History* op. cit. Vol. I, p. 153.

45. J. N. Farquhar, *Modern Religious Movements in India* (London, 1924) p. 43.

46. Wednesday was the day of worship in Debendranath's Brahmo Samaj.

47. S. Sastri, *History* op. cit. Vol. I, p. 155.

48. P. K. Sen, *Biography* op. cit. Vol. I, p. 347.

49. S. Sastri, *History* op. cit. Vol. I, p. 156.

50. P. C. Mozoomdar, *Life* op. cit. p. 105. Debendranath later relented and offered the younger Brahmos the use of the pulpit once a month, but they refused. S. Sastri, *History* op. cit. Vol. I, p. 160.

51. For an idea of the continuing closeness of their relationship see the letters written to each other during this period of conflict in the Appendix of D. Tagore, op. cit. pp. 22-34.

52. Keshub Chunder Sen, *The Brahmo Somaj: Discourses and Writings* (Calcutta, 1904), pp. 78-79. The underlined part was italicized in the original.

53. F. M. Müller, *Chips from a German Workshop,* new ed. (London, 1895) Vol. II, p. 63.

54. P. K. Sen, *Biography* op. cit. Vol. I, p. 191.

55. H. C. Banerjee, *Brahmo Theism in India* (Calcutta, 1869), p. 61.

56. W. S. Smith, *The London Heretics* 1870-1914 (London, 1967) is a study of dissenting movements in England in that period. In a discussion on the Theosophists under Besant he wrote

> As with every other heretical organization of the time the conservative forces ("Back to Blavatsky") and the liberal pressures of adjustment could not avoid open warfare. As with other movements, too, the nature of the cleavage was largely determined by personalities ..... (p. 162).

57. H. C. Banerjee, op. cit. pp. 58-59.

58. There is no text of this lecture available, but an account of it is given both in S. Sastri, *History* op. cit. Vol. I, p. 168 and in P. K. Sen, *Biography* op. cit. Vol. I, pp. 301-302.

59. Albion Banerji, *An Indian Pathfinder*, new ed. (Calcutta, 1971) p. 60.

60. S. Sastri, *History* op. cit. Vol. I, p. 168. The letter was signed by Keshub, Umanath Gupta, Mohendranath Bose, Jadunath Chakravarty, Nibaran Chandra Mukherji and P. C. Mozoomdar.

61. G. S. Leonard, op. cit. p. 126. This book was commissioned by the Adi Brahmo Samaj, so is generally accurate with regard to Debendranath, but is heavily biased against Keshub.

62. P. S. Basu, op. cit. pp. 81-84.

63. P. S. Basu, op. cit. p. 84.

64. P. C. Mozoomdar, *Faith* op. cit. p. 117.

65. From a letter from Debendranath to P. C. Mozoomdar in August 1881, reprinted in the *Sunday Mirror* 11 September 1881.

66. P. K. Sen, *Biography* op. cit. Vol. I, p. 301—a statement made by Debendranath to some friends after Keshub's death in 1884.

# CHAPTER FOUR

# A PERIOD OF CONSOLIDATION AND EXPANSION (1866-1869)

HAVING FINALLY separated from Debendranath Tagore in 1865, Keshub Chunder Sen was then ostensibly free to pursue his own course of development without restraint from any superior. This feeling of greater freedom was initially mingled with a sense of loss and uncertainty. Suddenly all his props had been removed, and Keshub, at the age of 28, had to stand alone as the leader of a group that had a reputation to maintain as progressive in its religious and social thinking. After the schism Keshub actually missed Debendranath's guidance. He had been a stable anchor, a source of constant support in the past. Keshub retired to his ancestral garden home in Calcutta to think in solitude, to sort out his new position, and to work out how best to cope with and use this newly won independence. Although Keshub had been very prominent in the Brahmo Samaj for the past five years, and although his rise to power was outstandingly rapid, he was not fully prepared to take over from Debendranath the position of the leader of the Samaj, an organization he himself had helped to make India-wide. Keshub's followers had been instrumental in causing the separation, but they now looked to him to point the direction in which they should channel their energy. There is no indication that his leadership was challenged or questioned, or that anyone other than he had any ideas on what shape the group was going to take. All seemed to subside into silence, while Keshub came to grips with the extent of his influence and responsibility, and the scope ahead for him to exercise that influence.

The first sign that Keshub was developing a new line of thought, and a very controversial one at that, came with his public lecture on 'Jesus Christ: Europe

and Asia' on 5 May 1866.[1]    This lecture is of major
significance, partly because it was an outline of Keshub's
preoccupations at the time, and partly because many
people based their estimate of Keshub on this lecture
for a long time to come.

The lecture was given at that particular time as a
direct response to a lecture by a Scottish merchant,
Mr R. Scott Moncrief, which had dwelt contemptuously
on the low character of the Indian people.    Keshub
took the opportunity to correct that view, and also to
point a moral to the so-called Christian community. He
was also influenced by currents of contemporary thought
in Europe, where there was a new interest in the personality and humanity of Christ rather than his divinity[2]
—a line of approach which was obviously much more
congenial to non-Christian Theists like Keshub.  He was
especially impressed by J. R. Seeley's *Ecce Homo*[3],
published in England towards the end of 1865.    *Ecce
Homo* was about the importance of Christ's moral
teaching in the history of civilization, and reinforced
the esteem Keshub already had for Christ and Christian
ethics: this bias towards morality was congenial to
nineteenth century thinkers in both England and Anglicized India as it measured up to their values of utility
and    improvement.[4]    It was    also    less    contentious
than a spiritual interpretation, and provided a much
broader basis for unity and exchange of ideas.  Apart
from these outside influences the lecture was the result
of long pondering over the subject in the author's mind,
not merely a response to immediate circumstances.

Keshub declared at the outset that he was going to
trace  "the gradual and steady progress of this grand
movement[5], and its influence on the character and desti-
nies of the European and Asiatic nations",   and show
how

> ..........under an overruling Providence,  it has
> brought the Asiatic and the European races together,
> and made the East and the West kiss each other in
> fraternal sympathy: how it has linked the best re-
> presentatives of the two continents in India, and
> come to affect our interests at this distance of time

and place. I shall compare the national character
of the two nations in relation to the high standards
of Christian ethics, and point out their respective
defects and shortcomings, which prevent their harmonious union and counteract the spirit of true
Christianity. I shall show the absolute necessity
which exists for a proper appreciation of Christ's
precepts by the Natives and Europeans in the present critical state of India, and impress upon you
those fundamental precepts, the observance of which
the present age seems specially to demand. In
addressing you on this momentous theme, I cannot,
however, forget that I am a Brahmo. I will not
dissemble my convictions, which differ, as you are
aware, from the orthodox opinions of popular
Christianity. Whatever differences, however, there
may be on strictly theological questions, I must say
I am no hater of Christianity—much less of Jesus
Christ. I cherish the profoundest reverence for the
character of Jesus, and the lofty ideal of moral
truth which he taught and lived........[6].

On a political level, Keshub gave a clear statement
of his position :—

While, through missionary agency, our country has
thus been connected with the enlightened nations
of the West, politically, an All-wise and All-merci-
ful Providence has entrusted its interests to the
hands of a Christian sovereign. In this significant
event worldly men can see nothing but an ordinary
political phenomenon, but those of you who can
discern the finger of Providence in individual and
national history will doubtless see here His wise and
merciful interposition. (Hear, hear)........[7].

Keshub went on to say how grateful India should be
for British rule, and that Indians should freely give
their loyalty to Queen Victoria. This belief aroused
no opposition, being the current position of most educated Indians at that time. His glowing devotion to
the British Queen and British rule, publicly expressed,
though not uncommon, endeared him further to the
British community and officials. It increased his influence with them too, as having unmistakably established his loyalty, he could then go on to criticize the
British without being accused of ingratitude.

Keshub first set out the history of Christianity—its trials and reforms—showing a remarkable acquaintance with biblical and ecclesiastical history. He then went on to the history of the church in India.[8] He praised the missionaries, and then proceeded to his main practical moral point of the evening—the relations between the British and the Indians. He acknowledged the low ebb of these relations (without mentioning Scott Moncrief by name) and discussed the common stereotypes each race had of the other—the Englishman typifying the Indian as a fox, the Indian typifying the Englishman as a wolf. He gave due attention to the unjustness of these, but acknowledged the misunderstandings which may have given rise to these stereotypes. He seemed to criticize both races equally, but his point was fairly plainly directed more towards the British, who were supposedly Christians:—

> I regard every European settler in India as a missionary of Christ, and I have a right to demand that he should always remember and act up to his high responsibilities. (Applause.) But alas! owing to the reckless conduct of a number of pseudo-Christians, Christianity has failed to produce any wholesome moral influence on my countrymen. (Hear, hear—"They are nominal Christians.") Yea, their muscular Christianity has led many a Native to identify the religion of Jesus with the power and privilege of inflicting blows and kicks with impunity! (Deafening cheers) ........[9].

During this lengthy lecture there were at least 70 points when the audience interjected with an appreciative response, ranging from laughter to deafening applause—a response which corroborates the frequent assertion, made by almost everyone who wrote about him, that Keshub was a great orator. The audience was largely drawn from the educated middle-classes, but also included many Europeans, most of them missionaries, probably attracted by the title. Keshub's chosen subject matter obviously struck a sympathetic cord. It fulfilled a placating, healing function whereby both Indians and Englishmen could affirm their as-

sent to the necessity for brotherliness and mutual regard. Keshub set himself above the racial discord he
described by addressing his audience as 'brethren', in
the manner of a Christian preacher.

The most significant and controversial point of the
evening, however, was Keshub's presentation of his
notion of the Asiatic Christ. This was not totally un-
heard of[10], but it had been largely forgotten until it
seemed that Christianity, like so many other new ideas
and inventions, belonged solely to the West. Keshub,
having already proclaimed his loyalty to Britain in no
uncertain terms, used the notion of an Oriental Christ
in an avowedly nationalistic way, designed to foster
national pride and self-esteem : —

> I rejoice, yea, I am proud, that I am an Asiatic.
> And was not Jesus Christ an Asiatic ? (Deafening
> applause.) Yes, and his disciples were Asiatics,
> and all the agencies primarily employed for the
> propagation of the Gospel were Asiatic. In fact,
> Christianity was founded and developed by Asia-
> tics, and in Asia. When I reflect on this, my love
> for Jesus becomes a hundredfold intensified; I feel
> him nearer my heart, and deeper in my national
> sympathies.[11]

His concept of nationalism was unusual in that it was
not narrowly confined. He saw beyond a merely Indian
Christ to an Asiatic one, and he identified himself as an
Asiatic. This represented a new awareness. Historically,
Indians had never considered themselves part of Asia.
When they talked of East and West it was usually India
and England that they were referring to. Keshub
himself, although he too showed little interest in, or
familiarity with, the rest of Asia, wished to make the
point that Christianity was not the exclusive property
of Europe, nor of India alone.

Although the audience seemed to like it, this lecture
was afterwards attacked from all sides, and had many
repercussions. The missionaries were tremendously excited by it, believing that it showed Keshub to be on
the verge of conversion to Christianity. Most of them
had none of his breadth of mind, and despite what Keshub

had said, they could not separate the personality of
Christ from the body of the Christian church. Debendranath and the Adi Brahmo Samaj found their suspicions
justified and confirmed—Keshub had no interest in the
reform of Hinduism, he was more concerned with the
spread of the Christian spirit.    Debendranath's view
of Jesus was that he was a dangerous 'finite God'.    A
third group, including many prominent English officials,
were highly impressed with Keshub from that time on.
These included the Viceroy himself,    Lord Lawrence,
who read the lecture and desired to make Keshub's
acquaintance—the beginning of a friendship which was
kept up until the death of the former in 1879.

Even though it was highly unlikely that Keshub
entertained any ideas of giving up the movement to
which he had contributed so much, and in which he
had such a prominent position, to become a humble
Christian convert, there were still some grounds for
the excitement of the missionaries. Here was a man
who personally had a deep feeling for Christ,  to the
extent that for a while after he called himself 'Jesu-
das'.[12]   In a personal letter to his close follower Protap
Chunder Mozoomdar, on 18 May 1866, Keshub intimated
that he would only preach Jesus Christ when he and
the country were ready for it, implying that he had
not said his all on the subject :—

> I have my own ideas about Christ, but I am not
> bound to give them out in due form, until altered
> circumstances of the country gradually develop
> them out of my mind. Jesus is identical with self-
> sacrifice, and as he lived and preached in the fulness
> of time, so must he be in turn preached in the ful-
> ness of time.  The more is sacrifice needed in India,
> and the more it is made, the more will Jesus find
> a home in this land.    I am, therefore, patiently
> waiting that I may grow with the age and the
> nation, and the spirit of Christ's sacrifice may grow
> therewith.[13]

Keshub was obviously open to the Christian spirit,
although he did not agree in detail with much of its
dogma.  The missionaries also found it hard to grasp

that, even apart from his rejection of certain fundamental tenents of Christianity, it was his independence,
and, despite his Anglicism, his sense of national pride,
that would always have prevented him from embracing
Christianity as a religion.    Keshub was, in fact, engaged in a tremendous effort to apply Christianity to
India and thereby create a new synthesis, and he was
using the Brahmo Samaj as the means for this.    This
was the first intimation of his future plans after he had
left Debendranath.

Keshub was well aware of the hopes and fears
aroused by his May lecture on Christ, and it was to
clarify his position that he delivered his next public
lecture at the Town Hall, on 28 September 1866 on
'Great Men'.[14]    This was addressed to much the same
audience as before.    There is little direct continuity
of thought with the previous lecture.    Keshub was
probably alarmed at the zeal with which the Christians
had got on to his trail, and felt that that part of his
theology should be cooled for the time being.    He had
also said that India was not yet ripe for Christ's teachings.

The substance of his lecture on 'Great Men' was to
explain that God revealed himself to man in three
ways—through nature, through history, and through
the soul.    Keshub's main interest was in the revelation
of God in history, which, he believed, was through the
lives of certain great men.    God existed in every man
to a degree, but in some chosen people he exhibited a
larger measure of the divine spirit.    His definition of
the Great Man was thus:—

> Great men are sent by God into the world to bene-
> fit mankind.    They are His apostles and missiona-
> ries, who bring to us glad tidings from heaven ; and
> in order that they may effectually accomplish their
> errand, they are endowed by Him with requisite
> power and talents.    They are created with a nature
> superior to that of others, which is at once the testi-
> monial of their apostleship and the guarantee of
> their success.    They are not made great by culture
> or experience : they are born great.    They succeed,

not because of any ability acquired through personal exertions, nor of any favourable combination of
outward circumstances, but by reason of their inherent greatness. It is God's light that makes them
shine, and enables them to illumine the world. He
puts in their very constitution something super-
human and divine; hence their greatness and superiority. They are great on account of the large
measure of divine spirit which they possess and
manifest. It is true they are men; but who will
deny that they are above ordinary humanity?
Though human, they are divine......[15].

Another definition he gave of great men seemed to
tally closely with the role he saw as his own, although
he did not specifically put himself forward as a great
man. His theory was that great men appear when
they are needed, and so are seldom born in ordinary
times.

Their lot is always cast in troublous days; for they
have to combat established errors and prejudices,
to revolutionize popular tastes and ideas. They
mark the transition state of society, the turning-point
in the career of nations. The preceding age ends and a
new epoch commences in them. In the established
economy of Providence they are special dispensations,
to meet the pressing wants of humanity....[16].

This description fitted his own role and his own era
very aptly. The idea expressed here was that it was
the task of the great man to fight against the ignorance
of the unregenerate masses, but elsewhere in this lecture he claimed that great men were also representative men, rulers and heroes:—

In him the people recognize their truest representative, and they spontaneously and trustfully throw
themselves on his guidance.[17]

The confusion apparent in presenting these conflicting
views reflected a basic uncertainty in Keshub himself,
wavering between a desire for public acclaim and
honour, and his firm commitment to religious and social
reform which alienated him from the rest of society.
Either position would have been possible for him, but

they were not compatible with each other. He had t
choose.

His lecture did not have the placating or clarifyin
effect he had aimed for, even though he had tried t
engage the sympathies of all sections of his audienc
by mentioning as great men Luther, John Knox, an
Chaitanya. Most people drew the inference that Keshu
had delineated an ideal type which was most perfectl
suited to himself. He was charged with setting him
self up as a great man, and people were on the lookou
for any further manifestations of his egoism to substan
tiate their charge. The Christian missionaries felt es
pecially bitter. They had hoped for further affirmatior
of Christ, but instead, although Keshub had acknow
ledged Jesus as 'the Prince of Prophets', his point wa
that the chain of prophets preceding and following hin
must be given due reverence. Having had their hope
dashed, the missionaries unfairly accused Keshub o
recanting, and taunted him with being scared of com
mitment to Christ because of the unpopularity it hac
caused him.[18] Adi Brahmos, like Rajnarain Bose, fel
the whole doctrine of great men was permeated with
*avatarism,* one of the doctrines they had broken away
from in Hinduism, and that it was also a distraction
from the main purpose of worship, which was the glorification of God.[19] The Christians were most frustrated
because Keshub was still hovering around the edge of
their doctrine by acknowledging Jesus Christ as a mani-
festation of God in history, but remaining beyond the
pale in not admitting that he was a unique revelation.[20]

The controversy stimulated by this lecture, supposedly a clarification of his ideas, was not congenial
to Keshub. Functioning more on an emotional than an
intellectual level, he did not welcome debate, expecting
an appreciative response. His personality seemed to
lean more to the representative man type, rather than
the lone battler which he was committed to being. The
controversy on this occasion made such an adverse impression on him that he decided rather conveniently,
that in future he would not even attempt to explain,

because of the impossibility of preventing further mis-understanding.[21] Keshub was by nature an autocrat, appreciating discussion only when it did not involve disagreement. He wanted the impossible—universal appreciation in a sharply polarized situation.

The range of ideas contained in these two lectures represented Keshub's basic doctrinal and practical position. His mission as he conceived it was to fight error and prejudice and to illumine the world with God's light. The response to the lectures showed the range of alternatives that he was pitting himself against. It was a situation which was almost conducive to delusions of grandeur, as the opposing forces were formidable. The main bastion was orthodox Hinduism—which now also found support from Keshub's one-time allies in the Adi Brahmo Samaj. Then there were the Christians, always aggressively on their guard against corruption of their doctrines, critical rather than understanding. There were some who diverged from this view, including the more enlightened missionaries and others like Max Müller, as they considered it a self-defeating attitude which overlooked a golden opportunity to respond to signs of an appreciation of Christianity.[22]     Another group, which Keshub railed against in 'Great Men', were those who had given themselves up to Materialism and Positivism. Numerically this group would have been small (although Keshub mentioned that Positivism counted its followers by the hundreds) but it did have a strong appeal to the same Western-educated group that Keshub was trying to reach. The attractions of Positivism were widely discussed in a series of letters between S. Lobb, Principal of Krishnagar College, and Grish Chunder Ghose, in 1867 :—

> I am glad to know that Positivism is gaining some attention in India, as I feel certain the system is thoroughly well adapted to satisfy the intellectual needs of a very large class. Brahmoism is very well but unstable, and if I may coin a word unnational. What is required is a system which can be grafted upon Hinduism, which Hindus can make their own and which by espousing they will not be obliged

to sacrifice any of their national customs or traditions—in a word a system which is national.... [23].

You are I think quite right in the view you take of
Positivism. It affords men who are emancipated from
the old beliefs a resting place and does not demand
that any violent innovation should be made in the
belief of the people—the change will come about
gradually, and in the meantime those who believe
they have a firm footing can do their utmost to
render it still more secure.[24]

The force of all this opposition made Keshub realize
that Brahmoism, to be effective, had to reach out actively
to people, as he was pressing something new which
required conviction and commitment, not just con-
venient acquiescence.

The first important requirement was an organization, so that Brahmoism would not present itself merely
as an abstract faith but as a community of fellow believers. With this object in mind, a meeting of the Pratinidhi Sabha was called, which resulted in the establishment of the Brahmo Samaj of India on 11 November
1866. A series of resolutions were passed, which formed
the basis of the new policy[25]—that believers of both
sexes were to be admitted as Brahmos and that the
purity and universality of Brahmoism were to be preserved. Mottos agreeing with Brahmic principles were
to be printed and published from texts of all nations.[26]
This was immediately embodied in the Slokasangraha,
a collection of scriptural texts from all major religions
which was to replace the Brahmo Dharma as the main
liturgical text. Gour Govinda Roy composed a motto in
Sanskrit, which graced the cover of the Slokasangraha
and of the Samaj's Bengali paper, the Dharmatattva.[27]
The new movement was suffused with a spirit of catholicism and eclecticism. There were no restrictive
membership requirements in the matter of sex, caste
or race. The very name of the Samaj showed its affi-
liation with all Indians as one nation. It aspired to
being a national religion, not a localized movement—
but its sources of inspiration went beyond even national
boundaries to embrace the main scriptures of the world.

The new church was based on the idea of harmony and respect for all religions. The *Slokasangraha* still included many Hindu texts, but the aim was to acknowledge that these were not the only true scriptures.

As no human being could be the real head of the church, God was formally declared to hold that position. Keshub was Secretary, and Protap Chunder Mozoomdar the Assistant Secretary.[28] Keshub was elected: no provision, however, was made for any future election of office bearers, challengers being neither envisaged or desired.

One of the reasons Keshub had parted with Debendranath was because of his autocratic rule, where Samaj members were not consulted in decision making. His real reason seemed more likely to be that he was chafing under Debendranath's authority and desirous of exercising his own, rather than objecting on principle, as the new Samaj was not founded on a constitutional basis either. Though all resolutions were passed by a vote, there was no obligation on Keshub to consult all members of the Samaj before making a decision on the running of Samaj affairs.

Keshub's acknowledged position as the leader of the Brahmos and as a progressive pioneer in society was evident in his role of guide to the strong-willed Unitarian, Mary Carpenter, on her first visit to Calcutta. She was most impressed by his "candour, spirituality and religious feeling".[29] Being a publicly active woman in the Victorian era, the cause which interested her most was that of female education and enlightenment. She was not disappointed in Keshub's achievements in that field. She attended a women's service conducted by Keshub, and, losing no opportunity to add to his zeal, invited these ladies, and what was most controversial, their husbands as well, to tea at the house of a Dr Chuckerbutty. Keshub endorsed the scheme by agreeing to send the invitations out himself. The evening proved very enjoyable (at least it was for Mary Carpenter) and also marked the passing of another social milestone, reflecting great credit on Keshub for his sponsorship of the event. It was, for him, a logical progression from the time when he was turned out of home for taking his wife to festivities at Debendranath's in 1861. The evening showed that Keshub's courageous spirit had influenced many others, who were willing to attend despite the social obloquy they knew this would, and did, provoke.

Miss Carpenter was by no means an uncritical observer. She soon saw the limits of charity in Calcutta, and concluded that the benefits of Western education had done little to help anyone beyond the middle-classes. She pointed out the need for improvement in prison conditions, for a school for low-caste boys, and for a Female Normal School. Fired by her enthusiasm a group of educated Bengalis, including Keshub, petitioned the Lieutenant-Governor with the object of setting up a Female Normal School in Calcutta. Both Keshub and Vidyasagar were on the Committee for deciding the matter, on which they held opposing views—but Vidyasagar withdrew his name in anger because of Keshub's autocratic disregard of his opinion, and his offhand dismissal of the regular channels when he found them standing in his way. Because the committee was taking time deliberating, Keshub and a following of Brahmos had sent a separate petition to the Government calling for the opening of a school.[30]

This remarkable woman seems to have goaded everyone into action. Reverend Long heard from her of the British Social Science Association, a philanthropic welfare body, and wanted to form a Bengali branch. He called a meeting to form a Provisional Committee for establishing such an Association. Long himself, Keshub, and other such notables as Justices Norman, Phear, and Seton-Kerr, and Peary Chand Mitra, Monomohan Ghose, Debendranath Tagore, Rajendralal Mitra and Vidyasagar were members,[31] although neither Long nor Keshub were on the committee of the Bengal Social Science Association when it was founded as an autonomous organization on 22 January 1867. The Association served to focus the attention of the elite on the most pressing

ocial problems of the day.    An instance of this was
when Koylash Chunder Bose read a paper on 'The
laims of the Poor'.    In response Keshub made a
speech in which he remarked sharply that his countrymen had a large proportion of camphor in their consti-
ution, for their zeal in a good cause evaporated in a
wonderfully short time.   Grish Chunder Ghose rounded
ff the topic with a 'stirring appeal to the rich on be-
alf of the poor'.[32]

Keshub was never a mere theoretician, but made a
enuine effort to live according to his beliefs. He con-
nued to foster the religious and social development of
ie Brahmikas. His daughter went to the Bethune
irls' school, and his wife was not confined to the
znana. An example of Keshub's overall thoroughness
a reform was recounted in an anecdote by his eldest
aughter, Sunity Devi:—

> One of our customs is for young girls to make vows
> as they worship before symbolic figures made of
> flour, or painted on the ground. "May I have a good
> husband," prays one. "May I be rich," sighs her
> worldly-minded sister ... My vows, ordered by my
> father, were planned on different lines, and usually
> excited pity or amusement. I promised to give
> money to the poor, never to tell a lie, to feed animals
> and birds, and to give people cool beverages during
> the hot weather.[33]

To part of the vows expressed went against the Hindu
radition, but the fact that she was made to say them,
ather than the customary romantic vows, set this apart
s a very conscious and earnest attempt to uphold and
istil moral principles in the face of indifference.
Keshub also re-opened the Calcutta Brahmo School, on
lternate Sundays, "to explain in a popular style the
heology and Ethics of Brahma Dharma".[34]

The social reform aspect of Brahmoism appealed to
large number of the educated middle-classes who
would not have been as keen on religion alone. A great
many reformers rallied around Keshub at this time, the
most noteworthy being Mr Sasipada Banerji. His main
reoccupation was the improvement of the condition of

women, especially widows.  His history indicates th
dilemma of the Brahmo social reformer.  To embrac
Brahmoism seemed a natural decision for one who ha
given up orthodox Hinduism and had little confidenc
in contemporary Hindu society, but taking this step a
most retarded the cause of reform.  Banerji seems t
have been persecuted more for his Brahmoism than fc
what he did in the name of it, at least initially, bu
with great courage he managed to continue his wor
by ignoring the orthodox opposition.  He was disinher
ted of his share in the joint family property, and o
one occasion he and his wife were stoned by cast
Hindus.[35]  He started a girls' school in 1865, but all th
pupils left when he became a Brahmo.  He took u
zenana teaching, but had to give it up when he wa
forced to leave home because of his Brahmoism.[36]  H
also organized widow-marriages, but the opposition t
this was so strong that often the poor women involve
had to be abducted and remarried in secret.  Eigh
widow remarriages took place under the auspices of th
Brahmo Samaj between 1864 and 1869.

The Brahmo Samaj of India would not have gon
far if it had depended for support on those who ha
devoted their lives to the cause of social reform alon
Keshub needed to help the new Samaj find its bearing
in the religious field.  He was aware of growing dis
content and restlessness among some of his follower:
Having gained their independence, they felt lonely an
uncertain of their aims and purposes, and perhaps als
felt excluded from Keshub's absorption in the semi-alie
Christianity.  They gave vent to their feelings in dis
agreement with each other.  It was up to Keshub t
unify them and recreate a sense of community. Socia
reform activity did not satisfy their emotional need:
Keshub's answer was to arouse enthusiasm and lov
amongst his followers by devotional methods.  He trie
to make the Samaj lively and attractive,  as well a
deeply spiritual.  His instrument in effecting th
change was the introduction of Vaishnava devotiona
methods.

Keshub regularized the use of *sankirtan,* a traditional Vaishnava way of worship, and introduced the basic and simple Vaishnava musical instruments of the *Khole, Karatal* and *ektara.* Although a Vaishnava by birth, Keshub had formerly despised these, sharing the upper-caste attitude of regarding them as rowdy and degenerate. His recognition and acceptance of them marked a change in his own attitude, an opening up to popular, vital sources within his own tradition. He was urged along this path by Bijoy Krishna Goswami, a former Vaishnava *guru,* and Trailokyanath Sanyal, a devotional singer who had joined the Samaj in 1867. Keshub was also shrewd enough to realize the publicity value of these new modes. Not only would they revitalize the flagging morale of current members of the Samaj, but they would popularize Brahmoism among the lower castes.[37] Not many of these people ever formally joined the Brahmo Samaj, but Keshub felt that they would be enlightened and improved by such contact with Brahmoism, and that they would be more sympathetic with its principles. Keshub also instituted daily prayers around September 1867[38], another way of increasing the cohesiveness and communal sense of his followers. They prayed with a new fervour : —

> From being regarded as a dreary duty, as an occasional impulse, prayer was explained and felt to be a deep, abiding, intense necessity, such as could be only wrung out from the deep-seated wants of a sinful penitent heart.[39]

The culmination of this overwhelming intensity was another of Keshub's innovations. He decided to organize an all-day *Brahmotsav,* or devotional festival, on 24 November 1867. This allowed for a complete release of pent-up emotion. It lasted from six in the morning to ten at night, and included repeated services, *sankirtan,* sermons, expositions of texts, and intervals of silent meditation. Hundreds of people were involved.[40] Keshub relaxed visibly in this atmosphere : —

> He loudly sang, a thing which his natural shyness had never permitted him to do before; he had

never been seen to weep, but streams of tears ran
down his handsome face......[41]

Keshub himself said that he had been given the title of
*Brahmananda* before he was really ready for it.[42]

To enhance the sense of unity and communion a
comfortably familiar touch was that Debendranath conducted the evening service.[43] This was a measure of
his deep feeling for Keshub, as Debendranath himself
disliked the emotionalism of *bhakti,* and was not a
populist in religion. He preferred quiet contemplation
in the hills to the colour and noise of a *sankirtan.* This
self-indulgent outpouring of emotion distracted attention from the more earnest and serious reforming
mission of the Samaj, but Keshub was well aware of
the psychological need for such a diversion. His own
reactions showed that he was not merely being mani-
pulative, but himself felt these outpourings of *bhakti*
as a welcome relief from his usual position of heavy
responsibility. It afforded a release from the inner
tension he underwent in trying to reconcile such different and seemingly opposed traditions reflected in his
personality—from the sophistication of a Westernized
English orator to the simplicity of a Bengali Vaishnava.

On achieving independence from Debendranath,
Keshub was able to give full attention to the Mission
Department of the Brahmo Samaj, the only part of the
old organization he was left with. In 1866 there were
54 branches of the Brahmo Samaj, most of which sided
with Keshub in the split. By 1870 there were 80
branches[44], the increase due entirely to the zeal of
Keshub and his missionaries. The original band were,
besides Keshub, Bijoy Krishna Goswami, Umanath
Gupta, Mahendranath Bose, Annada Prasad Chatterjee,
Jadunath Chakravarty and Aghorenath Gupta.[45]

Their first independent mission tour was of East
Bengal, in October 1865. Keshub, accompanied by Bijoy
Krishna Goswami and Aghorenath Gupta, visited Farid-
pur, Mymensingh and Dacca, stopping in Dacca for about a
month to give sermons and lectures and conduct divine
service. Keshub's main lectures were in English, but

he also gave some extempore lectures in Bengali, the first time he had done so.[46]  It was on this tour that he wrote the tract *True Faith*[47], setting out what was to be required of the missionaries.  He used an archaic, stern, biblical style, giving concise injunctions on moral principles.  In this he propounded such cardinal doctrines as that on 'Resignation': —

> It taketh no thought for the morrow and deemeth it scepticism to lay up provisions for the future.[48]

and on 'Wisdom': —

> Faith is true wisdom, which is noble and divine. It loathes prudence, which is earthly and mean. Prudence is the arithmetic of fools.[49]

These 'warnings' of austerity were not uncalled for on this tour.  Keshub and his band were treated as outcastes.  They had no cook, no fixed residence, and were generally regarded with disdain.  Undeterred, Bijoy Krishna Goswami, Aghorenath Gupta and Jadunath Chakravarty stationed themselves in East Bengal, with Barisal as their centre, while Keshub returned to maintain the central organization in Calcutta.

In December 1866 Keshub and four missionaries set out on a tour of Upper India.  Their route included Krishnagar, Bhagalpur, Patna, Allahabad, Cawnpore and finally Lahore.  They willingly underwent great hardship, with little money, poor food, and light clothing which could not withstand the cold chills of the North-West.  They stayed in Lahore for a month, and then went on to Amritsar and Delhi, from whence they returned, via Monghyr, in April 1867.[50]

The third major tour was in 1868.  Leaving Calcutta in February, Keshub and Trailokyanath Sanyal made their first stop at Santipur, the home of Vaishnavism.  Here Keshub gave a talk on *bhakti* and Chaitanya, which ensured him of an enthusiastic reception by the Vaishnava leaders, who declared him to be the reviver of their religion.  They went on via Bhagalpur, Monghyr, Patna, Allahabad and Jubbulpore to Bombay, where Keshub joined in celebrations marking the first

anniversary of the Prarthana Samaj. They spent a
fortnight in Bombay before returning to Monghyr to
collect Keshub's family.[51]

These tours seem impressive merely for the sheer
amount of territory that they covered, but they were
much more than mere geographical feats. Their main
purpose was to spread Brahmoism as a national religion. In 1866 there were also 37 periodicals to supple-
ment this aim.[52]    Brahmoism as a national religion
may have seemed like an impossible dream, but it is
remarkable how much success Keshub did have in
spreading the influence of the Brahmo Samaj in India,
especially in Bengal.

Keshub's lectures were intended mainly for an
English-educated middle-class audience. On his tour of
East Bengal, only four out of 25 public lectures were
in Bengali, and the remainder were in English.[53]    At
Monghyr in 1868 he gave divine service more than once
each day, with separate services in English and Bengali.
The Bengali service would have appealed to those who
were less educated and not so familiar with English,
with an added possibility of indicating an awareness of
the new patriotism and defence of vernacular languages.
English was useful outside Bengal as it was the only
means of reaching across local linguistic barriers. The
use of English also made it easier for Keshub to keep
his British contacts informed of the success of his
mission. Speeches made by him in Bombay were reported in the London Daily Telegraph.[54]

In the rural towns of Bengal, Keshub's core audience
was made up of government servants and professional
men, who were always eager for intellectual stimulation and guidance from Calcutta, and many school students, idealistic youths going through a crisis of faith,
"balanced between orthodox idolatry and absolute unbelief".[55]    Mary Carpenter noted that the most socially
progressive sector of the townsfolk was the Brahmos,
as for instance in Utterparrah,   where Brahmos were
responsible for the Benevolent Institution,   the girls'
school and an outstanding library.[56]   The number of

practising Brahmos was usually small, although there was often a large group of sympathizers who attended services and talks and contributed to Samaj funds, as in Dacca.[57]

Keshub's audience outside Bengal would have included some of the local middle-class, but the main support was from Bengalis. Because of the shortage of suitable employment, Bengali graduates went all over India in search of jobs, taking their religious interests with them. (It was said of Brajasundar Mitra, Brahmo deputy-magistrate, that wherever he went on official duty he founded a school and a Brahmo Samaj.[58]). In 1872 the Brahmo Samaj had a branch in Gaya, at which the members were all Bengalis. In Cuttack, however, the younger branch run by the Brahmo Samaj of India, although led by Bengalis, attempted to reach local people by holding services and printing a monthly paper in Oriya.[59] Bengalis also monopolized government positions in the North-West provinces, and formed a large part of Keshub's audience on his tours there.

As one of the main areas of employment of Brahmos in rural districts was teaching, and one of the major fields of benevolent activity was the founding of schools, students were naturally one group that were very affected by the new ideas. In his official reports W. W. Hunter stated that "every Kayath boy attending the Government College becomes a member of this new sect".[60]

Bipin Chandra Pal, whose home was at Sylhet in Assam, vaguely recollected hearing a lecture on Rammohun Roy given by the Brahmo missionary Gour Govinda Roy, although it made very little impact on him. His main source of information on Brahmoism at the time was his school-friend Sitanath Datta (later Pandit Sitanath Tattvabhushan). Sitanath, who had a cousin in Calcutta, Sreenath Datta, who was actually a covenanted member of the Samaj, became "a centre of Brahmo propaganda" at the Sylhet Government School.[61] Sitanath himself recalled that his interest in the Brahmo

Samaj was reinforced by coming into contact with Keshub and hearing him preach in Dacca in 1869. He wrote : —

> The *Bhakti* movement was then going on and Keshub's advent simply set the Dacca Somaj on fire. The Somaj services of those days were quite unlike the quiet and placid things they have become in these days. They were then full of sobs, cries and rapturous singing of hymns. I caught the frenzy in my boyish way and indulged every day in a flood of tears the meaning of which I could not always understand. My stay at Dacca was very short and Keshub's visit lasted only a few days. But those few days made a lasting impression on me. I heard from his own lips the story of his early life and the missionary zeal which characterised it...[62]

Where it was possible, the initial enthusiasm was reinforced by the activity of a resident missionary. (In the case of Dacca this was Banga Chandra Ray.)

This kind of fervour erupted sensationally for the first time at Monghyr, in Bihar, on Keshub's return from Bombay in March 1868. Keshub's audience at Monghyr consisted largely of a number of semi-educated Bengali clerks who worked for the East India Company Railway there. They were men whose faith had been shaken, and were thus open to new ideas, but they were only semi-Westernized and therefore less inhibited and closer to popular Hindu beliefs than most Brahmos. Keshub realized that Brahmoism usually only appealed to the educated, but his social consciousness and religious zeal, as well as his devotional affinities with the less educated, prevented him from ignoring them altogether.[63]

Vaishnava methods, especially the *nagar sankirtan* (street processions), had been used very effectively already on the laying of the foundation stone of the Brahmo *Mandir* on the 38th anniversary of the Brahmo Samaj. This brought Brahmoism to a wider range of people, and facilitated their participation. Similar methods were used in the three momentous *Brahmotsavs* at Monghyr, on 19 April, 23 May and 7 June.[64] These produced a huge welter of emotions, often bordering on hysteria. People fell into fits of unconsciousness, and some saw visions. Some threw up their jobs and left home to sing and dance kirtan in the streets.[65] Not surprisingly, this outburst of emotion found a suitable outlet in expressions of love and devotion for fellow-worshippers. Keshub, who by his presence and oratory had worked them up to such a pitch—not entirely unknowingly, as being a good orator involved being a good manipulator of crowd responses—found himself the chief object of their devotional feelings. Their closeness to traditional Hindu religious thought immediately led them to see him as a holy man, an *avatar*, talking of him as Lord, Master and Saviour, and prostrating themselves before him. Their cultural confusion is strikingly evident in that some of them connected him with Jesus, as the younger son of the Father.[66] The revival itself reflected a mixture of ideas—Vaishnava expressions of devotion were engendered by an Evangelical conviction of sin, repentance and salvation through God's grace.

Most educated people were alarmed, and singled Keshub out for blame. They traced his ego-mania back to 'Great Men'. Keshub had aroused their indignation by passively accepting all forms of devotion and not forbidding them. His possible reasons for doing so were varied. According to Rajnarain, he justified his actions by saying, "I don't want to stop the flow of *bhakti*".[67] This seemed understandable, although it did ingenuously ignore the fact that he had himself created that flow. It is probable that he did not realize, however, how intense the flow of *bhakti* could become, and as he was not himself detached from the excitement, he too got carried away and was not able to exercise much control over the situation. It was also true that he did have an egocentric personality, desirous of recognition and appreciation. The kind of recognition he got normally was because of his position as the leader of the Brahmo Samaj, and must have seemed mundane and unsatisfying compared with the extreme adulation he received from those whose lives were less governed by rationality than the educated classes. He might not have intended to produce such a reaction, but he must unconsciously have been pleased with it, as he took steps to explain and justify it rather than to stop it. There were also more rational and 'respectable' reasons for his being pleased with the Monghyr campaign. It popularized the Brahmo Samaj of India, and many were publicly initiated into the Samaj as a result. It heightened Keshub's awareness of the value of popular tradition, as well as demonstrating forcibly to him the reverence accorded to the figure of the *guru* in Hinduism, an attitude which gratified his sense of his own importance.

Debendranath had grown away from Keshub to the extent that he reluctantly but fully believed that Keshub was making unjustifiable claims for himself. He expressed this opinion to Rajnarain Bose : —

I can't understand why Keshub aspires to being an *avatar*—in our country even fish are *avatars*, even turtles are *avatars*.[68]

However, there is no evidence that Keshub actually believed that he was an *avatar*. He was too practical and rational ever to consciously arrogate divine honours, and although he may occasionally have unconsciously delighted in playing the exalted roles his devotees provided him with, he did not keep this performance up for long enough for it to be proof that he really believed in his own divinity. He was conscious of himself as an important, singular, person but the word *avatar* was an emotional exaggeration, as it was not even a concept that Keshub believed in.

Many of his followers were highly indignant over the outcome of the Monghyr revival. He had shocked them by his acquiescence in Hindu manifestations of devotion which the Samaj was supposedly fighting against, and by the emotionality and irrationality of the whole campaign. Underneath this they may have also been jealous of his egoism in focusing the whole revival around his own personality, giving little credit to the missionaries who had prepared the ground for him. Two of the missionaries, Bijoy Krishna Goswami, always an activist, and Jadunath Chakravarty, a deist who had strongly objected to the lectures on Jesus Christ and great men, rushed into press with a letter of protest dated 20 October 1868, which was printed in the *Indian Daily News* :—

> We are astonished and grieved to observe that some Brahmas have begun to acknowledge Baboo Keshub Chunder Sen, *as a saviour of men,* commissioned by God....
> Even to divine service they have given an objectionable form. They now offer up their prayers to God, through Keshub Baboo....
> This sort of proceeding on the part of certain Brahmas has given a shock to almost all Brahma Samajes, as has been brought to notice during a tour in the Mofussil, and many are jumping to the conclusion that Keshub Baboo is propagating his own worship and not that of God. But we would advise them to wait till we hear anything from him for or against this practice.
> In conclusion, we beg of our Brahma brethren, who have thus begun to worship Keshub Baboo, to think what they are about; what a dangerous doctrine they are preaching to the world, a doctrine which has been the cause of all bitterness and antipathy between religious sects, and which has ultimately led men to pseudo-divine honours. We also beg of Keshub Baboo to direct his efforts to put a stop to the above practice, and disabuse the public mind that is prejudiced against him.[69]

Keshub's dislike of explanations was fully evident in the letter he sent from Monghyr as a private reply to the two missionaries :—

> Dear Vijaykrishna and Jadunath,
>
> Truth will prevail; don't be anxious about that; God will Himself take care of His beneficent kingdom of heaven. I only beseech you, let not the present agitation deviate your heart from unswerving devotion to the feet of the Merciful. From a long time you are bound to my heart; may nothing harm you—this is my earnest desire. For a good many years I have served you; speak and act as you think best in defiance of me, but see that you do not forget my Merciful Father. He knows what I have to say

regarding the present happenings. I live on the faith
that He will preserve His Truth. May my heart
enjoy peace at His feet and in His sweet name.

Keshav Chandra Sen[7]

In this reply Keshub had absolved himself of all need
for explanation by taking refuge in the notion of God's
'Providence'. Keshub put his accusers in the difficult
position of having to level their charges against God
as he disclaimed responsibility for his own actions. It
is hard to tell whether Keshub actually believed this,
or whether he was using it as a sure way of getting
out of an uncomfortable situation without damaging his
prestige. He also turned the case against the missionaries by implying that it was they who were deluded and
had become godless, and he was magnanimously concerned for their well-being. His letter bordered on
emotional blackmail as he reminded them of how he
had served them in the past, although it is understandable that Keshub was genuinely hurt by the attacks of
his missionaries, supposedly his closest sympathizers.

To quell the rising opposition and to avert serious
disruption within the Samaj, a public-spirited Brahmo,
Thakur Das Sen, sent an open letter to Keshub asking
for some clarification of his position. The tone of
Keshub's reply (which Thakur Das Sen printed as a
pamphlet entitled The Refutation of the Arguments of
the Opponents of Bhakti) was hurt and indignant, but
it did provide an explanation of his actions which was
satisfactory to most.

> Those to whom I have opened my whole mind and
> heart have tried to make me guilty before the public
> of the most frightful and soul-rending charges.
> I have been charged with trying to destroy loving
> prayerfulness unto God, the only Saviour, a principle
> which has been the object and faith of all my life.
> Very near friends now charge me as proud and hypo-
> critical, the robber of God's supremacy, the propa-
> gator of my own worship. I have no wish to defend
> my character. It is enough that I am guiltless before
> God...[71]

He stated unequivocally that man-worship was against
Brahmo Dharma, and then went on,

I have never approved of the manner in which some
of my friends honour me.  Because in the first place
I am not worthy of such honours...In the second
place external honours are, in my judgment, unnecessary and improper.  Real love and honour lie
in the heart, and if their outward expressions dec-
rease, there is not much harm.  While on the other
hand too much expression may do mischief to weak-
minded men ; I have repeatedly expressed my hesita-
tion to receive such honours.  But I have no right
to interfere with the freedom of others.  It has
ever been against my taste and conviction to bring
men to do what I like by command or entreaty.[72]

Although Keshub had given no guarantee that he would
discontinue these *bhakti* revivals, his reply stating his
disapproval of man-worship satisfactorily established
his innocence of those charges against him.[73]    Bijoy
Krishna Goswami and Jadunath Chakravarty retracted
their accusations—although the latter did not return to
the missionary fold.  Another missionary, Annada
Prasad Chatterjee, and some other young Brahmos also
left the Samaj, their reason being that they could not
accept Keshub as anything *less* than an *avatar*. Obviously
it was impossible to satisfy everybody.   The controversy ended there, and in fact Monghyr over time became a hallowed memory to later generations of
Brahmos.[74]

The kind of dual role Keshub assumed was exaggerated when he left Monghyr between the first and
third festivals to meet with the Viceroy, Lord Lawrence,
at Patna.   Keshub advised him of the need for a
Marriage Bill to legalize Brahmo marriages that were
not, he had found, considered legal by the law as it
was then defined.  As Keshub had been one of the fore-
most supporters of inter-caste marriages, widow
marriages and marriages according to Brahmo rites, he
felt a strong responsibility for this matter.

Not being entirely unmindful of democratic proce-
dures, Keshub returned to Calcutta in July 1868 and
called a general meeting of Brahmos to get up a petition
urging the need for legalization of Brahmo marriages.
He took the petition back with him to Simla, the sum-

mer seat of the government, in August. Keshub must
have made a very favourable impression on the Viceroy,
as he went to Simla, along with his family, as his invited
guests. They stayed at a government guest house, and
Lord Lawrence sent Keshub a 'present' of 500 rupees to
cover expenses.[75] His time was spent divided between
prayer and meditation inspired by the Himalayas, and
discussion with various officials in the Viceroy's Council about the proposed Bill. He may have won some
over by sheer force of personality—he made himself
known by giving lectures on 'The Rise and Growth of
the Brahmo Samaj' and 'The Prodigal Son', which were
very well received. J. C. Oman was present at one of
these lectures, and described Keshub's style as characterized by "showy eloquence and emotional fervour".[76]
It was a tribute to Keshub's flexibility that he could
so successfully pitch the level of his approach, from a
religious revival at Monghyr to the 'little England'
that was Simla—and it also showed the kind of pressures he must have been subject to in having to made
these adjustments, although on the surface he certainly
did not even appear to perceive any incongruity in his
position.

The Marriage Bill was introduced into Council by
the Legal Member, Sir Henry Maine, on 10 September
1868. His opinion was that the creed of the Brahmos
lacked stability, and that it was difficult to define a
Brahmo—and therefore a Civil Marriage Bill would be
more widely acceptable.[77]   A commission was set up
to consider this, and Keshub let the matter rest there
until such time came for a renewal of debate. In his
anniversary address for 1869 on 'The Future Church'
Keshub gave a grand summary of his beliefs, and of his
aims for the Brahmo Samaj.[78] He reiterated the cardinal doctrine of universality—the Fatherhood of God
and the Brotherhood of Man—and emphasized the residue of truth and purity that existed in each and every
religious system. Then he outlined his special plan for
India : —

But the future church of India must be thoroughly
national ; it must be an essentially Indian Church.

The future religion of the world I have described will be the common religion of all nations, but in each nation it will have an indigenous growth, and assume a distinctive and peculiar character...[79]

Keshub was firm in seeing India as a united whole, and he saw the idea of Brahmoism, or a universal but national faith, as being the basis for identity.[80]

The new Brahmo *Mandir* was opened on 22 August 1869. The Trust Deed for this was similar to that of Rammohun Roy, but with some interesting differences. Topically, it put an official ban against man-worship:—

> ..No man, or inferior being, or material object shall be worshipped here, as identical with God, or like unto God, or as an incarnation of God ; and no prayer or hymn shall be offered or chanted unto, or in the name of, any except God. No carved or painted image, no external symbol which has been or may hereafter be used by any sect for the purpose of worship, or the remembrance of a particular event, shall be preserved here...[81]

The new declaration expressed open and egalitarian sentiments, giving due respect to all creeds and scriptures, and ensuring the right to worship of men and women of all castes and races. The declaration was issued first in Bengali, then in English and Urdu. Divine services in the new *mandir* were to be in Bengali, but the principle of universality was being upheld in the form and content of the service. It was also reflected in the architecture of the new *mandir*, which combined the Gothic windows and spire of Europe with the shape of a Hindu temple and the dome of a mosque. The opening of the *mandir* was marked by the public initiation of 21 young men, including Ananda Mohan Bose, Sivanath Sastri, and Keshub's younger brother, Krishna Behari Sen.[82] What was most outstanding was the initiation of two women—Svarnaprabha, the wife of Ananda Mohan Bose, and the nine-year old wife of Krishna Behari Sen, Jadumohini.[83] Sastri gave up his sacred thread on this occasion as he felt it would be hypocritical for him to retain it.

The period 1866-1869 was thus one of great hope

and enthusiasm in the Brahmo Samaj of India. Owing
to the activity of Keshub and his missionaries, the
Samaj had gained numerous converts. Towards the end
of 1869 Keshub went to Dacca to consecrate the new
*mandir* there, and at the same time initiated 36 young
men. In May of the same year he had a telegram from
Mangalore asking him to go down and initiate 5,000
members of the low Billawa caste, who were ready to
become Brahmos.[84] Both the zealous efforts of the
official missionaries, and the enthusiasm of Brahmo
converts on service outside Calcutta spread Brahmoism
throughout the rural areas of Bengal and the major
towns all over India. There were 37 new Samajes
founded between 1867 and 1870.[85] By that date there
were 10 missionaries, including Keshub.[86]

Progress had been great, reforms seemed to be
gathering momentum, but the opposition had by no
means been destroyed. The forces of social persecution
were most powerful in rural areas where Brahmos were
an isolated group. There were many instances of vic-
timization. When Bijoy Krishna Goswami preached
at Santipur, he was caught and smeared with treacle,
and wasps were set on him.[87] In Harinabhi, Umesh
Chandra Datta was grabbed and thrown into a thorny
bush while he was praying.[88] Brahmo meeting places
were set fire to in a number of places, including Mymensingh[89] and Chittagong.[90] A more intellectual approach
was that of the orthodox Hindu community of Dacca,
who started a parallel organization and newspaper,
the Hindu Dharma Rakshini Sabha and the
*Hindu Hitaishini,* to attack Brahmoism and defend
Hinduism.[91] The tension was greater in the rural
towns than in Calcutta because Hindu society in the
former was more stable and conservative and the new
ideas of Brahmoism therefore seemed more threatening.
Excommunication from the family and caste group was
used as a weapon against conversion. For instance, in
Mymensingh and Barisal, the orthodox Hindus organized a systematic boycott of Brahmos—cooks, washer-
men, barbers, servants, boatmen all refused to make

their services available.[92]  This was only an effective
weapon, however, in the smaller Brahmo communities
which could provide little support or security for the
individual thus outcasted.   It was less effective in
larger, self-sufficient communities,  where the result
was often to increase solidarity and determination within the group.  Those who had taken Brahmo principles
no longer believed in caste values anyway.   Sitanath
Tattvabhushan resisted all opportunities presented to
him to re-enter his caste.[93]  Brahmoism in rural areas
was not self-generating,  but depended on stimulation
from Keshub and Calcutta, so the social tensions were
not permanent.   In weaker areas the Brahmo movement often disbanded after the founder had been posted
elsewhere.[94]

In Calcutta the Brahmo Samaj had become an
accepted institution, with an estimated membership of
between 5,000 and 6,000 people.[95]   Keshub was thus a
very prominent personality in society.  The two main
sources of Keshub's inspiration, and that of the new
Brahmo Samaj of India, had been established.  These
were a great reverence towards the personality of
Christ on the one hand, and the *bhakti* doctrine of
Vaishnavism on the other.   Keshub had defined the
areas that he drew on when he envisaged a new, universal religion.  It was not so much universal as an
attempt to synthesize and harmonize Hinduism and
Christianity,  using particular parts of each to make
his possible, but not without much tension and conflict
is well.  In the years immediately following the split
there was a heady sense of freedom, as Keshub had full
opportunity to develop and play out his remarkable
visions of a new religion which would shape society not
only in India, but throughout the world.  Being fairly
satisfied with his achievements in India over these
years, Keshub felt the need of wider fields to reach
out to.   As well as this, although he had successfully
weathered the man-worship controversy, he may have
felt a need to escape the pressures of his position in
India by leaving for a time.  In the *Indian Mirror* of

13 August 1869 Keshub announced, to the surprise of even his closest friends, his intention of visiting England the following year.[96]

## NOTES AND REFERENCES

1. Keshub Chunder Sen, *Lectures* (1954) op. cit. pp. 1-36.

2. Strauss's *Leben Jesu* (1835), E. Renan's *Vie de Jesu* (1863) and J.R. Seeley's *Ecce Homo* (1865). For a full account of the development of this school of thought see Owen Chadwick, *The Victorian Church* (2 vols, Oxford, 1970), Part II, pp. 60-75.

3. P. C. Mozoomdar, *Life* op. cit. p. 115. *Ecce Homo* was lent to Keshub by Dr George Smith, editor of the *Friend of India*.

4. Anon. *Credentials of Conscience* (London, 1868) gave this and other reasons for the popularity of *Ecce Homo*.

5. Keshub was referring to Christianity.

6. Keshub Chunder Sen, *Lectures* (1954) op. cit. pp. 1-2.

7. Keshub Chunder Sen, *Lectures* (1954) op. cit. p. 15.

8. ibid. p. 13. There were 154,000 native converts, 32 Missionary Societies, and 519 foreign missionaries. £ 250,000 was spent on missions annually.

9. Keshub Chunder Sen, *Lectures* (1954) op. cit. p. 24.

10. Monier Williams, *Religious Thought and Life in India* (London, 1883), Part I, p. 483 gave an anecdote about Rammohun Roy. It is said that when he was shown a picture of Christ he remarked that the artist had falsely given him a European countenance, forgetting that he was an Oriental.

11. Keshub Chunder Sen, *Lectures* (1954) op. cit. pp. 25-26.

12. M. C. Parekh, *Brahmarshi Keshub Chunder Sen* (Rajkot, 1926) p. 31.

13. Quoted in P. C. Mozoomdar, *Life* op. cit. pp. 114-115.

14. Keshub Chunder Sen, *Lectures* (1954) op. cit. pp. 37-73.

15. Keshub Chunder Sen, *Lectures* (1954) op. cit. pp. 46-47.

16. ibid. p. 51.

17. ibid. p. 53.

18. P. C. Mozoomdar, *Life* op. cit. p. 116.

19. Rajnarain Bose : —"I am sick of the excessive glorification of great men. Brahmo brethren ! let us cease altogether for a time from glorifying great men. Let us now only glorify the great God to our heart's content....". Quoted in P. K. Sen, *Biography* op. cit. Vol. I, pp. 344-345.

20. F. Lillingston, *The Brahmo Samaj and Arya Samaj in their bearing upon Christianity* (London, 1901).

21. P. C. Mozoomdar, *Life* op. cit. p. 116.

22. T. E. Slater, *Keshab Chandra Sen and the Brahma Samaj* (Madras, 1884), p. 64 and M. Muller, *Chips* op. cit. (London, 1875), Vol. IV, pp. 273-275.

23. M. N. Ghose, *The Life of Grish Chunder Ghose* (Calcutta, 1911) p. 230. Letter dated 24 September 1867.

24. ibid. p. 231. Letter dated 29 September 1867.

25. G. S. Leonard, op. cit. p. 135.

26. Rajnarain Bose was very disapproving of this. He wrote in *Brahmic Questions of the Day answered by an old Brahmo* that there was absolutely no need to quote from the scriptures of all nations, as there was nothing in them which did not have its counterpart in the *sastras*. Quoted in P. K. Sen, *Biography* op. cit. Vol. I, pp. 342-343.

27. P. K. Sen, op. cit. p. 351. The motto was :—"The wide universe is the temple of God ; Wisdom is the pure land of pilgrimage ; Truth is the everlasting scripture ; Faith is the root of all religion ; Love is the true spiritual culture ; the Destruction of Selfishness is the true asceticism ; So declare the Brahmos".

28. P. C. Mozoomdar, *Life* op. cit. p. 110.

29. Mary Carpenter, *Six Months in India* (London, 1868), p. 169.

30. S. C. Mitra, op. cit. p. 463.

31. For a full list of members see J. Long, *Selected Papers* (Calcutta, 1968), p. iii.

32. M. N. Ghose, op. cit. p. 134.

33. Sunity Devee, op. cit. p. 19.

34. P. S. Basu, op. cit. p. 123. See Keshub Chunder Sen, *Lectures* (1904) op. cit. pp. 206-221 for the lecture delivered by Keshub on this occasion.

35. Albion Banerji, op. cit. pp. 13, 18.

36. S. Natarajan, op. cit. p. 47.

37 By the 1880s Surendranath Banerjea was using the *sankirtan* to attract crowds to political meetings in rural areas. It became an accepted means of political propaganda. S. N. Banerjea, *A Nation in Making* (Madras, 1925), p. 94. Native Christians also used the *sankirtan* as a means of propagating Christianity.

38. P. C. Mozoomdar, *Faith* op. cit. p. 105.

39. ibid. p. 106. This was an extract from his private notebook.

40. P. C. Mozoomdar, *Faith* op. cit. p. 108.

41. P. C. Mozoomdar, *Life* op. cit. p. 122.

42. P. S. Basu, op. cit. p. 454. From the *Jeevan Veda*.

43. S. Sastri, *History* op. cit. Vol. I, p. 221.

44. S. Sastri, *History* op. cit. Vol. I, p. 181. In the second volume of his history Sastri gave a statistical table of the number of Samajes in 1877, with the dates of their foundation. This showed that there were only 43 branches founded on or before 1866, so a number of branches must have closed down altogether between 1866-1877 and were consequently not mentioned in the later statistics. (Vol. II, pp. 548-550).

45. S. Sastri, *History* op. cit. Vol. I, p. 170. In a later volume, N. Niyogi *The Apostles and Missionaries of the Navavidhan* (Calcutta, 1923), the list also includes P. C. Mozoomdar, Amrita Lal Bose and K. Sridharalu Naidu from Madras. It leaves out Bijoy Krishna Goswami, Annada Prasad Chatterji and Jadunath Chakravarty, all of whom later left Keshub.

46. P. S. Basu, op. cit. p. 84.

7

47. ibid. pp. 85-95.

48. P. S. Basu, op. cit. p. 89.

49. ibid. p. 91.

50. ibid. pp. 120-121. For Keshub's comments on this tour see the Bethune Society's *Proceedings and Transactions* (1859-1869) op. cit., pp. cxiii-cwv.

51. P. S. Basu, op. cit. pp. 155-156.

52. S. Sastri, *History* op. cit. Vol. I, p. 181.

53. P. S. Basu, op. cit. pp. 120-121.

54. P. S. Basu, op. cit. p. 155.

55. P. C. Mozoomdar, *Faith* op. cit. p. 122.

56. M. Carpenter, op. cit. pp. 239-248.

57. A. Seal, op. cit. p. 206.

58. P. Sinha, *Nineteenth Century Bengal* (Calcutta, 1965) p. 86.

59. A. Seal, op. cit. p. 207.

60. From W. W. Hunter, *Statistical Account of Bengal,* quoted in A. Seal, ibid. p. 207.

61. B. C. Pal, *Memories of My Life and Times* (two Vols., Calcutta 1932) Vol. I, pp. 136-137.

62. G. C. Banerji, *Keshub as seen by his opponents* (Calcutta, 1930) p. 20.

63. P. C. Mozoomdar, *Faith* op. cit. p. 125. Missionaries had also tried to reach this group, and the Samajes at Bagachra and Amragori were composed almost entirely of 'unlettered men'. This was rare. Even at Monghyr there were only occasional visitors from amongst the 'ignorant people' of the *bazaar.*

64. S. Sastri, *History* op. cit. Vol. I, pp. 226-227.

65. (T. N. Sanyal) *Keshab-charit,* third ed. (Calcutta, 1931) p. 137.

66. P. C. Mozoomdar, *Life* op. cit. p. 124.

67. Translated from Rajnarain Bose, op. cit. p. 127.

68. Translated from Rajnarain Bose, op. cit. p. 127.

69. Extracts from the full text of the letter given in J. C. Oman, *The Brahmins, Theists and Muslims of India* (London, 1907) pp. 122-123.

70. P. S. Basu, op. cit. p. 160.

71. S. Sastri, *History* op. cit. Vol. I, p. 232.

72. This and the previous passage are extracts from portions of the letter quoted in P. C. Mozoomdar, *Life* op. cit. pp. 126-127.

73. An even more unequivocal reply was given to Bijoy Krishna Goswami. Quoted in P. K. Sen, *Biography* op. cit. Vol. II (1954) p. 12.

74. P. K. Sen, op. cit. p. 14. "To the man of true faith, Monghyr has ceased to have a mere local, geographical or temporal significance. It is a name to conjure with, an idea that fills the soul, a landmark of Brahmo history never to be forgotten What the Jordon is to Christendom, the Nairanji to the Buddhist, and Keshub Bharati's Asram to the Vaisnava, that is Monghyr to the Brahmo. It marks a conversion, a fulfilment a transfusion, of *Bhakti* into life." Even so, by 1881 the

Monghyr Brahmo Samaj was practically deserted—see *Theistic Quarterly Review*, January 1881.

75. P. S. Basu, op. cit. p. 158.

76. J. C. Oman, op. cit. p. 118.

77. ibid. p. 119.

78. Keshub Chunder Sen, *Lectures* (1954) op. cit. pp. 99-124. The anniversary lecture for 1868 was on 'Regenerating Faith'.

79. Keshub Chunder Sen, *Lectures* (1954) op. cit. p. 122.

80. He had made a more specific statement on the need for unity in a lecture on 'Religious and Social Reformation' given in Bombay the previous years :— "...I look hopefully forward to the day when all the educated Natives of this country will combine together to show by their actions what enlightenment dozen men in Bombay, a dozen in Madras, and a dozen in the Punjab, and we shall form the nucleus of a general confederation—one caste for all the educated natives of India—and then we shall gradually take in all other classes of the Native communities, and unite in a vast and mighty op. cit. pp. 417-418.

81. P. S. Basu, op. cit. p. 175.

82. P. K. Sen, *Biography* op. cit. Vol. II, pp. 269-270 gives a full list of those initiated.

83. J. C. Bagal, *Keshab* op. cit. p. 44. Evidently Keshub had not yet convinced his family of the desirability of reformed marriages.

84. P. S. Basu, op. cit. p. 174. When the missionaries were finally able to go in response to this call, in 1870, there were only a handful instead of the promised 5,000, but those few formed themselves into a strong branch which was still going in 1940.

85. S. Sastri, *History* op. cit. Vol. II, pp. 548-550.

86. S. N. Dutt, *The Life of Benoyendra Nath Sen* (Calcutta, 1928), p. 193. This represented a net gain of five new missionaries, as two left, for opposite reasons, during the man-worship controversy.

87. A. C. Gupta, *Studies in the Bengal Renaissance* (Bengal, 1958), p. 491 in an essay on the Brahmo Samaj by Jogananda Das.

88. S. D. Collet, 'Indian Theism and its Relation to Christianity', *Contemporary Review*, XIII (1870), p. 239 and A. Gupta, ibid. p. 491.

89. K. Mitra, op. cit. p. 59.

90. *Liberal and New Dispensation*, 4 May 1884.

91. A. Seal, op. cit. p. 207.

92. S. Sastri, *History* op. cit. Vol. II, pp. 351, 369-370.

93. S. Tattvabhushan, *Autobiography* (Calcutta, no date) pp. 47-48.

94. See note 44 on the apparent disappearance of a number of Samajes.

95. S. D. Collet, op. cit. *Contemporary Review*, XIII (1870), p. 238.

96. P. S. Basu, op. cit. p. 177.

# CHAPTER FIVE

# ENGLAND : MARCH-SEPTEMBER, 1870

KESHUB CHUNDER SEN'S visit to England was the apex of his career. It was an immensely bold stroke, one without precedent, for an Indian in 1870 to decide to embark on a lecture tour of Britain to proclaim a new, non-Christian creed. The novelty of his undertaking did not deter Keshub. His self-confidence left no room for doubt on the success of his mission. He would, in fact, have had less reason for misgivings than most of his Indian contemporaries, as he was already known and respected by many prominent personalities in England, mainly Theists like himself. His relations with the British in India, even with his rivals the missionaries, had been on equal terms. Thus he had no cause to expect bad treatment, or even condescension. The activities of the Brahmo Samaj had gained sporadic mentions in many British journals and papers. Many of Keshub's tracts were available from a London book company, and his most important lectures to date were published as a book entitled *The Brahmo Somaj—Lectures and Tracts*.[1]

During his time in England, Keshub met nearly all the notable intellectuals, churchmen, and public leaders of the period. He travelled around the provinces, attracting large audiences at all his numerous public meetings and sermons. In six months he had addressed 36 public meetings and preached 24 sermons, in 14 principal towns. Even allowing for some overlap, the number of people who heard him was over 40,000[2]. Despite murmurs of opposition from some quarters of the church, the visit was undoubtedly a great success. Although Max Müller was exaggerating when he said that Keshub's name was almost a household word in England,[3] through his constant public appearances Keshub had reached and impressed a large sector of the English middle-class, and smaller numbers from the upper and lower classes. Most of the major newspapers and journals, especially those run by religious bodies, covered his visit[4].

What were the reasons for the warmth of this reception ?  The most obvious one, evident from his previous experience in India, was Keshub's own charisma
—his compelling personality and magnificent oratorical
skills.  His looks were arresting, and most descriptions
of him comment on his handsome appearance.  His
daughter remembered him as tall and broad-shouldered,
giving an impression of great strength[5].  Frances Power
Cobbe wrote that

> In his outward man Keshub Chunder Sen was the
> ideal of a great teacher.  He had a tall, manly figure,
> always clothed in a long black robe of some light
> cloth like a French *soutane,* a very handsome square
> face with powerful jaw ; the complexion and eyes
> of a southern Italian ; and all the Eastern gentle
> dignity of manner.[6]

The *Pall Mall Budget* reported that

> His appearance is striking, and has a certain quiet
> dignity, in harmony with the simplicity of his dress
> and the absence of any forced gesticulation.  His
> features are well cut, and combine a certain sweet-
> ness with an expression of marked decision.[7]

Indians were still a comparatively rare sight in England
at that time. People were drawn to hear him out of superficial curiosity as to his appearance and way of speaking, and
they were usually favourably impressed by what they encountered.[8]     Another point singled out for comment
was his perfect command of the English language.  Miss
Cobbe said he had not "a single betrayal of foreign
accent", though the writer in the *Pall Mall Budget* did
notice a slight trace of one, while still acknowledging
that he spoke "with perfect fluency, with complete gra-
mmatical accuracy, and apparently without even the use
of a note". Not only was he completely fluent, but his
use of rhetoric was powerful and stirring.  It was said
that his style was 'Carlylese'.[9]

Another important reason was that that hardly tangible phenomenon, 'the climate of the times', was right
for Keshub's visit.  He must have been aware of this
through his correspondence with his Theistic friends,

but what was remarkable was the way that this intellectual interest had filtered through the whole educated population. The interest displayed came from different sectors of the church and community. It came mainly from the growing influence of the Freethinking movement, the Broad Church movement in the Church of England which found support from some of the Nonconformist churches, and the Evangelicals.

The Freethinkers represented a tendency to move further and further away from orthodox Christianity to a looser form of faith—Theism. Some went even further, on to Atheism, but they were still beyond the pale as far as Keshub and most of the British public were concerned. Theists like Frances Power Cobbe, social worker, author, journalist and religious thinker, and Mr James Martineau, the influential Unitarian philosopher and preacher, believed in God and Christ, but not that Christ was the unique revelation of God in history. Martineau even disliked the label 'Unitarian' because it entailed formulation of a set dogma, whereas he felt that belief should never be static. They were totally against both the idea of divine revelation in the Church or in the Bible. Their religion was of a non-traditional, personal kind and hence they shared much common ground with Keshub—understandably, as they had been influenced by the same sources as Keshub and had in turn influenced Keshub's own religious development. They were tolerant in their approach to other religions, and welcomed the progress of Theism the world over. The Brahmo Samaj excited them, being a sign of the possiblity of universal Theism. Because of the fundamental closeness of their beliefs it was the British and Foreign Unitarian Association which organized Keshub's itinerary when he got to England. The Unitarians were not numerically a large group,[10] but they were influential in social reform activities and in theological circles, and had the reputation of being the least bigoted of the Christian sects.

The main representative of the Broad Chruch was Dean Stanley. He stood for the greatest latitude in the Church of England, wanting to break down narrow sectarianism by overlooking differences in form and reducing Christianity to its lowest common denominator of dogma, which was that Jesus was the son of God. They felt sure that Brahmos, at heart, believed this, or at any rate were so close to this belief that they needed to be encouraged on their way towards it. The evangelical Nonconformists, and many others too, were interested in the Brahmos as the means of the conversion of India. While they were somewhat doubtful about some of their beliefs, they felt that Brahmoism was moving towards Christianity, and that being an indigenous movement, it would have greater power than proselytization by foreign missionaries to rescue and convert the masses from the depths of idolatry. Idolatry was one of the most abominable vices conceivable for most low churchmen.

Max Müller was renowned for his belief that every religion had a core of truth, and he saw Brahmoism as centring on that core in the Hindu religion. Like many others he also saw the Brahmo Samaj as a step towards an Indian Christianity, as even though he believed in the truth of all religions, he felt that the moral beauty of Christ and Christianity was the summit of civilized belief. Interest in India was often linked with desire for converts in this way. Monier Williams, Sanskrit Professor at Oxford, gave his inaugural lecture on 'The Study of Sanskrit in relation to missionary work in India'.[11] All groups except the Freethinkers, although genuinely interested in Keshub's visit for independent reasons, cherished some hopes for his ultimate conversion.

There was also a natural interest in India, its religious life and social conditions, which was the interest taken by the ruling nation in the ways of its subject people, so as better to understand and rule over them. Keshub's audiences would often include people who had served in 'India, as missionaries or government servants, who maintained a continuing interest in Indian affairs.

The Victorian era generally was one of abounding intellectual curiosity and activity. People felt it their duty to extend their knowledge of fields unknown, and so for this reason, too, Keshub's lectures on a wide range of subjects were always well attended. The intellectual curiosity of the English was matched by that of Keshub, who threw himself into all branches of public interest and activity, acquainting himself with and speaking forth on most topical issues of the day during the course of his short visit.

In Calcutta, the few months following Keshub's announcement of his plans were spent making detailed arrangements and raising funds. Most of the money was his own, but he also raised contributions from friends and from the audience present at his talk on 'England and India' prior to his departure.[12] He gave some parting instructions to his followers which revealed a residue of apprehension at a possible flaring up of conflict over the position he assigned to himself in the Samaj. He told them that a religious teacher could be compared to a pair of spectacles, as an aid in seeing, or to a gatekeeper, who leads men to his master and then himself departs.[13]

Keshub set out on his journey on 15 February 1870, accompanied by an entourage of five men[14] They went via Madras, where Keshub was shocked to find that the Samaj had dwindled away to one member—the resident Brahmo missionary—and noted that "immediate steps should be taken to strengthen our mission in this part of the country".[15] Keshub kept a diary beginning from the time he set out, which is a valuable source of information on his doings, but otherwise disappointing.[16] He recorded only very brief comments on the people he met, and his remarks were largely observations on the novelty and peculiarities of the scene he had entered into. A surprising simplicity emerges from these personal jottings, very different from the rhetoric of the pulpit or the lecture hall. Given that European thought and ideas were not at all alien to him, it is understandable that it was the physical appearance of Europe that he found most outstanding. He freely admitted, in his diary, his amazement at Marseilles,, their first European port of call : —

> The brilliance of the city, especially the shops, dazzles
> me. It is the first European city we pass through ;
> I cannot help being struck with astonishment, every-
> thing is so unique, so peculiarly beautiful, so per-
> fectly *bilaiti*.[17] The hotel is a grand thing, being a
> six-storied richly furnished house with innumerable
> rooms and attendants. Of course we conduct our-
> selves in an imperial style.[18]

Protap Chunder Mozoomdar mentioned, presumably from
further impressions conveyed in letters home, that
Keshub had been alarmed at the spring mattress. He
felt he was going to sink through to the floor, and called
his companion to see if he was still visible on the
surface.[19]

The party reached London on 21 March. Keshub
had received offers of hospitality, from Sir John Bow-
ring and from the British and Foreign Unitarian Association, but initially preferred to retain some independence by finding his own lodgings close to his Bengali
friends in London.[20] He did not get involved in public
engagements immediately, but spent the next three weeks
in paying and receiving calls from various prominent
people. On his first day in London he called on his main
British contacts —Miss S. D. Collet, whose mind was of
"an eminently historical or rather statistical type ; she
is ever gathering facts and eliciting information", Lord
and Lady Lawrence, and Frances Power Cobbe, "a most
lively and earnest-minded person".[21] Even in the inti-
macy of his diary Keshub left out all mention of an
amusing 'newcomer' incident  which he had related at
length to Miss Cobbe. He had made up his mind to call
on Lord Lawrence when he arrived, and so simply called
a cab and told the cabman to go to Lord Lawrence's
house. Of course the man did not have a clue as to
where it was, but he drove vaguely all over London
for three hours, finally bringing Ksehub back to his start-
ing-point and charging him 14 shillings for the ride.
Keshub, on realizing his mistake, referred to an old letter
from Lord Lawrence which gave his address as Queen's
Gate. He directed the next cab to that address, only to
find that it might be any one of a row of about 185 houses !

The cabman in this case helped him out, by suggesting that the nearest butcher might know which house belonged to Lord Lawrence. His intuitions proved right, and it was the butcher who finally directed Keshub to Lord Lawrence—who was at home, and gave him a very warm welcome. Apart from this human, humourous side to him—he was the only Indian she knew who could enjoy a joke in 'the English way'—Miss Cobbe was most impressed by Keshub's saintliness. In a letter to a friend she described him as Christ-like, one who lived in God. She was also amazed at the striking similarity in the beginning of their religious lives. A deep sense of correspondence and sympathy sprang up between them, as Keshub had also felt drawn to her, thinking "How can this English woman have felt all this just as I ?"[22]

The list of people he met in the following few weeks was extensive. It included the Reverend R. Spears, Secretary of the Unitarian Association, who took charge of ensuring his comfort and fostering his interests; Miss Elizabeth Sharpe, a young Theist who had been corresponding with Rajnarain Bose; and the Queen of Holland. A fruitful contact was the American Theist, Moncure Conway, in charge of Finsbury and South Place Chapels, where Keshub later preached. In Conway's services he dropped formal prayer and read devotional passages from the world's religious literature, including the Hindu scriptures.[23] He also met the aged philanthropist, Lord Shaftesbury, and Mr Seeley, author of Ecce Homo- (although unfortunately he did not record anything beyond the fact that he was delighted to meet him). Lord Lawrence took him to the Indian Office, and introduced him to the major officials there, showing that he was seen as an important Indian visitor as well as a purely religious leader.

He was taken sightseeing, and was an observant and interested tourist. He was impressed by the Crystal Palace, but not by the session he attended on the Irish Land Bill in the House of Commons. His keen awareness of the shortcomings of Britain came out in his comment on the ladies' gallery, hidden from public view.

which he termed a 'parliamentary zenanah', seeing it as rather incongrous in a country that had hitherto impressed him as the land of female liberty".[24]

His first public engagement was a sermon on 'The Living God' at Mr Martineau's chapel at Little Portland Street, on 10 April. It was based on the text "In Him we live, and move and have our being".[25] Keshub's diary entry mentioned that the congregation numbered about 500, and, it being his first sermon in an English chapel, he felt a little awkward. The congregation included Members of Parliament, and many important scientific and literary figures, all waiting eagerly to hear what the Indian Theist had to say. Martineau's impression was that

> His preaching (quite extempore) is simple and affectionate ; highly interesting from its religious tone, but not marked by any striking intellectual force.[26]

The opinion of the correspondent of the *Pall Mall Budget*, on Keshub's second sermon at Conway's South Place Chapel a week later, would have been applicable to the first sermon as well.[27] This observer said that Keshub's awkwardness did communicate itself to his audience, who were slightly disappointed, although the calmness of his style was attributed to his not being sufficiently at home with an English audience. The audience was looking for answers to questions like "Would he throw any light upon that difficult problem why our spiritual influence seems to have lagged so far behind the material conquest ? Looking at our society from a point of view so entirely novel, would he throw new light upon the peculiarities of our creed as they strike a race so different and yet so closely connected with us ? ". Keshub gave no answers, but it was felt that he would be more forthcoming later in his stay. This sermon was extremely simple, and contained nothing startling—Keshub spoke "with much quiet fervour upon the goodness and mercy of God", which they could "expect to hear from Mr Martineau or from any able Unitarian preacher" —quite a disappointment. However, the congregation came away with feelings of warm respect for Keshub. He wrote in his diary that after the

service many came forward to shake hands, and a large
crowd (South Place Chapel seated about 1,000 people)
followed him to the cab.

Although Keshub did, at a later date, give a sermon at
South Place on 'Theism in India and in England', thus
departing from the ranks of Mr Martineau, in general in
his sermons he took a biblical text as his starting point
and expounded on that. It was not surprising that what
he had to say in this field sounded familiar, as he had
drawn heavily on British and American sources in forming
his own Theistic ideas. His first occasion for presenting a
broader view encompassing secular matters, came at the
Welcome Soirée arranged for him by the British and
Foreign Unitarian Association at their Hanover Square
rooms, on 12 April. It was a rare ecumenical gathering,
which testified to the Victorian desire for unity and harmony, and their remarkable tolerance for new ideas, especially in the religious sphere. It is to be hoped that the
presence of most people was not based on such ignorance
as that inferred in a rather laboured poem printed in
*Punch* on the occasion, which began : —

> Who on earth of living men,
> *Is* BABOO KESHUB CHUNDER SEN ?
> I doubt if even one in ten
> Knows BABOO KESHUB CHUNDER SEN.[28]

The significance of Keshub's visit was evident from the
composition of the welcome gathering. It included leading churchmen of ten denominations (among whom were
Dr Cappel, representing advanced Roman Catholicism,
and Dean Stanley and Reverend Stopford Brooke of
the Broad Church Movement), Dr Marks, the leader of
reformed Judaism, and a group of politicians headed by
Lord Lawrence. Many others were unable to attend but
sent letters of sympathy. Dean Stanley of Westminster
Abbey, whom Keshub had already met twice, moved the
welcome resolution.[29] In his speech he showed his concern
to impress Keshub with a united Christendom, "that
amidst and athwart all the divisions which he may
find amongst us in England, there is still a common
Christianity to which he would look with reverence".

His speech followed by others from Lord Lawrence, Mr Martineau, Reverend Dr Mullens (Secretary of the London Missionary Society) and the Jewish leader Dr Marks. Keshub's speech in reply conveyed the gratitude of 180 million Indians for the revolutionary reforms that Britain had carried out in India. He reiterated his cherished belief that England and India were connected not merely by human circumstances, but by God in history, by Providence. From that political union came intellectual union, and although physical and material improvements had been many, the grandest achievement was the moral and religious reformation that was being accomplished, of which the Brahmo Samaj was the most prominent result. He predicted that India would accept the true spirit of Christ in an Asiatic form of Christianity. He urged his audience to press on with the "great work of Indian regeneration". The vote of thanks to Keshub was proposed by Lord Hughton, who thanked him "politically, socially and religiously".

Keshub attracted the notice of many eminent Victorians. John Stuart Mill was one of those who had been unable to attend the welcome soiree, but he had called on Keshub earlier that day. Keshub's diary showed that he was impressed by the call from "the greatest thinker of the age",[30] but he was not so overawed by anybody as to let them interrupt his normal routine. Prosunno Coomar Sen related that Mill had called without an appointment, at a time when Keshub was busy with his Indian correspondence, so Keshub asked him to wait till he was finished. Keshub's companions were apprehensive as to how Mill would respond to this, but he took it very well, spending his waiting time reading the newspaper.[31] After their talk, which was mainly on politics —the education cess, income tax, the administration of justice, the character of Anglo-Indians—Mill was greatly embarrassed by Keshub's courtesy in showing him to the door himself, as a mark of respect. The interview showed that the English saw Keshub not merely as a representative of the Brahmo Samaj, but as a representative of the whole of India, and that Keshub saw him-

self in that role too. He had avoided direct political
involvement when in India, but he felt quite unperturbed about discussing Indian politics overseas. When
the Government proposed to remove its contribution to
schools and colleges and to further mass education in
India by imposing a tax on the *zamindars*, Kristo Das
Pal wrote to Keshub in London asking him to point out
the defects of the scheme to India Office officials. Keshub
had many meetings with the Duke of Argyll and Sir
Erskine Perry on this and other political issues.[32]   He
was also invited to breakfast with the Prime Minister,
Mr Gladstone.

Keshub had already met another famous admirer,
Professor Max Müller, at Dean Stanley's shortly after
his arrival in London. Of this interview Keshub noted
only that they had conversed on Indian subjects, especially the Vedas. Max Müller's interest in Keshub was
made plain in a letter to his wife, saying "We soon got
into a warm discussion, and it was curious to see how we
almost made him confess himself a Christian".[33]   Müller
referred back to this point again in a protrait of Keshub
in his book *Auld Lang Syne*.[34]   He said that he had
asked Keshub why he did not publicity declare himself
a Christian, seeing that he was at heart a true follower
of Christ. This direct question was indicative of Max
Müller's naivete and enthusiasm, as it should have been
obvious to him that if Keshub had really wanted to
become a Christian he would have done so by then.
Keshub's tactful reply, given in a grave and thoughtful
tone, was "Suppose that thirty years hence people find
out that I was a disciple of Christ, what would be the
harm ? Only were I to profess myself a Christian now,
all my influence would be gone at once". Keshub renewed his contact with Müller in a visit to Oxford. Müller
took him to see the famous Tractarian leader Dr Pusey,
a strong advocate of the all-embracing power of the church
as an institution for reaching salvation. Müller's record
of the interview corroborated other English accounts in
testifying to the impact Keshub made on those who met
him : —

Dr. Pusey was at first reserved till the conversation turned on prayer. Keshub Chunder Sen, while defending his own position towards Christianity, burst out into an eloquent panegyric on prayer which ended with the words, 'I am always praying.' This touched Pusey's heart, and he said, 'Then you cannot be far wrong.'[35]

As Pusey then went on to describe a very English form of Church-centred Christianity, Müller (whose beliefs were probably more in harmony with Keshub's than with Pusey's) asked him whether if at the time of Christ a man had held a belief such as Keshub's he would have been received as a disciple. Pusey's answer was yes, a great concession to the impression Keshub's spirituality made on one so renowned for his dogmatism.

Keshub also visited Cambridge, where he met an old Calcutta friend, E. B. Cowell, Professor of Sanskrit —a former Principal of the Sanskrit College, Calcutta. He also met F. D. Maurice, the main exponent (along with Charles Kingsley) of the doctrine of Christian Socialism and founder of the Working Men's College in 1854. Later, in Bristol, he met his early correspondent, Professor F. W. Newman, the freethinker, who was also at the time an anti-vaccinationist, anti-meat-eater, and anti-Christian. Being the author of *Against Hero-Making in Religion,* he was naturally opposed to Keshub's views on Christ and great men.

Keshub made a point of seeing as much of English life and institutions as he could. He was present at the Lord Mayor's Easter banquet, and at the opening of the new building of the University of London by Queen Victoria. He attended a grand musical entertainment at the Crystal Palace, and went to an exhibition of paintings at the Royal Academy. In a more serious vein, he went on a tour of the Sussex County Lunatic Asylum, the Asylum for the Blind, Newgate Prison and the Carterlane Mission School for poor children. His attempts to try to reach the British working-classes did not meet with much success. He preached in the East End, the poorest quarter of London, but there were few workingmen present in the congregation.[36] However, he had

a captive audience of working-class children when he
gave an address to Sunday School children at Unity
Church, Islington. There were about 700 children, from
the mission schools run by the Unitarian church. They
listened with concentration as Keshub talked on the
text "Suffer the little children to come unto me and for-
bid them not, for of such is the kingdom of heaven",
finishing with the Hindu legend of Dhruba, "the devout
child who sought and found God".[37] Despite this enthusiastic reception by their young, Keshub obviously had little
appeal for the working-classes, who could barely be made
to take an interest in Christianity, let alone an Indian
variant of it.

While in England Keshub became very enthusiastic
about the cause of temperance. He had always been
an advocate,[38] but had not made it a prominent part of
his teaching in the past. More zealous was the one-
time drinker Rajnarain Bose, who founded the first
Temperance Association in Bengal in the early 1860s.[39]
Keshub threw his weight behind the British Temperance Movement, by supporting a resolution condemn-
ing legislation by which the sale of liquor was maintained for purpose of revenue in England and India, at
the annual 'demonstration' of the United Kingdom Alliance on 19 May, at which thousands of people were present. The audience rose and cheered him en masse
before he spoke. His speech was a fervent and emotional plea to end the liquor traffic, in which he freely
criticized the British Government for introducing brandy
along with education, thus causing the premature deaths
of hundreds of promising young Indians.[40] He gave
another address on the same subject at Shoreditch on
22 May, and again on 25 June at Manchester. He also
made a speech furthering this cause to the annual fete
of the National Temperance League, the Evangelical
counterpart of the secular U. K. Alliance, at the Crystal
Palace in September.[41] Over 50,000 people attended the
fete, and after the midday meeting there was a procession
and choral singing by 5,000 children of the Band of
Hope, who had signed the teetotaller's pledge.

Keshub also gave his valued support to the Peace Society, speaking at its 54th anniversary meeting on 17 May.[42]   He registered a protest against war, speaking as one who came from a race well-known to be quiet and mild.  As a Hindu, he looked upon war as a great anomaly in Christendom (and he was shortly to be given tangible evidence of the anomaly with the outbreak of the Franco-Prussian war in Europe during his visit).  One of the most surprising points of the address was his quotation of a Sanskrit couplet, with a translation—which he had never done in his lectures in India. It was significant enough for him to have entered the fact in his diary.  He could have felt that at that time the support from Indian antiquity and tradition would carry more weight in England than in India.  Keshub's support for a cause was much valued by British leaders as being an independent, outside endorsement of their activities. He was called on to give his opinions of British Ragged Schools at the annual meeting of the Ragged School Union on 9 May.  He said that he had been most impressed by what he had seen, as in India education floated on the surface of society, amongst the upper and middle classes only.

Keshub gave an address on the social progress that had been made in India to the East India Association on 13 May.  His speech was on 'Female Education in India', and followed the main speech given by Mary Carpenter on her experience of the subpect, and a speech thanking her for her efforts made by the Honorary Secretary of the Association, Dadabhai Naoroji.  Keshub stressed the need for *zenana* education for women, and urged English women to follow Miss Carpenter's example and go to teach in India.  He recommended the establishment of a society to promote female education in India, differing from the Christian societies already established in that it would be non-sectarian.  Keshub gave another address along similar lines to the Victoria Discussion Society on 1 August.[43]  He chaired the meeting and then made a speech in which he gave a detailed picture of the condition of women and the need for reform.  The reforms he thought most urgent were the allowing of widow remarriage, the abolition of early marriage, and suppression of bigamy and polygamy. The root of these evils was want of enlightenment. Women accepted their condition passively, because they knew no better. It was not a result of Hinduism, because he claimed that the Hindu scriptures said that a man must love and respect his wife, that girls should be educated and that they should not marry young. Hindu women had some sterling qualities—their devotion, modesty and gentleness—which he did not want them to lose through the introduction of English customs. Sharing the same attitude as many other Victorian gentlemen, his comments on the problem of women's rights showed a lack of proper understanding of it, and his adherence to the traditional stereotypes—"In all that is manly and vigorous men excel, and must continue to excel, but in all that is soft, and tender, and gentle, women must continue to surpass men...". He did not really approve of the movement for women's rights : —

I would proscribe and denounce class legislation and class agitation. Why should we get up an exclusive movement for the purpose of obtaining women's rights, so-called ? If women are fit, they must have their rights and privileges. I do not see why they should be excluded from positions which they are entitled to occupy. If they are not fit they ought not to occupy them, but if they are fit, then let their fitness be proved, and vindicated and declared throughout the length and breadth of the land...

He wound up with a humble appeal to his 'English sisters' to do all in their power to effect the elevation of Hindu women, the best way being to go to India and teach an unsectarian, liberal and useful education, "calculated to make Indian women good wives, mothers, sisters, and daughters". This lecture had the desired effect on many. Miss Annette Ackroyd, an educated Unitarian, was not present at the lecture but heard about it, and was so inspired that she tried to see and hear Keshub as much as possible in the few months before he left, eventually going out to India to teach in answer o his appeal for volunteers.[44]

Although Keshub made a good impression on most eading men of the time, it was the women whom he had nost to do with in England. It is difficult to give a recise explanation for this. Possibly his strikingly andsome appearance had its charms for them, or per-aps they had more spare time for entertainment of visi-ors. Middle-class women found a useful outlet for their nergy in philanthropic works, and may have been in-erested in India as a widening of their sphere of activity. The condition of women naturally aroused their special oncern, and was also one of Keshub's main preoccupa-ions. Keshub was not an intellectual, so perhaps his imple sweet spirituality was more attractive to women han to their intellectually precise husbands. Whatever he reason, Keshub was 'lionized' by London female society. Apart from his closeness to women of public stature like Frances Power Cobbe and Mary Carpenter, he was in-vited to family gatherings which he enjoyed, and to be the guest of houour at numerous 'At Home' parties held by ladies of high social standing—including the Unitarian Mrs Manning, Mrs Russel Martineau, whose husband was Professor of Hebrew at Manchester New College and son of James Martineau, Mrs Moncure Con-way, and Lady Lyell, wife of the famous scientist. A very satirical article in the *Saturday Review* filled in the background to this 'lionizing' phenomenon. It was a recognized pastime of middle-aged women to take up controversial figures and show them off as their own pet discoveries. The article, entitled 'Lions and Lion Hunters' described one lion as the "distinguished re-ormer of Indian religion", the Bengalee Conundrum Baboo—an unmistakeable (though very unfair) carica-ure of Keshub : —

Nobody takes the posture you want like a Bengalee, and that distinguished reformer of Indian religion, Conundrum Baboo, answers every string his hostess pulls with a perfect adaptability. It is amazing to compare his performance with the clumsier gambols of his Western rivals. A flow of pietistic enthusiasm gilds the vagueness of his dogma ; the Bible, in-

stead of being vulgarly reduced to arithmetic
disappears in a cloud of Vedas ; a gentle, pitiful shake
of the head expresses the regret of the distinguished
stranger over the blind antagonism of Western
faiths ; there is something irresistibly winning in his
invitation to throw everything overboard, and exchange the convictions of Christendom for the
dreams of a handful of Hindoos.   There is something
exquisite in the perfect absurdity which expresses
itself with such an air of prophetic persuasion, in the
delicious way in which the shock is administered—not
in the coarse, concrete fashion of Occidental heretics.
but with a gentle titillation, which creeps through
one's frame to the very fingertips.  Unquestionably,
if one is to try the *leo hereticus*, there is no lion
like Conundrum Baboo.[45]

Keshub himself found the social atmosphere relaxing,
and behaved in a much less temperamental manner than
he had done in India.  In England he was an important
man in society, but one among many, not the major
leader.  He did not have to struggle to prove himself,
but was easily accepted by English society, whereas in
India he had always been too much of a radical, an out-
caste, to gain such acceptance. In England he was considered to be a 'gentleman'.[46] In many ways his English visit
removed some of the strain he had been undergoing.
He had been given the highest recognition, but was regarded as one of a large fraternity of distinguished men
rather than a single outstanding individual, as he appeared to be in Calcutta.  Also, being thrust into an
entirely English atmosphere, he was totally shut off
from the conflicting attractions of popular Hinduism.
He could throw himself wholeheartedly into the English
situation, fulfilling entirely the most Anglicized side
of his personality.  He fitted in perfectly, and the old
tension subsided for a time, as Indian culture was absent
in England, although English culture was still a powerful
and confusing force in India.  In England he fitted easily
into the Theistic community—in India he had to work
to create such a community.  In England he was not
trying to introduce Hindu ideas, whereas in India he was
trying to introduce Christ, and so obviously his struggles

n India were going to be greater.

The most controversial of Keshub's London lectures were not the strictly religious ones in which he followed the lines of British Theism with little originality. It was his quasi-political lectures, on 'England's Duties to India' and 'Christ and Christianity' that raised a storm—of interest in England, and of wrath in the English community in India.

'England's Duties to India' was delivered at Spurgeon's Metropolitan Tabernacle.[47] Keshub had attended a normal Baptist service there previously, and, finding its capacity to accommodate 6,000 in the congregation 'tempting', he had asked Spurgeon if he would consent to Keshub's giving a secular lecture there. Spurgeon, the famous Victorian popular preacher who could draw crowds of 10,000, agreed to this, so Keshub used the Tabernacle as the venue for his lecture on 24 May. A large audience was attracted. Keshub declared that he spoke as a representative of India, all India, not any particular sector. He saw the British as trustees of India, and therefore governing for the good of India, and thus felt it incumbent on himself to set out a list of Britain's duties, or much-needed improvements in Indian administration. The first of these was to promote education, especially education of the masses, which would in turn promote a grand reformation and loyalty to Britain. It was the Government's duty to find a way to finance this. This led on to a much more topical, and specifically middle-class, issue—that education should have its rewards, meaning that educated Indians should be given high posts in the Government. Keshub shrewdly used the technique of pointing out advantages accuring to Britain from these changes, going beyond an appeal to their humanitarian instincts alone. In this case, he said the reforms would mean a much cheaper machinery of administration. He lodged a protest against the abolition of the two year state scholarships to England. Education of females was another duty—partly so as to solve family problems caused by the difficulties encountered by educated husbands marrying uneducated wives. The final duty was to abolish

the liquor and opium traffic, his arguments for th
covering the same ground as he had in other discus
sions of the matter. He also protested against the racis
behaviour of many 'nominal Christians' in India, in muc
stronger terms than in 'Jesus Christ : Europe and Asia
his last lecture on the topic. He hoped that Britis
men would go and found hospitals, workhouses an
ragged schools in India, and that women would go ther
to help in education. Keshub had never spoken out i
such a political manner in India—he must have fe
that speaking forth in England would have more direc
results, and also that English public opinion was a mor
effective pressure group on the Government than India
public opinion. The thousands of people in his audienc
must have agreed with Keshub's suggestions, as the news
paper report said that he was "frequently loudl
cheered".[48] The meeting had been presided over b
Lord Lawrence, who, at one remove from the welter o
Indian politics, did not raise any objections to Keshub'
proposals, implying his concurrence. The British i
England, removed from direct blame or responsibilit
for the condition of India, could afford to applaud, bu
not so the British in India, who through their direct in
volvement were highly sensitive to criticism. Their re
action was alarming, and afforded further proof of th
accusations Keshub had made against them. Every
English subscriber to the *Indian Mirror* withdrew hi
name.[49] In England Keshub had been treated as ar
equal in the highest intellectual circles, which was ob
jectionable to the Englishmen in India who had alway
felt themselves to be above the native community and
its interests. For him then to presume to lecture them
on their duty seemed to them like gross impertinence
One Englishman in Bombay publicly threw out a chal
lenge of 500 rupees to anyone who would read the lec
ture in his presence while he stood by with a horse-
whip.[50] While indignation raged in India, Keshub's popu
larity in England was undiminished, proving that the
Englishman at home and abroad were almost two different species.

His next lecture on 'Christ and Christianity', on 28 May, viewed Christianity from the standpoint of a Hindu Theist.[51] This was a slightly more touchy subject, but still well received by a "large and mixed audience",[52] who were fairminded enough not to have taken offence at this attack on their beliefs and practices. Keshub described his own spiritual history and acknowledged "candidly and sincerely" that he owed a great deal to Christ and his Gospel. He challenged Christians to examine their own actions, on doing which most would be sure to find that there was little to choose between them and a non-Christian. He told them that to be a Christian meant becoming like Christ, and he meant it literally. The main 'test' of being a Christian that he put forward was whether they could forgive their enemies —if not, they were not true Christians. Lastly he accused them of being materialistic and said that they had to learn to give up worldliness, yet remain cheerful. Surprisingly, he did not take this opportunity to say that this attitude could be learnt from India, probably because he was then more concerned with analysing English society on its own terms. He commended English philanthropy, which was to him the shining ray of proof that England was a Christian country. Nonetheless, England was not a *true* Christian nation, because the English were not forgiving. They had not absorbed the spirit of Christ, only the dogmas of High, Broad and Low Church, all separate facets of religion. Keshub stood for a religion of love and unity, marking the death of sectarianism. What he said was basically ecumenical, not asking people to give up their present religion, but to overcome their bias and stand united in the spirit of God. He spoke as a Theist, not an Indian. His criticisms were valid, but he seemed to be excessively vehement in insisting that anything short of perfection was non-Christian, and that therefore England was not Christian. He had expected to find England more suffused with the Christian spirit than he did, and was consequently disillusioned. He may also have been angry at being 'duped', as he had always heard that England was much more advanced than India, as a justification of English contempt for Indian religion and society, and he had now found that there was little foundation for British arrogance and superiority.

In an address to the Swedenborg Society Keshub threw some light on the reason for his outburst against British Christianity.[53] He had become hardened against attempts to convert him. He hated sectarianism, but was continually drawn into it in England, when becoming identified with any one sect meant separation from and hostility to many others. His diary revealed that he had been shocked early in his visit by two particularly blatant attempts to proselytize. The first time a Mrs Bevan wrote and invited him to lunch, saying she had something important to communicate to him, which was only to interrogate him on why he could not accept orthodox Christianity. The second occasion was after dinner at the home of a retired Anglo-Indian, when a group of men cornered him and expounded a chapter of the Bible, preached a sermon, and offered a prayer, all entirely without warning, and quite out of place in such a social situation.[54] He gathered from the churchmen that he had met that their sympathy with him was due partly to seeing him as the agent for the conversion to Christendom of the 180 million idolatrous masses of India.

The assertion of independence can be traced through his lectures, culminating in his criticisms of Christianity in the lecture on 'Christ and Christianity'. In a speech after this, at the Independent Union Chapel at Islington on 7 June, the Minister made an announcement wishing it to be understood that Keshub Chunder Sen was not a Christian but a Hindu Theist. In his speech Keshub harked back to the good that existed in ancient Indian religion. This again was something he had not touched on in India itself. He criticized the missionaries for not cooperating more with Brahmos in attempting to build on the good existing in traditional religion, in the simplicity and devotional fervour of the people, rather than

just seeking numerical conversion and denationali-
zation : —

> Truth is not European, and it would be a mistake to
> force European institutions upon the Hindus, who
> would resist any attempt to denationalize them.[55]

More and more lectures were on these themes. In
'Religious and Social Liberty' at a Unitarian meeting
on 9 June, he reiterated that though Christianity was
a better religion than Hinduism, professed Christians
were no better than idolatrous Hindus.  His point was
that nations and religions should learn from each other,
and that *all* men must be made free.  Keshub was himself aware of his growing assertiveness, as before speaking he excused himself for stepping into 'forbidden territory'; that of criticising his hosts.

Interest in Keshub was not confined to the intellectual centre of London alone.  Many provincial centres
had expressed a wish to hear from him, and he accepted
as many invitations to speak as he could.  Welcoming
committees were set up in advance to make arrangements for his reception.  Rev. R. Spears, Secretary of
the British and Foreign Unitarian Association, circulated
handbills amongst his hosts giving instructions on his daily
schedule and diet.  His daily schedule showed the metho-
dical and organized way he planned his days : —

> Mr. Sen desires to retire at 10 o'clock p.m.  He takes
> a cup of tea (no bread) at 8 in the morning.  His
> devotions, correspondence, and bath, till half-past 10.
> He takes breakfast at half-past 10, enjoys private
> study till 1.  From 1 till 7 enters on engagements,
> which may be arranged by friends.  At 5 he dines,
> and from 6 to 10 he is open to engagements.[56]

Nor did he ever compromise his vegetarian diet :—

> Mr. Sen and his cousin Mr. Prosonno are vegetarians,
> and so abstain from all animal food and eggs, and
> all alcoholic drinks as well.  Their drink is water
> or lemonade, they also enjoy warm milk.  For break-
> fast, the following may be prepared : boiled rice
> and sliced potatoes fried in butter ; also vegetable or
> peasoup.  Dinner the same as breakfast, with fruit,

puddings and sweets; no eggs in the pastry. In all cases they desire to be entertained together.

Keshub's first stop was at Bristol, the home of his old friend Mary Carpenter, and the burial place of his renowned predecessor, Rammohun Roy. He visited Rammohun's tomb at Arno's Vale and had a quick look at the philanthropic institutions Mary Carpenter had initiated—girls' schools, a Ragged School, a Workmen's Hall, an Industrial School and Reformatory School for girls. Although Mary Carpenter showed no awareness of it (and her friend Miss Cobbe said that she was not very sensitive to other people's feelings), seeing her at such close quarters dampened the affection and respect Keshub had formerly held towards her. She said in a letter about his stay with her that

> It is the first English home he has lived in, and he fully admired it, and seemed quite happy and comfortable here with his friend, especially as I had just the curry and rice prepared for him which I knew he liked. My friends in the country sent me plenty of choice flowers, fruits, vegetables, and Devonshire cream for him; and I got up a splendid soiree for him in the Elizabethan drawing-room at the Red Lodge. In fact, I could not have done more than I did for the most distinguished guest. I told him that he had been a great 'lion' in London, but that here he was a valued friend.[57]

Keshub must have put up a good front, for in fact he was highly irritated by her continual instructions on English etiquette, and her constant criticisms of his way of doing things, even down to objecting to the way he combed his hair.[58] However, he was favourably impressed by her institution of daily worship, where morning prayer was a pious habit involving the whole household. The other fruitful result of his visit was the plan to form an association which would support the reforms Keshub was working for in India.

His next stops were Bath, Leicester, and Birmingham. In the first two towns he lectured on England's duties to India, covering familiar ground. In Birmingham, however, he made his most pointed critical speech to

date, on 'The Duties of Christian Missionaries in India'.[59]
He set out his reasons for visiting England—to study it,
to survey Christian life in all aspects, to analyse the
Christian character, and to carry home practical lessons
of Christian civilization to India.  He had also come to
plead the cause of India before the British people, to
inform them of India's wants and England's duties.  He
stated emphatically that he had no intention of embracing any one Christian sect in England, as he in India
had his own Christ, which was as good as theirs.  His
criticism of the missionaries was related to a specific
incident that had recently taken place in Calcutta, the
Gunesh Soondery case.[60]  The report in *The Times* had
said that the young widow was a relative of Keshub's,
and had commented archly on the inconsistency of his
liberalism beside the intolerance of the rest of the Brahmos.  In his lecture Keshub referred to the report as a
vilification of the Brahmo Samaj.  He said that as Brahmos had a profound reverence for Christ, it was impossible that they should presecute Christians.  He believed that the missionaries were at fault in affording
protection to young converts against parental wishes.
The issues and implications involved in this case were
argued about at length in England.  The report from the
Calcutta correspondent of *The Times* was obviously hostile to the Brahmos, but the *Pall Mall Budget* came to
their defense.[61]  Their writer saw no reason why Brahmos should welcome converts to Christianity.  Miss Collet
had been troubled by the whole affair, and was thus
pleased to get Keshub's clarification of certain points—
he had never heard of the girl before, though she may
have been a very distant relative, being a Vaidya and a
Sen, and she was not a Brahmo.  He thought the confusion probably arose because his cousin, Norendranath
Sen, was attorney for the prosecution.[62]  In the lecture
Keshub said that he was not opposed to missionaries,
only to some of their modes of conversion.  The
missionaries in Calcutta reacted in a militantly aggressive
way.  They circulated a leaflet to discredit Keshub,[63]
saying that he allowed idolatry in his own home.  This

was strictly true, because he lived in a joint family, but
he had no control over anyone outside his own nuclear
family, and he had nothing to do with those idolatrous
observances. The missionaries were obviously trying to
destroy the good reputation Keshub had built up in
England, because he had dared to criticize their work.

From Birmingham Keshub proceeded to Nottingham,
Manchester and Liverpool. His welcome at most places
was organized by a committee composed mainly of churchmen but also including many civil officials, aldermen
and city councillors, and even the Lord Mayor. About
this time the warnings from Calcutta Evangelicals
began to take root in some parts of the church. At a conference of the Church of England Clerical and Lay
Association, remarks were made objecting to the warm
reception given to Keshub by some leading Evangelical
Nonconformists. In most towns there had been heated
discussions over just what claim he did have on the
sympathies of Evangelical Christians, carrying the hint
of a suspicion that some were letting the aim of conversion be superceded by an independent interest in what
he had to say, which was heretical. A prominent Baptist in Liverpool protested against exchange of pulpits[64]
with Keshub because of his criticism of Christian missionaries in India. Christian solidarity meant to some
extent a closing of the ranks against him. One Presbyterian minister declared it Christian duty to denounce
Keshub and his doctrines, and another proclaimed
derisively that Mahomet was more of a Christian than
Keshub.[65]

It was not entirely coincidental that, as the opposition seemed to be mounting, Keshub's health suddenly
deteriorated. There was every reason for him to feel
exhausted because of the tremendous pace of public life
that he had been keeping up, coupled with continual
travel and little opportunity for real relaxation. He was
having problems with the food—watery milk and taste-
less boiled vegetables—and so was filling up on biscuits,
which would not have provided much sustenance or
nourishment.[66] Although his body was overtaxed, it is

also probable that he stopped his tour in Liverpool because he did not feel he had added strength needed to
withstand direct opposition. He had never liked public
controversy, and although he had numerous people in
England who would have supported him, he did not feel
like entering the fight. He had a severe attack of ver-
tigo, accompanied by fever and retching. His English
friends were not too alarmed by his illness, but Keshub
himself was probably haunted by visions of meeting the
same fate as Rammohun Roy and Dwarkanath Tagore.
It was clear that he needed a rest, so he stayed con-
valescing with a Liverpool family for about three weeks
before returning to public life in London, at a slightly
less strenuous pace than before, on 14 July.

His first public engagement after his illness was
one designed to cheer his spirits, as it was a meeting
to promote the formation of a Theistic Society in London on 20 July.[67] A meeting had been held prior to this
one, where the intentions of the proposed Society were
described. The second meeting put forward more definite
resolutions Keshub could not but have concurred with
its object : —

> ...to unite men, notwithstanding any differences in
> their religious creeds, in a common effort to attain
> and diffuse purity of Spiritual life by (1) investigat-
> ing religious truth, (2) cultivating devotional feelings,
> and (3) furthering practical morality.

In his address Keshub told them that they must not
make the mistake of trying to abolish individual liberty
in belief and custom, but that all sects would be united
on a grand scale in their common belief in the Fatherhood of God and the Brotherhood of Man.

The most gratifying occasion of Keshub's whole tour
was his interview with Queen Victoria on 13 August.[68]
Her Majesty was in residence at Osborne, so Keshub was
received there. Even the palace had heard of his strict
vegetarianism, and a vegetarian lunch was provided for
him before his audience in the afternoon. The Queen
was accompanied by Princess Louise. They had what
seemed like an ordinary conversation, the Queen showing

interest in the condition of women, and pleasure at the knowledge that it was improving, but to Keshub the interview was of climactic significance. He had always held the position of the Queen as Empress of India to be symbolic of the bond ordained by providence uniting England and India. An interview with the Queen also amounted to an official endorsement of his stature in society.[69] Keshub modestly gave the Queen two pictures of his wife only, but was later informed by the palace that she would like some photographs of himself too. Before he left England Queen Victoria presented him with a large engraving of herself, and two books—*The Early Years of the Prince Consort* and the *Highland Journal*—personally inscribed.

By this stage Keshub had recovered sufficiently to resume his provincial tour, and proceeded to Edinburgh, Glasgow and Leeds. He then returned to London briefly, before making a second visit to Bristol to inaugurate the Bristol Indian Association on 9 September. This Association was to promote reform in India (especially mass education, women's education, sanitary improvements, improvement of prisons and the establishment of juvenile reformatories) and also to pay special attention to and to welcome Indians who were being educated in England.[70]

Keshub's English visit was finally coming to an end, and he was due to leave from Southampton on 24 September. He could have stayed longer as he had been unable to visit 40 towns which had invited him, and he had even been invited to America—he wanted to go on, but finally decided that his commitments in India were more important. It must have been quite a struggle to give up the chance for world fame to go back to hardships and responsibilities. He delivered a farewell sermon at Unity Chapel, Islington, and his popularity was still such that the church was packed and many had to be turned away. He also gave last sermons at the Effra Road Chapel, Brixton, and at the Unitarian church at Southampton. His most significant parting remarks, however, were those made at the Fare-

well Soiree held on 12 Sptember by the British and
Foreign Unitarian Association, to round off his visit in
the same way that it began. This time 11 Christian denominations were present, and it was said that those
present were fifty times more commited than those at
the previous occasion, as Keshub had publicly stated his
views many times in the intervening period.[71]   The Rev.
R. Spears, protocol manager of Keshub's tour, read a
report detailing the extent of Keshub's activities. He
included mention of his interviews with statesmen on
the legal disabilities under which his co-religionists
laboured, which had fair prospects of removal, so evidently Keshub had not passed over the opportunity to
speak in favour of the Brahmo Marriage Bill. Many of
the clergymen, and representatives of Theistic movements as far distant as France and Germany, paid their
tribute to Keshub. He replied in 'My Impressions of
England'. This was a very easy, familiar kind of talk,
showing much more casual ease and confidence than that
given on his arrival. He started off very lightly, saying
that his first impression was of the vast number of shops,
then the art of 'puffing' or advertising, then thirdly the
sheer mechanical activity of the English. He jokingly
condemned the English dinner party as being more like
a hunting party in its carnality : —"My flesh creeps on my
bones when I see a huge piece of roast English beef
on the table", and made a few passing criticism of the
'Girl of the Period' with her head (chigon) and her tail
(the bustle). He wittily protested that

> In these days of "woman's rights" may I not seriously
> suggest that women ought not to occupy more ground
> than men. (Laughter) It is a fact that a civilized
> and refined lady of the West occupies five times as
> much space as a gentleman. The fair sex ought to
> be fair.[72]

In a more serious vein he commented on the vast
amount of poverty and pauperism in London, and the
moral destitution and physical suffering caused by intemperance. The British Government needed to crack
down on drunkenness and prostitution. He had not been

blind to English faults—for instance, he mentioned that caste was almost as bad there as in India—but he softened the criticism by including a goodly amount of praise. He had great admiration for the London charities, a result of the Christian spirit. He had also been delighted by "the happy English home", or at least that of the middle-class Victorian, in which warmth and affection were mixed with a strict piety and religious observance. He also commended the power of British public opinion, and expressed a hope that these virtues could be transferred to India.

These were his secular impressions. The deepest part of his talk was reserved for his impression of Christianity in England. Its major drawbacks were sectarianism, muscularity and warlike militancy, and materialism, without any time for meditation.

He summed up the result of his visit to England thus :—

...as I came here an Indian, I go back a confirmed Indian ; I came here a Theist, I return a confirmed Theist. I have learnt to love my own country more and more. English patriotism has by a sort of electric process quickened my own patriotism. I came here a believer in the Fatherhood of God and the Brotherhood of Man, and I shall return confirmed in this belief. I have not accepted one single new doctrine that God had not put into my mind before ; I have not accepted new dogmas or doctrines, but I have tried as far as possible to imbibe the blessed influence of Christian lives. I have placed myself at the feet of Christians of all shades of opinion, and tried to gather from their lives and examples all that was calculated to enlighten me and to purify me, and to sanctify my native land ; and I have been amply repaid for all my exertions. I am now, thank God, a man of the world, and can say that England is as much my Father's house as India...

Despite his firm avowals to the contrary, Keshub was not the same man when he left England as when he arrived. Although Keshub fitted very well into English life (some thought almost too well—in a review of his Calcutta lectures the *Saturday Review* said that his

doctrines were taken too much from the West, and even
the earnestness of his tone was more Western than Oriental[73]), he was keenly aware of its shortcomings. He
had gone to England expecting to find a great Christian
nation, but the actuality did not support this. Martineau wrote that "I hardly know whether our social
formality, or our religious hardness and divisions, offend
him most. It is easy to perceive that he is profoundly
disappointed by the aspect of our religious life".[74] The
fact that England was far from perfect, although disappointing, at the same time served to boost his confidence. The British had always made unfavourable
comparisons between England and India, implying that
England was above reproach. When Keshub went there
he found that in many ways Britain's problems were
as great as those of India—there was certainly plenty
of room for criticism and improvement. Again, despite
his own Anglicism which was commented on by all,
having seen England he seemed to realize more fully,
in the light of England's defects, India's own claims to
greatness. In his lectures in England he mentioned
ancient Indian religion, and the Indian socio-political
situation much more than he had ever done in India.
This would have been partly because he realized that
the British public wanted to hear about something more
exotic than simple Theism, but it was also because he
was there in the role of a representative of India, which
developed and heightened his sense of nationality and
national pride.

His English visit shattered some of his illusions
about Christianity.[75] He had come across nominal Christians in Calcutta, but England, supposedly a Christian
nation, was full of them. Those who were not nominal
tended to be over-zealous, and tried to convert him. In a
flow of national pride, Keshub repaid the criticisms that
had been heaped on Hinduism by the missionaries, and
made extensive criticisms of English Christianity. Having seen what the West had to offer, he felt that the
time had come to reverse the trend, and let the West
learn from the East, to achieve a harmonious connec-

tion of the two traditions.

Although he aggravated some churchmen, the English seemed to appreciate Keshub's fearless championing of his religion and his country.[76] His visit to England was of no lasting importance there, but he did make a significant impact at a time when people were looking for a common faith and wider understanding among different sects and religions. As one speaker at a Unitarian meeting said,

> We are thinking less of the superficial waves tossed up by the uncertain gales of the human intellect, and are sinking down into the deep, calm, and unruffled ocean of religious faith and religious love, and, having felt in our own souls what it is to have faith in and to worship God, and having acknowledged in our hearts and by our actions what it is to love our fellow-men simply because they are men, we feel we are not giving way to loose and vague sentimentalism in extending our sympathies broadly to men of all religious persuasions, but yielding to the imperative call which has come to us from the God and Father of us all...[77]

Everything Keshub said was listened to with the greatest of interest, and his opinions and comments were taken very seriously.[78] After his departure, Mr Martineau stressed the importance of his visit for English Christianity : —

> It appears to me that the visit of Keshub Chunder Sen was a demonstration that our churches are wrong in their definition of Christianity (Applause) and that the very essence of it lies, not in the doctrinal and historical machinery, but in the spirituality of which this machinery is the mere vehicle to our souls. If this be so, I think it a lesson of the deepest moment to our Christian churches.[79]

Personally, Keshub responded with great affection to the way he was received by the British people. His own diary, and the many descriptions of him available from English sources, give an entirely different picture of him from that hitherto seen in Calcutta. In England he seemed more worldly-wise and assured, more relaxed and genial. His confidence increased through being taken so seriously. Being given full recognition and 'lionized' gratified the demands of his ego. The main sources of his former tension were not present—he was away from the burden of responsibility entailed by his position as leader of the Brahmo Samaj, and there was no conflict involved in the role he had to play in England. He was riding on the crest of a wave, having accomplished what he set out to do—to put the case of India before England—without encountering any major setbacks and with much personal satisfaction.

## NOTES AND REFERENCES

1. Keshub Chunder Sen, *The Brahmo Samaj—Lectures and Tracts* ed. S. D. Collet (London, 1870).

2. Keshub Chunder Sen, *In England* op. cit. p. 474.    Statistics taken from Reverend R. Spears' speech at the Farewell soiree.

3. F. M. Muller, *Chips* op. cit., Vol. II, p. 72.

4. I was able to find coverage of Keshub's visit in the *Illustrated London News*, the *Pall Mall Budget*, the *Saturday Review*, the *Contemporary Review*, and *Punch*.

5. Sunity Devee, op. cit. p. 8. Lord Dufferin once said to her, "I did not know you were Mr. Sen's daughter. I've travelled far and seen many handsome men, but never one so handsome". Daniel E. Bandman, an American actor, remembered him as "....fully six feet high, broad shouldered, deep chested, of slightly olive complexion, mild, eloquent eyes, firm set lips, genial chin, black moustache, and long black hair, which hung carelessly over a well-developed forehead...he certainly was the handsomest man I saw in India". *Liberal and New Dispensation*, 6 April 1884.

6. F. P. Cobbe, *The Life or Frances Power Cobbe by herself* (2 Vols, London, 1894), Vol. II, p. 130.

7. *Pall Mall Budget* (a weekly collection of articles from the daily *Pall Mall Gazette*), 23 April 1870, p. 24.

8. The *London Daily News* (in his obituary) said that Keshub had "a majestic presence, and that rapt look which of itself exerts an irresistible fascination over impressible minds....". Reprinted in the *Liberal and New Dispensation*, 10 February 1884.

9. *Pall Mall Budget*, 25 June 1870.

10. W.S. Smith, op. cit. p. 250.    There were only 26 Unitarian churches in 1870, with an average attendance of about 2,500.

11. O. Chadwick, op. cit. Vol. II, p. 38.

12. The money raised was only enough for his fare, as he arrived in England penniless and was supported by English hospitality. Keshub Chunder Sen. *In England* op cit. pp. 494-495.

13. S. Sastri, *Atmacharit,* new ed. (Calcutta, 1952), p. 107.

14. J. C. Bagal, *Keshab* op. cit. p. 45. He was accompanied by D
    Krishna Dhan Ghose (father of Sri Aurobindo), A. M. Bos
    Rakhalchandra Ray, Gopalchandra Ray and Prosunno Cooma
    Sen, who had left his post in the East India Railway Compan
    to go with Keshub as a missionary.

15. Keshub Chunder Sen, *In England* op. cit. p. 4. From Keshub
    diary.

16. Unfortunately the extant copy of his diary (in Keshub Chunde
    Sen, ibid. pp. 1-59) only goes to 21 May. The rest has eithe
    been lost or Keshub was too busy to keep it up.

17. *Bilaiti* means English, or foreign.

18. Keshub Chunder Sen, *In England* op. cit. p. 25.

19. P. C. Mozoomdar, *Life* op. cit. p. 137.

20. Also in England at the time were R. C. Dutt, S. N. Banerje
    Krishna Govind Gupta, and Keshub's nephew, Behari La
    Gupta. See Keshub Chunder Sen, *In England* op. cit. p. 26
    and and H. Das, 'The Early Indian Visitors to England', *Cal
    cutta Review*.   Third series, XIII (1924), p. 111.

21. These, and other impressions, are taken from his diary.

22. Keshub Chunder Sen, *In England* op. cit. pp. 131-132.   Mis
    Cobbe's impressions are recorded in her *Life* op. cit pp. 129-132

23. W. S. Smith, op. cit. p. 113.

24. Keshub Chunder Sen, *In England* op. cit. p. 36.

25. ibid.  pp. 61-70.

26. J. Drummond and C. B. Upton, *The Life and Letters of Jame
    Martineau* (2 Vols, London, 1902), Vol. II, p. 2. From a lette
    to Rev. Charles Wicksteed, dated 11 April 1870.

27. The *Pall Mall Gazette* (and *Budget*) were edited by W. T
    Stead, a freethinker, and were thus sympathetic to Brahmos
    There was a long article on the impact Keshub made in hi
    second sermon, entitled 'Baboo Keshub Chunder Sen' in the
    *Pall Mall Budget*, 23 April 1870, p. 24.

28. *Punch*, 16 April 1870, p. 155. The poem continues : —

    Have *you* heard—if so where and when—
    of BABOO KESHUB CHUNDER SEN?
    The name surpasses human ken—
    BABOO KESHUB CHUNDER SEN !
    To write it almost spoils my pen :
    Look—BABOO—KESHUB CHUNDER—SEN !
    From fair Cashmere's white-peopled glen
    Comes BABOO KESHUB CHUNDER SEN ?
    Or like "my ugly brother BEN"
    Swarth BABOO KESHUB CHUNDER SEN ?
    Big as ox, or small as wren,
    Is BABOO KESHUB CHUNDER SEN ?
    Let's beard this "lion" in his den—
    This BABOO KESHUB CHUNDER SEN.
    So come to tea and muffins, then,
    With BABOO KESHUB CHUNDER SEN.

29. Keshub Chunder Sen, *In England* op. cit. pp. 71-108, gives al
    the speeches made on this occasion.

30. Keshub Chunder Sen, *In England* op. cit. p. 38.

31. P. K. Sen, *Biography* op. cit. Vol. II, p. 27.

2.  *Liberal and New Dispensation,*    25  May  1884—'Our  Minister'.

3.  M.  Muller,  *Life  and  Letters  of  F.  M.  Muller*  (2  Vols,  London, 1902),  Vol.  I,  p.  374.

4.  F.M.  Muller,  *Auld  Lang  Syne,*  2nd  series,  'My  Indian  Friends' (London,  1902)  p.  101.

5.  F.M.  Muller,  *Chips*  op.  cit.  Vol.  II,  pp.  73-74.

6.  Keshub  Chunder  Sen,  *Keshub  Chunder  Sen's  English  Visit,* ed.  by  S.D.  Collet  (London,  1871)),  p.  137.

7.  Keshub  Chunder  Sen,  *In  England*  op.  cit.  p.  187.

8.  He  was  a  member  of  Peary  Charan  Sarkar's  Temperance  So- ciety,  founded  in  1864.  Bagal,  *Keshab*  op.  cit.  pp.  52-53.

9.  Rajnarain  Bose,  op.  cit.  p.  82.

0.  Keshub  Chunder  Sen,  *In  England*  op.  cit.  pp.  179-186,  and  the *Liberal  and  New  Dispensation*  4  May  1884—'Our  Minister'.

1.  *Pall  Mall  Budget,*  3  September  1870,  p.  33.

2.  Keshub  Chunder  Sen,  *In  England*  op.  cit.  pp.  173-178.

3.  Keshub  Chunder  Sen,  *In  England*  op.  cit.  pp.  386-396.

4.  Lord  Beveridge,  *India  Called  Them*  (London,  1947),  pp.  83-85.

5.  *Saturday  Review,*  11  June  1870,  pp.  763-764.

6.  "His  manners  have  also  not  so  much  of  the  ordinary  Eastern softness  and  somewhat  exaggerated  courtesy,   as  of  the  easy inborn  dignity  and  simplicity  of  a  wellbred  man  of  high  Euro- pean  birth.  In  a  word,  and  in  the  most  strictly  conventional sense,  Keshub  Chunder  Sen  is  a  gentleman ...".  From  *Cassell's Magazine,*  reprinted  in  B.  Mozoomdar,  *Mahayogi  Keshub  and Europe*  (Calcutta,  no  date)  p.  19.

7.  Keshub  Chunder  Sen,  *In  England*  op.  cit.  pp.  195-226.

8.  *Pall  Mall  Budget,*  28  May  1870,  p.  33.

9.  P.  C.  Mozoomdar,  *Life*  op.  cit.  p.  142.

0.  loc  cit.

1.  Keshub  Chunder  Sen,  *In  England*  op.  cit.  pp.  227-245.

2.  London  *Spectator,*  quoted  in  P.  C.  Mozoomdar,  *Life*  op.  cit.  p.  143.

3.  Keshub  Chunder  Sen,  *In  England*  op.  cit.  pp.  252-269.

4.  ibid.  pp.  39,  42.

5.  Keshub  Chunder  Sen,  *In  England*  op.  cit.  pp.  271-275.

6.  P.  C.  Mozoomdar,  *Life*  op.  cit.  pp.  143-144.  The  following  ex- tract  is  taken  from  the  same  source.

7.  J.  Estlin  Carpenter,  *The  Life  and  Work  of  Mary  Carpenter* (London,  1879),  p.  380.  From  a  letter  to  Sasipada  Banerji dated  24  June  1870.

8.  P.  C.  Mozoomdar,  *Life*  op.  cit.  p.  145.

9.  Keshub  Chunder  Sen,  *In  England*  op.  cit.  pp.  318-328.

0.  The  report  in  *The  Times*  (London)  13  June  1870,  p.  7  gave the  case  history  as  a  young  widow  aged  16,  of  a  Brahmo  family, who  had,  along  with  her  mother,  been  receiving  *zenana*  edu- cation  from  a  Christian  lady.   She  managed  to  convert  the daughter,  who  then  left  home  to  live  with  the  missionaries against  her  parents'  wishes.   Her  parents  took  the  case  to court,  but  the  judge  decided  against  them,  as  the  girl  was  old enough  to  choose  for  herself.

61. *Pall Mall Budget,* 25 June 1870, pp. 6-7. Ironically the after
    math of this case was that the girl soon wanted to return t
    her home, but her Hindu relatives refused to take her back
    Sivanath Sastri took her into his own home and later arrange
    a good marriage for her—so the Brahmos were in fact he
    saviours! H. Sarkar, *Sivanath Sastri* (Calcutta, 1929), pp. 17-1{

62. Keshub Chunder Sen, *English Visit* op. cit. pp. 375-377, in
    footnote by the editor, S.D. Collet.

63. P. C. Mozoomdar, *Life* op. cit. p. 146.

64. Exchange of pulpits was a customary demonstration of unit
    amongst low churchmen. K. Heasman, *Evangelicals in Actio*
    (London, 1962), p. 16.

65. *Pall Mall Budget,* 2 July and 9 July 1870.

66. (T. N. Sanyal), op. cit. p. 164.

67. Keshub Chunder Sen, *In England* op. cit. pp. 376-385. S. N
    Dutt op. cit. p. 192 mentioned that in the 1870 *Maghotsa*
    (January) report an English Theistic Church, England's 'Ban
    of Faith', was given as a branch of the Brahmo Samaj of India
    It is uncertain which body this referred to, as this Theisti
    Association was never developed, and Charles Voysey did no
    open his Theistic Church in London till 1871.

68. Keshub Chunder Sen, *In England* op. cit. pp. 397-398.

69. He asked Rev. Spears to telegraph his family after the inter
    view to tell them of the honour that had been done him, s
    they could share in his joy. From Rev. Spears' reminiscence
    of Keshub in *Liberal and New Dispensation,* 24 February 188∢
    p. 8.

70. Keshub Chunder Sen, *In England* op. cit. pp. 469-471. A com
    mittee was formed in October 1870. Its report mentioned th
    there was already a gentleman near Calcutta, Sasipada Baner
    jee, carrying out many of their aims.

71. ibid. pp. 472-496.

72. It is interesting to note the different reactions of *Punch* an
    the *Pall Mall Budget* to this speech. *Punch* of 24 Septembe
    1870 published a letter protesting against the Baboo's unfair
    ness in his criticism of women's fashions, whereas the *Pa*
    *Mall Budget* of 17 September 1870 took each criticism seriously
    and called for improvements in the situation.

73. *Saturday Review,* 4 June 1870 in a review of Keshub's boo∤
    *The Brahmo-Somaj.*

74. J. Drummond and C. B. Upton op. cit., Vol. II, pp. 2-3. From
    a letter to Rev. Wicksteed of 5 May 1870.

75. Despite this, apparently two of his travelling companions (no
    mentioned by name) were later baptized.    Monier Williams
    op. cit. p. 506.

76. Rajnarain Bose, op. cit. p. 172. In a letter to Rajnarain, th
    Theist Miss Elizabeth Sharpe mentioned that the English res
    pected Keshub for his resistance to being denationalized.

77. Keshub Chunder Sen, *In England* op. cit. p. 278.

78. His visit was even reported in Europe. When Annette Ack
    royd heard about his idea of forming a Theistic Association
    she was in Switzerland. Beveridge, op. cit. p. 83.

79. Quoted in P. K. Sen, *Biography* op. cit. Vol. II, p. 49.

# CHAPTER SIX

# ACTIVITY AND ASCETICISM (1871-1877)

KESHUB'S RETURN to India was triumphant. His grand reception in England, as a representative of India, boosted Indian pride and self-confidence. He had been treated not only as an equal, but honoured as an important person. This enhanced his image in the eyes of his fellow-Indians, and also helped them to realize that India did have valid claims to world recognition. Even sections of the native press, usually hostile to the Brahmos, praised his success in England. The *Amrita Bazar Patrika* and the *Dacca Patrika* roundly condemned the *Somaprakash* for not doing so.[1] Keshub's successful English visit gave Bengalis, and Indians, a new pride, which was a factor in accelerating the beginnings of the nationalist movement.

He landed in Bombay, where a Welcome Soiree was held in his honour on 16 October 1870, at which he spoke on his impressions of England and the English.[2] Keshub's talk was jovial and entertaining, but he was in earnest. He was, on the one hand, fostering patriotism by saying that India was no worse than England--a major revelation at the time--but he harboured no ill feeling towards the English, as he told his audience that they could always appeal to the English people and to the Queen to see justice done. He was a patriot with pride in his own country, but not a nationalist. For him loyalty to Britain was of the utmost importance. His ideal went beyond national awakening to a vision of universal harmony. The only improvement he sought was greater mutuality, because

> ....England has yet much to learn from India, as India has yet much to learn from England. If we enter into a sort of moral and spiritual covenant with each other, mutually and independently resolving to supplement our respective deficiencies by receiving and accepting from each other—if we determine not to flatter ourselves nor to flatter the other

party, but dispassionately and calmly to receive all
that is good in each nation—then I say a glorious
result will accrue to both.

He commended English charity, and singled out for
special mention the "sweet English home".

In Calcutta the excitement on his return was even
greater. He was greeted by cheering crowds at Howrah
station on 20 October, and was given two public recep-
tions, by the Brahmos and Brahmikas respectively.
Keshub's enthusiasm and energy were such that he
wanted to put into practice straight away those aspects
of English life which he felt would be beneficial to India.
He called a meeting of the Indian Reform Association,
formally founded on 2 November. The first meeting of
the Association was held on 7 November, and at this
the structure of the Association was agreed on and the
office-bearers were elected. It was an Association with
grand aims, covering a total reformation of society and
the furtherance of a puritanical, industrious middle-
class. It was open to non-Brahmos, and as religion did
not play a major role in it, it had a wider appeal than a
purely Brahmo organization would have. Christians
welcomed the Association as promoting accepted Western
ideals, and some, like Rev. Dall in the temperance movement, gave it their active support. However, the Association was primarily an Indian one, with few English
members, as patriotism was one of the factors providing
renewed impetus for reform. It was unique for that
time in that it aimed at action rather than theoretical
discussion, unlike the Bethune Society and the Bengal
Social Science Association. It was divided into five sections:
—Charity, Female Improvement, Education, Temperance
and Cheap Literature. Each of these had a Vice-President
and a Secretary, the President of the whole being Keshub
and the Honorary Secretary Gobind Chunder Dhur.[3]
Keshub had given some attention to all of these sectors
in the past, but his present inspiration was based on
what he had seen in England, and wanted to experiment
with and implement in India.

The Charity section was probably the most conventional, almsgiving having been an established Hindu tradition. It provided assistance to small groups of schoolboys, widows, poor families and blind people, and more widely, provided medical relief, treatment, and food, for victims of epidemics.

All other areas of reform were more controversial. The Female Improvement Section found many ready sympathizers among the more enlightened middle-class gentlemen. Their first activity was to found a much-needed Female Normal and Adult School, which opened on 1 February 1872[4]. Mary Carpenter had promised a grant of 200 rupees a month, but this was reduced and finally discontinued when she found that the Government was not giving supplementary aid—a vicious circle, as the Government withheld aid because the school was run by a non-secular body and thus not eligible for a grant. The Government was prompted to found its own institution but it was a failure, presumably because the need for such a school had already been satisfied by the Brahmos, so they finally conceded to giving the school a grant of 2,000 rupees per annum from 1872.[5] A Girls' School was attached to the Normal School from September 1871. There were some lady teachers, but those chiefly responsible for teaching initially were Bijoy Krishna Goswami and Aghorenath Gupta. Miss Ackroyd was expected to teach there when she came to India, but she withdrew her co-operation because of a personality clash with Keshub.[6] (She taught instead at the rival Hindu Mahila Vidyalaya, founded in November, 1873.) It is noteworthy that even at this early stage none of the female emancipationist party which had grown up in the Brahmo Samaj, for instance Dwarkanath Ganguli or Durga Mohan Das, were involved in Keshub's projects for female improvement, where the stress was on development of womanly virtues rather than high-level education. It would be unjust, however, to see Keshub's education scheme only in the denigratory terms of the female emancipationists, as his scheme was probably of greater benefit than theirs, enabling the spread of basic knowledge among a wide circle of women and giving them some stimulation even if it did not provide for those who wanted to go further. The syllabus for the highest class included the study of Bengali grammar and literature (ranging from the *Megnadh Badh Kabya* by Michael Madhusudhan Datta to Valmiki's *Ramayana*—presumably in a Bengali translation), History, Geography, Natural Philosophy, Arithmetic and English. The students were tested by external examiners, most of whom expressed great satisfaction with their prowess in all subjects (although perhaps being more astounded at the neatness of their handwriting than the actual content of their work!)[7] The ladies held discussions on various topics at meetings of their Bama Hitaishini Sabha, founded in April 1871. Keshub presided over the weekly meetings where the women gave talks on such appropriate subjects as True Modesty, Female Liberty, Charity, Sisterly Love, Gratitude, Dress, Pride and False Refinement—topics which now appear very limited but which were presumably similar to those discussed by most middle-class society ladies Keshub met in England. He had, of course, also met many publicly active women there too, but evidently found their type either untimely or undesirable in India. Literature was considered a suitable feminine field, and many of the group's discussions and literary compositions were published in the *Bamabodhini Patrika,* which had a circulation of 500 and was read by many more.

The Education section was composed of the Working Men's Institution and Industrial School—both direct imports from Britain.[8] They were opened on 28 November 1870.[9] As this kind of education was foreign to the Indian tradition and to the system the British had set up in India, keeping it going was bound to be a struggle, and the number of pupils always fluctuated widely. Out of the six departments of the Industrial School—Carpentry, Tailoring, Clock and Watch Repairing, Printing, Lithogrophy and Engraving—the latter three were closed down within the first year because of the low attendance. The purpose of the Working Men's Institution was to spread knowledge among the working-classes, but failed to take into account the fact that there was no class in India (small even in England) corresponding to the English industrial worker anxious to improve his position by self-help, who could appreciate such "rational recreation" as the school provided. It is unclear as to what kind of working men Keshub had in mind to benefit from the Institution, as the introductory lectures were on magnetic electricity, oxygen and atmospheric pressure, and on the Diurnal and Annual Revolutions of the Earth, Solar and Lunar Eclipses of the Seasons, and on the rudiments of Geology Surveying and Geometry. The Industrial School was founded to give the middle-classes training in the useful arts, and to provide respite from the ceaseless toil of the *keranee's* desk, which repressed "all the noble aspirations of their minds", and also exercised "a deleterious moral influence on them".[10] For some, the School was to offer an alternative to white-collar employment, for others of the higher classes it was more of a pastime, for utility and pleasure. It was an idealistic project in India at that time, where caste was still firmly entrenched, and arts and crafts did not rank highly in the caste occupational hierarchy. The whole operation was not only influenced but fostered by England, especially by the British and Foreign School Society which made contributions of educational apparatus. The Committee sagely perceived the middle-class nature of the Schools :—

> The Working Men's Institutions and Industrial Schools are not much appreciated by the classes for whom they are intended, and that a considerable length of time must elapse before they elicit sufficient public interest and take root in this country. The committee must therefore 'learn to labour and to wait', and patiently persevere in their work till the full measure of success is achieved.[11]

The Calcutta School was placed under the Education Section in July 1872. It was a school for middle-class boys, its distinguishing features being moderate fees and the stress on moral discipline and physical sciences.[12]

The aim of the Temperance section was twofold—to cooperate with the United Kingdom Alliance in petition-

ing for the suppression of the liquor traffic in India and
to make people aware of the evil effects of intemperance
through lectures, tracts, and the foundation of societies.
It also issued a monthly journal, *Mad na Garal?* (Wine
or Poison). Keshub's activities in this field were undoubtedly given great impetus by the zeal for the cause
of temperance that he had come across in England.
English temperance bodies sent literature to India to
further the cause. Originally Keshub seemed to have
been most worried by the effects of alchohol on the youth
of the middle-classes, who had succumbed to it under the
guise of being 'civilized', but in England he was made
aware of the demoralizing effect it was thought to have
on the lower classes, as there it was seen by many middle-
class philanthropists as being the root cause of the pro-
belms of the working-class. With this heightened consciousness of the problem, in September 1872 Keshub
circulated a questionnaire among prominent Indian and
European citizens[13] soliciting their opinions on seven
questions regarding the extent of intemperance and the
measures needed to combat it, as a prelude to a memorial
to the Government suggesting reforms. Probably in
some measure owing to Keshub's exposure of the Indian
situation in England, the Government ordered an inquiry
into the working of the liquor policy, but this did not
produce many changes. However, the Victory, Lord
Northbrook, agreed with Keshub's remarks and so in
1876 when the excise system was revised there was some
reduction in the number of liquor shops.[14]

   Keshub had mentioned in his speech at the Farewell
Soiree in England that he had been impressed with the
power of English public opinion, as expressed through
the press. In England he had also become more conscious of the need to 'elevate' the working-classes. He
initiated reform to cover both these fields under the
auspices of the Cheap Lietrature section of the Indian
Reform Association, by starting a weekly paper costing
only one pice, the *Sulabh Samachar* (Cheap News) on
16 November 1870. This turned out to be one of his
most successful enterprises, both in terms of its sales

(281, 149 copies in 14 months) and its example. Its circulation fell from its peak of 27,202 in February 1871, to 14,273 in December 1871, because of competition from other cheap vernacular papers on the market[15] but in 1877 it still had the highest circulation of all vernacular newspapers.[16]  The number influenced was even greater than the sales figures indicate, as each copy was passed on to a wide circle of readers, and the information contained would have filtered down to the illiterate masses by word of mouth.  Keshub was responsible for most of the articles in the paper.  He saw himself as a popular leader, calling on the masses to be aware of their rights and inciting them to rise up, though in the English sense of self-help rather than in any revolutionary way.[17]  In 1871 the *Indian Mirror*, formerly a weekly, became a daily paper, and thus increased its influence as a channel of public opinion.  It had the distinction of being the first daily paper in English to be conducted by an Indian.[18]

In the first few months after his return Keshub had already set in motion a tremendous range of reforms, based on his observations of England, but not always fully thought out in the Indian context.  This was intentional, as Keshub did not want to 'waste' time in theoretical discussion.  He felt that the suitability of reforms could only be judged from their practical effects.  The Indian Reform Association, despite its failures, was one of the highest testimonies to Keshub's capacity for quick, practical action to bring about a state of affairs which he considered desirable.  It was also a concrete example, albeit not always a successful one, of his constant desire to harmonize East and West, and to introduce into India those institutions which he had admired in England, following his idea that India could learn most from England in practical matters, while offering the way to spiritual fulfilment to England in return.  His enterprise was lauded by leading representatives of the Indian and English communities alike as showing the possibility of an active, practical and progressive reform association, open to all but run entirely by Indians and thus not reliant on the British Government for aid of any kind.[19]

The most lasting reform accomplished in this period was the passing of the Native Marriage Act as Act III of 1872, on 19 March 1872. This was the culmination of lengthy and persistent agitation on the part of Keshub. The British sympathized with him and saw the need for such a reform, but their co-operation represented a tribute to Keshub's persuasive powers rather than their interest in the cause alone, as a previous petition from over 400 Bengali gentlemen in 1956, calling for a similar Act, had been fruitless.[20] The British shared Brahmo objections to Hindu marriages, and as the Advocate-General also declared that Brahmo marriages were invalid because they did not conform to Hindu law, and that therefore reformed marriages were illegal and their offspring illegitimate, it was clear that something had to be done to rectify the situation. The Bill in its original form as a Civil Marriage Act was rejected by the Select Committee for its consideration in 1871, because of pressure from orthodox Hindu all over India, and even from the British Indian Association.[21] As the bride and groom were only required to declare that they were not Christians, and objected to the *marriage forms* of the Hindu, Muhammedan, Buddhist, Parsi and Jewish religions,[22] the opposers of the Bill felt that there was a loophole whereby people could remain Hindu while disregarding Hindu law and custom, in effect opening an avenue for the undermining of traditional Hinduism.

The matter did not rest there. The Select Committee rephrased the Bill, saying that

> It is the unanimous opinion of the Local Government that the Bill as introduced should not be passed. They all, on the other hand, agree that the Bill would be unobjectionable if confined to the Brahmo Samaj, for whose benefit it was originally designed. We have, accordingly, narrowed its operation to the members of the sect..[23]

In its second form the Bill was called the Brahmo Marriage Act, thus placating the Hindus and other religious denominations. However, the Committee reckoned without the objections of the Adi Brahmo Samaj. The

Adi Brahmo insisted that its marriages were valid according to Hindu law, even though Keshub had obatined the
opinions of *pandits* from all over India who contradicted
this. The Adi Brahmo Samaj had always maintained
that it was merely a reformed version of Hinduism, and
so was loath to separate itself from the Hindu community.
As one of the basic causes of former disputes had been
the question of how far marriage reform could be taken,
it was predictable that on this issue they would not
side with the Brahmo Samaj of India. The Adi Brahmo
Samaj's form of marriage involved reformed non-idolatrous rites, but avoided breaking caste rules, whereas
Keshub's kind of reformed marriage involved a ceremony
with an exchange of vows very similar to that of the
Christian marriage, and also ignored all caste rules. As
they departed less from orthodox Hinduism the Adi
Brahmos were naturally more confident of being accepted
within its fold. Rajnarain Bose issued an appeal to the
Brahmos of India expressing his indignation at the im-
position of a civil ceremony of marriage as the essential
one, almost superceding the religious ceremony which
had no legal validity on its own.[24] He felt this to be an
historic interference with the religion of India on the
part of the Government, as in all other forms of marriage
the legal and religious ceremonies were one. The Government was aware of the various complications. Sir
Fitzjames Stephen (Sir Henry Maine's replacement as
Legal Member of the Viceroy's Council) diagnosed the
problem thus :—

> By recognizing the existence of the Hindu religion
> as a personal law in this matter of marriage, I think
> that we have contracted an obligation to enforce its
> provisions in their entirety upon those who choose to
> live under them, just as we have, by establishing the
> general principle of religious freedom, contracted a
> further obligation to protect anyone who chooses to
> leave the Hindu religion against injury for having done
> so, and to provide him with institutions recognized by
> law and suitable to his peculiar position. I think that it
> is hardly possible for us to hold other language on
> the subject than this—'Be a Hindu or not as you

please ; but be one thing or the other, and do not
ask us to undertake the impossible task of cons-
tructing some compromise between Hinduism and
not-Hinduism which will enable you to evade the
necessity of knowing your own minds ?'....[25]

The new Bill, accordingly, included a proviso that it
was confined to persons who were not Hindus, or members of any other established religious denominations.
Sir Fitzjames Stephen expected that the Adi Brahmo
Samaj would accept this but that it would be rejected
by the Brahmo Samaj of India, which he believed belonged to that indeterminate religious position he had
mentioned. To his surprise they forestalled any such
criticism by writing a letter to the Government before the
Bill had even been presented in this form, renouncing
the term Hindu because they denied the Vedas, they were
opposed to every form of Brahmanical religion, and were
eclectic in their beliefs. Thus the Bill was finally passed
in its third formulation.

Not only did the Act confer legality on Brahmo
marriages, it also defined the character of such marriages,
as certain rules applied to those who got married according to it. Perturbed about the evil of early marriage, in
1871 Keshub had sent out a circular to a group of doctors
asking for their views on the minimum marriageable
age of girls.[26] In reply he got a very detailed series of
reports on the average age of menstruation of Indian girls,
which most of them said was around the age of 13. They
did not wish this to be taken as the minimum marriageable age, however, as the age of menstruation was partly
determined by the custom of early marriage, and was
therefore a forced puberty. Apart from the consideration that a girl of 13 was still not fully developed physically, she was not psychologically ready for adulthood,
and so marriage at such an age would not be congenial
to producing healthy offspring. Of the 12 doctors involved in the survey only two set 14 as the minimum age.
Two others felt that 15 was reasonable, and one hopefully put down 20, but the majority agreed that 16 should
be the minimum. Despite their verdict Keshub felt that

it was necessary to make a practical compromise. As
he did not want to make the Act totally inaccessible and
as he knew that in India marriage commonly took place
under 13, he set 14 as the minimum age for the bride,
"leaving it in the hands of time to develop this reform
slowly and gradually into maturity and fulness."[27] The
minimum marriageable age of the groom was set at 18,
because he had to cope with the responsibility of providing for the family. The Act prohibited bigamy and
polygamy, and sanctioned inter-caste and widow
marriages. It prevented secret marriages, as the civil
ceremony required two weeks advance notification. It
also allowed for the possibility of divorce in extreme
cases.[28] The most contentious part of the Act was the
total renunciation of the Hindu faith. In his eagerness
to accomplish such a major reform Keshub felt that this
was only a minor point, the logical result of the path
the Brahmo Samaj had taken under him, always changing and progressing in directions which could not possibly
be confined within orthodox Hinduism. The significance
of this total break with Hinduism was only realized later,
in a more nationalistic era, when it became a factor which
discouraged people from joining the Brahmo Samaj.

In both 1871 and 1872 Keshub was Chairman of the
Education Committee of the Bengal Social Science Association. In February 1871 he gave an address there on
'The Improvement of Indian Women'.[29] He began by
using examples from ancient Indian literature to show
that Hinduism was not in principle opposed to female
education—thus showing, unwittingly, the need for establishing legitimacy in Hindu terms—then detailed the
progress that had been made both in female schools and
in *zenana* education. A number of women had written
books in Bengali—the vernacular being the usual medium
for female education. Keshub felt that there was still
room for greater progress, and made six suggestions to
this end, which included the establishment of Normal
Schools; school inspectresses; adult classes in the
*zenana* for those who had to leave school for early marriages; secular *zenana* teachers;[30] and visits to places

10

like the Asiatic Society Museum and the Botanical
Gardens, along the lines of the outings organized by the
Working Men's Institutes in England. Keshub's speech
was an earnest plea to raise the intellectual level of
women in order to promote general enlightenment and
reform in the country. He approvingly quoted J. S.
Mill's dictum, "The time has come when if women are
not raised to the intellectual level of men, men must be pul-
led down to the mental level of women".[31]    In fact Keshub
was not a thorough follower of Mill's ideas on women,
although Martineau had got the impression that he was in
favour of giving women the vote.[32] His ideas on the
question of female education, although undoubtedly advanced in the Indian context, were those of mainstream
conservative Victorian thinking, and were soon openly
challenged by those more radical. Keshub had been
greatly impressed by the "accomplished and devout"
women he had met in England, and was desirous that
Indian women should follow their lead,[33] but in spirit
rather than in outward form, thus setting limits on their
chance of participation in public affairs.

At the same time as he was making great efforts in
the field of basic female education Keshub was engaged
in a controversy with some fellow members of the
Brahmo Samaj on whether or not their wives and daughters should be allowed to sit with them amongst the
congregation and not in the special closed ladies' gallery.
He did not object in principle, but was concerned because
it would upset many less progressive members of the
congregation. He was adamant in his opposition to the
move, and when Durga Mohan Das and Annada Charan
Kasthigir actually sat in the congregation with female
members of their families they were forced to leave and
set up their own services.[34]. The rebels eventually returned to Keshub's fold when he agreed to allow ladies
to sit openly in the general congregation, though in a
special reserved area, in June 1872. Keshub expressed his
position regarding female emancipation in part of another address to the Bengal Social Science Association in
March 1872, on 'The Reconstruction of Native Society'.[35] He

said of the emancipationists:

> These men would give the first place to freedom and
> emancipation, and they believe that all other reforms
> would follow. I should, however, place education,
> moral training, and social reformation first, and these
> will, in the natural course of things, lead to what is
> called the emancipation of women. It is impossible
> to immure a Native woman in the zenana if she has
> received a sound education. But, then, do not bring
> about violent changes in this matter. It is a most
> delicate experiment, and ought to be tried in a most
> delicate manner.

As Keshub was never habitually so cautious this appears
to have been an excuse to cover his own inability to
endorse the advanced ideas of the emancipationists.

In his capacity of President of the Indian Reform
Association and head of the Education section of the
Bengal Social Science Association, Keshub wrote nine
open letters on education to Lord Northbrook in the
*Indian Mirror* between May and August 1872, under the
pseudonym of Indophilus.[36] In the seventh letter he gave
a detailed list of suggestions for the spread of education among the masses which displayed his practical
aptitude when applying his mind to a concrete problem.
His ideas were both novel and sensible. He suggested a
Native Inspector for vernacular schools and evening
schools for workers. He felt that a useful and relevant
education should be given to the masses—a *ryot* should
be able to write a business letter or draw out a bond,
and an artisan should have enough scientific knowledge
to arouse his interest in his occupation and enable him
to improve it. He also suggested Government grants to
poor schools, popular lectures on basic science, and the
distribution of cheap literature, as well as a system of
rewards to landholders who had established a large
number of schools, as an incentive for more to follow
their example. For the upper and middle classes he
thought that teaching should be made more stimulating
and less geared to cramming for examinations, and recommended that science should be taught on a larger
scale (a far-sighted observation, as science was not yet

widely taught even in England at that time). He was
in favour of greater emphasis on morality in education,
through such subjects as Ethics and Natural Theology.
The latter suggestion met with approval, and was taken
up by the University of Calcutta.

This very wide range covered the bulk of Keshub's
reform activities after his return from England. After
1872 there was a noticeable slacking off. Most activities were still kept up, but Keshub was less active and
innovative, continuing old projects rather starting new
ones. So much energy had already gone into laying
the foundations of his reform programme that it was not
to be expected that he should continue to maintain such an
active pace. His motives for reform were also an important reason for the change. Although very mindful of the
need for social reform, his primary interest was in religion, and the Brahmo Samaj was primarily a religious
institution. He realized that in order to achieve the
kind of religious state he envisaged, reform of society
would be necessary.[37] Once he had set up the conditions
for an improved society, as he felt he had done during
the period following his English visit, he lost interest
in pursuing those reforms for their own sake, and devoted
his energies to religious inquiry. His main aim was
to spread his idea of religion, though social reformation
was necessary for the ultimate fulfilment of his ideals.
The division between the two spheres was never entirely
clear-cut. As in Hinduism religion and society were
inseparable, so they were, theoretically, in Keshub's
Brahmoism, but as religious changes seemed to be more
easily accepted than changes in social custom, he concentrated his energies on what seemed to be a less difficult
area.

The combination of religious and social aims was evident in the establishment of the *Bharat Ashram* in February 1872. Keshub had been impressed with his observation of the communal harmony of the English home, as
distinct from the communal living of the Indian joint
family, which he knew from close experience to create
all kinds of divisive jealousy and bitterness. The English

family system accorded more closely with his ideals of
piety combined with earnestness and industry, ideals
which he had imbibed from his English education in the
first place. Keshub had enumerated the qualities which
attracted him about the institution of the English home
in idyllic terms :—

> ....You see there the spirit of moral righteousness
> and purity infused into the daily life, even into the
> petty details of daily transactions. This domestic
> life in England is not only sweet, but pure ; there is
> not only joy and happiness on the one hand, but
> there is also a stern and severe moral discipline
> exercised by the elder members of the family, by
> parents over children.[38]

To experiment with that ideal in India Keshub established
the *Bharat Ashram,* a religious boarding house, at Bel-
gharia, about seven miles from Calcutta. About 25
families lived there according to certain rules and guide-
lines. He meant it to be "a modrn apostolic organization"[39], where all individual selfishness was subsumed in
a desire to realize the common good. The community
shared some advanced views. The *zenana* system was
discarded, and men and women joined in the daily
worship conducted by Keshub. It was a social experiment, intended to establish a religious community, or
as Bijoy Krishna Goswami expressed it,

> The *upasanas* (divine services) held there were cal-
> culated to bring salvation by means of united wor-
> ship of the merciful Father to Brahmos bound together
> by heavenly bonds of brotherhood, and to realize the
> ideal of the Kingdom of Heaven on earth....[40]

Its resemblance to a traditional Hindu *ashram* was in
name only, as it was not a solitary, other-worldly type
of spirituality that was aimed for. Sivanath Sastri, who
lived in the *Bharat Ashram* with his family for some
years, said its aim was to train its inhabitants in the
English religious habits of order, neatness, punctuality,
and daily domestic devotions.[41] The Female Normal and
Adult School, and the Girls' School were on the premises,

so they could learn from and participate in this model community too. It also provided the core of pupils and teachers for both schools.

To live in such an intense community atmosphere entailed a great deal of commitment, not merely to Brahmoism, but to Keshub and his socio-religious ideals. Keshub was concentrating his efforts on building up a small community based on his ideas, headed and guided by him. Inevitably, the creation of the *Bharat Ashram* gave birth to a distinction between Brahmos in general and this special group. There was bound to be cause for resentment and criticism from those who were not part of the group—and because it required such goodwill in order to succeed, its stability was also easily threatened from inside by those who disagreed with Keshub or with each other.

Keshub's appeal to the younger generation was waning. One reason may have been that he no longer addressed himself to young people in particular, as they were (obviously) no longer his contemporaries. Another reason was that many active young men found his religious piety overwhelming and uncongenial, and directed their energies to other fields, especially politics. In 1872 he had established the *Brahmo Niketan* as a boarding house for schoolboys with nowhere to stay in Calcutta. Bipin Chandra Pal remembered that it did not appeal to him because he felt the inmates were more religious than human, cultivating an "excessive and abnormal religiosity".[42] For most of these boys, the highest object in life was to become a missionary.[43] The atmosphere in the Sylhet Students' Mess where Bipin Chandra Pal lived was anti-Brahmo for this reason. Although his younger following may have diminished, Keshub was more popular than ever with the bulk of the middle-classes, as their ideas were beginning to catch up with his. At an anniversary meeting attended by Miss Ackroyd on 26 January 1873, Keshub had an audience of about 2,000 people. She said they were "of quite the lowest classes". but her judgements, coming from a dogmatic English newcomer, cannot be relied on as accurate. Keshub was in his element in such a gathering, and she said he:

> ....looked very imposing, indeed a splendid figure in his white robes and with his graceful and passionate gesture. He spoke of the general attributes of Deity—then rested and then again spoke of practical reforms of life. The people were very attentive and frequently applauded.[44]

His major public statements on his religious beliefs were delivered in his anniversary lectures. That of 1872, 'Primitive Faith and Modern Speculations', contained nothing exceptional.[45] In it Keshub emphasized the possibility of seeing God, in the sense of spiritually perceiving his presence, in the modern world. His 1873 lecture on 'Inspiration' was more controversial,[46] proclaiming that God gave literal answers to men's prayers, and guided the actions of the spiritual man who listened for his voice—the actions of such a man were God's actions. This appeared to many as suspiciously like the doctrine of papal infallibility, abnegating the need for personal responsibility for one's actions. It also raised the question of what happened in cases of conflicting inspiration in different people. Both lectures were based on Western rather than Indian experience especially in the lament over modern materialism and the lack of primitive directness of devotion—the former not particularly prevalent in India, the latter present as a common feature in popular Hinduism. He strongly denounced the cardinal Upanishadic doctrine of *"Aham Brahma"* as a degrading and revolting doctrine.[47] Examples from the Bible and the life of Jesus were used with much greater frequency than references from Hindu texts. The 1874 anniversary lecture was again unexceptional, being about establishing the kingdom of heaven on earth, and the need for unity and harmony.[48]

In 1871 Keshub had revived the Brahmo School for training young men in Brahmo theology. Judging from the type of examination questions, the school curriculum followed the kind of beliefs that were part of universal Theism, and the study was firmly based on Western sources and concepts. The questions included such as these : "Give a philosophical analysis of the text 'In Him we live and move and have our being'. Coleridge says,—'It is not the motive that makes the man, but the man the motive'. What light does the principle stated here throw on the subject of free will ? Reconcile the justice and mercy of God, and show that vicarious atonement contradicts both these attributes. Explain the philosophy of the adage,—vox populi, vox Dei. In what shape does Idealism prevail in India ? How far are the mystics right ?"[49] Even though some of the questions did apply to India, the framework—the very fact of answering questions on religion in an examination—was not Indian.

Doctrinal questions aside, the course of Brahmonism was also being shaped by the behaviour of its adherents. The first incident to openly disrupt the peaceful flow of existence within the *Bharat Ashram* was the departure of Haranath Bose.[50] It was the practice for families in the *Ashram* to donate part of their salaries to cover the expenses of the *Ashram*. Haranath Bose had not done so, and had contracted debts. This situation may have been tolerated in a Hindu joint family, but here it was felt that he was not participating as a responsible member of the community. It was decided that if his wife and children were moved out, he would then be forced to follow. Just as his wife and children were about to leave, the manager of the *Ashram* stopped them at the gate, insisting on immediate payment of Haranath's debts before they would be allowed to leave. Having no money, his wife had to part with her own jewellery. When Haranath heard of the heavy-handedness of their approach, he was furious—especially as the story had been reported in the newspapers. His antagonism was probably spurred on by a residual resentment at having been replaced as head of the Calcutta School by Keshub's brother, Krishna Behari Sen. The furor he managed to work up against Keshub through the press was so vehement that Keshub felt obliged to prosecute. The matter was finally settled out of court, and Keshub's honour was vindicated y a public apology to him by the paper concerned.

Keshub's prominence and the acclaim given to him
as a source of much personal jealousy, both amongst
is followers and in the community at large. Not only
as he a famous popular preacher, he was also favoured
ith recognition and respect from the highest of Anglo-
idian officials, the Viceroy. Lord Northbrook presented
ie prizes to the pupils of the Female Normal School in
873, and afterwards visited Keshub's house, conferring
n him the distinction of being the first Indian to have
eceived the Viceroy at a private function in his own
.ome.[51] Keshub was not a society man, but he was
orldly enough to realize the value and prestige accruing
rom such influential contacts. He mixed easily in the
ighest circles of English society. His behaviour belied
is claim that:

> Where I perceive the dazzling garments of riches and
> rank, my nature shrinks therefrom. The rich, the
> respected, and the learned—to these three classes
> of people my spirit does not go with alacrity, does
> not like to approach..[52]

A major source of disruption was the continual wrang-
ing between Keshub and his loyal missionary followers
on the one hand, and the small group of new 'progres-
ives' that had formed in opposition to Keshub, initially
ver the question of the seating of women in the *Mandir*.
These men, such as Dwarkanath Ganguli, Durga Mohan
Das, Ananda Mohan Bose, Nagendra Nath Chatterjee, and,
on the fringe, Sivanath Sastri, were primarily reformers
who took reason as the decisive guide to their actions.
They felt, in an inversion of Keshub's scheme of thinking,
that to go with their kind of reformed society, they needed
a reformed religion—and Brahmoism seemed to be the
natural choice. They soon found that their aims were
n conflict. For instance, Keshub was not interested in
pushing female education beyond the point he saw as
necessary for an enlightened society, whereas they wanted
to take it to its furthest limits. Co-operation was made difficult because   Keshub believed that his actions   were an expression of God's will, an idea formulated in his doctrine

of *Adesh*—or as he put it in English, Inspiration. For th
*Samadarshi* group (called after the journal they founde
to express their views in 1874) rational criticism
analysis of the situation was made impossible by Keshub
invocation of *Adesh*. This became a major issue whe
they criticized the *Bharat Ashram's* handling of th
Haranath Bose affair, and were told that the missionarie
were above criticism from outside because they wer
appointed by God.

The rift with Keshub over the position of wome
also widened. The new progressives felt that Keshub
idea of women's education was too narrow. Sivanat
Sastri, who taught at the Female Normal School, argue
with Keshub over the necessity of teaching geometry t
his pupils. Keshub's objection was that it would be c
no use to them. Sastri wanted to teach geometry, logi
and metaphysics, but settled for Keshub's ruling tha
the elementary principles of science were enough—an
he managed to bring in mental science and logic unde
that heading.[53] The reformers snapped up Annie Ackroy
after she had parted with Keshub, to teach at thei
*Hindu Mahila Vidayalaya*.[54] Their only point of contac
left with Keshub and his band was as fellow-member
of the congregation of the Brahmo *Mandir,* with share
religious views. However, as Keshub's religious view
continued to develop, even this was open to question.

In the 1875 anniversary lecture on 'Behold the Ligh
of Heaven in India' Keshub's ideas took on a more insis
tent, definite and personal form.[55] The lecture had adde
significance in being the first occasion on which the term
New Dispensation was used by Keshub to mean a new
road to salvation especially shown to India by God'
Providence, which had also helped Indian redemption by
sending British rule. He felt that the history of India
was sacred, and every event contributing to the country'
advancement was fraught with religious significance—
good illustration of the inseparability of the spheres of
religion and society in his way of thinking. His message
for Indian salvation was idealistic, but not startling—the
Gospel of love. The most interesting part of the lecture

consisted of Keshub's allusions to himself and the Brahmo
Samaj. Apprehensive of being accused of seeking personal power, he denied all claims to being even a teacher
of men, because the authority of God was above him.
He also lashed out at his detractors, or 'persecutors'. He
rhetorically reiterated the charges that had been laid
against him—of infusing youthful minds with dangerous
doctrines calculated to jeopardize the moral and social
interests of the country ; and of being actuated by sordid
motives, preaching like a hollow-hearted hypocrite, and
impostor. His reply to all this was that no accusations
could impede his work, as it was God's work. He called
on all to unite in working for the "high objects of the
present dispensation", which were left unspecified except
that they were to represent to total unity. On the same
anniversary Keshub also delivered an unusual address in
Bengali on 'Beholding the Universal Mother', incorpora-
ting an age-old Indian tradition into his religious scheme.
This Hindu idea accorded well with the emotional side
of his nature, as the mother-child relationship was one
which allowed for effusive devotional expression. Victorian puritanism had closed off, for him, the common
Radha-Krishna devotional relationship of Vaishnavism.

Keshub met the Hindu mystic Ramakrishna in 1875.
He had not known him before this. The meeting was
sought for by Ramakrishna, who had heard about Keshub,
and had even heard him preach in the Adi Brahmo
Samaj.[56] There has been much dispute over how much
influence Ramakrishna had on Keshub's ideas.[57] From
what has been discussed hitherto, it is obvious that Keshub
had already developed the idea of using Hindu devotional aids in Brahmoism before his meeting with Ramakrishna. He continued to develop these ideas over the
ensuing years in a logical chain of development, so the
meeting with Ramakrishna should not be seen as a major
turning-point in Keshub's career. In a comparison
between Keshub and Ramakrishna, the differences are
more apparent than the similarities. Although in all
externals they formed a total contrast with each other,
they found great affinity in their devotional natures, in

the warmth and fire of their religious feeling. Keshub
admired Ramakrishna for his "primitive direct vision"
of God—which was a part of the Hindu tradition unknown to Keshub who had had little contact with Hindu
mystics. Ramakrishna was attracted to Keshub by the
spirituality that he perceived in him, although he was
also aware of the more worldly side of Keshub's nature.
Keshub had met another great Hindu figure, Swami
Dayananda Saraswati, in 1872. He admired him, but
Dayananda's stern, dogmatic and solitary character prevented them from establishing a warm personal relationship. Keshub organized public meetings where Dayananda addressed his audience in simple Sanskrit, leading
Keshub to advise him to use Hindi for greater accessi-
bility. As the two had similar organizational aims,
Keshub advised him that another prudent improvement
in his tactics for gaining public recognition and respect
would be to wear clothing.[58] Keshub made no such suggestion to Ramakrishna, who was not concerned with
methods of public propaganda as he did not consider that
he had an urgent message to convey. However, Keshub felt
that Ramakrishna did have much to teach people, and
so brought him to the notice of the public through mentions in the *Indian Mirror* and the *Dharmatattva*. Keshub's
enthusiasm for Ramakrishna was an important factor in
elevating him into a person to be taken seriously by the
middle-classes, beginning with the Brahmos and extending through the rest of educated society.[59]

Keshub felt that his acquaintance with Dayananda and
Ramakrishna gave him an added appreciation of the
depths and potentialities of Hinduism. He wrote in the
*Indian Mirror* of 28 March 1875 that

> We met one (a sincere Hindu devotee), not long ago,
> and were charmed by the depth, penetration and
> simplicity of his spirit. The never-ceasing metaphors
> and analogies in which he indulged, are most of
> them as apt as they are beautiful. The characteristics
> of his mind are the very opposite to those of Pundit
> Dayananda Saraswati, the former being as gentle,
> tender, and contemplative as the latter is tardy,
> masculine and polemical. Hinduism must have in it

a deep source of beauty, truth and goodness to inspire such men as these.[60]

Keshub began to explore this Hindu greatness more fully
for himself.   In August 1875 he drew up a list of 108
names of God, which was turned into a hymn, and later
a Sanskrit verse, taking a Hindu idea and moulding it
into Brahmo material.

The Haranath Bose case of the previous year had
served as a warning to Keshub that his *Ashram* experiment was not working as well as he had hoped, being
marred by petty personal conflicts over worldly matters.
He therefore instituted a strict programme of asceticism
in the middle of 1875, to instil habits of piety and humility.   He purchased a garden estate, which he called
*Sadhan Kanan,* for this purpose.   Keshub, who lived in
the *Ashram* only periodically, came to join them there for
some time, setting an example to them by cooking his
own morning meal himself.   More time was devoted to
organized prayer, and strict poverty was required.   This
comparatively mild asceticism (when compared to Hindu
asceticism) alarmed some of his English supporters, who,
being used to a comfortable Christianity, feared a leaning
towards the fanaticism of "mortification of the flesh".[61]
Their alarm was unnecessary, as it was not in Keshub's
nature or scheme of religion ever to renounce the world.
Keshub regarded asceticism as a remedy, or an antidote,
for too much worldliness.[62]   For him, a period of asceticism was a necessary prelude to any change and development in religion,[64] but the change was not necessarily
towards asceticism.   In fact, Keshub was still as much
involved as always in a normal round of activity.   In
November 1875 he went on a mission tour to Upper India
(he had recently visited there both in 1873 and 1874)
covering a large number of centres including Lucknow,
Allahabad and Lahore. Using good missionary technique,
he had begun to lecture his audiences there in Hindi for
a wider dispersal of his message, from 1873.   In December
1875 he sent an address of welcome to the Prince of
Wales on behalf of the Brahmo Samaj of India.

Some of the Indian Reform Association projects

started earlier had faded out owing to lack of response, but this was because of their nature rather than a falling off of enthusiasm on the part of their organizers. For instance, the Industrial School was left with only the Clock and Watch Repairing Department by 1872, because of "the absence of sustained interest in the manual arts or an appreciation of their utility among those for whom the School was intended".[64] The Female Normal School was still thriving, as both Miss Mary Carpenter, on her 1875 visit, and the 1875-76 School Report, testify.[65] Miss Carpenter gave an idea of the extent of progress that had been made by remarking that the ladies she had seen on her first visit, nearly 10 years before in 1866, now had a small society (probably the Bama Hitaishini Sabha) and that she could converse with many of them in English. She thought that Keshub's schools were the only ray of hope for women, as in general she felt that the cause of female progress had regressed over the time she had been taking an interest in it.

In adopting asceticism, Keshub had not manifested a real change of heart or attitude. Both the reform and religious sides of the Samaj were still operative and harmonious. He was merely acting consistently with his policy of taking what was needed, from whichever tradition was most applicable, at whatever time it would have most effect. In previous years he had concentrated his attention on examining Christianity. From 1876, possibly because of the living inspiration of Ramakrishna before him, he took a greater interest in Hinduism than he had in the past. He may have seen Hinduism as having more relevance for India, and thus having greater potential for attracting converts to Brahmoism.

However, despite the annual *Hindu Mela* and Rajnarain Bose's continued championing of Hinduism, the real rival to Brahmoism at the time was neither Hinduism, nor Christianity, but the widening sphere of political activity in the 1870s. By 1876, Sastri said that there were no new candidates for initiation to Brahmoism.[66] Politics represented a serious challenge to Keshub's sway over the public mind. Political activity at that time was much

ss demanding than Keshub's form of Brahmoism, and
ᴇe charisma of Surendranath Banerjea vied with Keshub
ɔr the captivation of the student body. Politics implied
ᴀtional concrete thinking (although it was made mysti-
ᴀl by being linked with Hindu revivalism) and so stood
ᴀ opposition to Keshub's espousal of the emotionality
: devotion and intense religious feeling. Patriotism be-
ᴀme a substitute for religion.

Around this time Keshub began to use Bengali almost
ꭓclusively in his preaching, although the major lecture
: the year, the anniversary lecture, was always delivered
ᴀ English. He was reputed to have developed a beauti-
ᴀl Bengali style, acknowledged even by Bankim Chandra
hatterjee.⁶⁷ Bipin Chandra Pal was drawn to hear him
ᴇcause he was "universally recognized as a master of
ᴇngalee diction and oratory".⁶⁸ This signified a height-
ᴀing of Keshub's national consciousness, an attempt to
ᴅentify himself with his own tradition through the use
f Bengali. This was a far cry from the days when he
ᴀd been unpopular because of h̄is limited ability to
ɔmmunicate in his own language, and showed what a
ᴇtermined and persistent effort he had made to over-
ɔme this disability.

In 1876 Keshub further utilized Hindu terms and
ɔncepts in his fourfold classification of devotees under
ʜe headings of *Yoga* (Aghorenath Gupta), *Bhakti* (Bijoy
ᴋrishna Goswami and Trailokyanath Sanyal), *Jnana*
Gour Govinda Roy) and *Sheba*.⁶⁹ These devotees had
ᴏffered themselves for the disciplines they wanted to
ᴘursue, and Keshub gave them a course of religious ins-
ʀuction according to their choice of discipline. In 1877
ᴀe extended his classification to include other religions.
ʜe four areas of study were Hinduism, Christianity,
ᴍohammedanism and Buddhism. The deeper under-
ᴛtanding of Hinduism, and the eclecticism shown in such
ᴄlassification could have been due to the influence of
ᴀamakrishna, but they can just as easily be fitted into
ᴋeshub's own development. Keshub's use of such classi-
ᴀications was not that of the Hindu tradition of master-
ng each discipline on the path to salvation, but was done

in a spirit of scientific experiment, as 'research aids'
the realization of his religious goal. The division
religions, in particular, was like appointing a team
research assistants with very productive results. Go
Govinda Roy was assigned to the study of Hinduism, an
was original and influential in the approach he too
He wrote a Sanskrit commentary on the *Bhagavat Gi*
being one of the first to popularize it as a major Hin
text, and wrote one of the first lives of Krishna, in t
historical personality style of nineteenth century studi
of the life of Christ. Protap Chunder Mozoomdar, t
most thoroughly Westernized of the missionaries, havir
travelled extensively in Europe and America, develop
one of Keshub's earlier ideas into a full-length study
his book *The Oriental Christ*. Girish Chunder Sen trar
lated all the major Islamic texts into Bengali, an
Aghorenath Gupta wrote a life of the Buddha
Bengali.[70]

In his anniversary lecture of 1876, 'Our Faith ar
Our Experience',[71] Keshub showed his growing sympath
with Hinduism by modifying his earlier pronouncemen
against Hindu idolatry. He still did not sanction it,
that would have been a renunciation of his idea of Theis
but he commended its spirit, its Puranic breadth of re
gious feeling. The lecture was also exceptional in i
use of numerous quotations from Sanskrit in referen
to the Hindu Scriptures. He chose the occasion to rea
sess the position of the Brahmo Samaj, haranguir
against nearly everyone who claimed the Brahmo nar
for their various shortcomings. The only signs of ho
he saw were not in the Brahmo Samaj at all, but in t
broader doctrine of Theism, which met with the approv
of all educated people who had not succumbed either
Christianity or materialism. He noted that the influen
of the Brahmo Samaj among women had been salutar
even though there was only a handful of women wl
actually claimed to be Theists. He prayed for a show
of Pentecostal grace to save the Samaj from stagnation
perhaps a vindication of the changes he was introducin

The anniversary lecture for 1877, 'The Disease ar

the Remedy',[72] began with an examination of a singularly
Christian preoccupation, man's sense of sin. This was
ever-present in Keshub's consciousness, and recurred with
increased intensity at most crisis periods in his life (as
it had done before he joined the Brahmo Samaj, and
after the split with Debendranath). Keshub did not
believe that man was born in original sin, but that he
succumbed to the temptation to sin brought on by his
carnal nature. The truly sanctified man, for him, was
not the sinner who repented, but the man who was above
the liability to sin. He thought that everyone should
strive for this rare quality by disciplining themselves to
a higher spirituality, through asceticism—not self-morti-
fication, but the cultivation of an attitude of mind not
tied to worldly concerns. Such a man would become like
a child, a drunkard, and a madman, in his behaviour.[73]
Although he did not refer to Ramakrishna by name, he
instantly springs to mind as wholly embodying these
three personalities. Though some people accused Keshub
of retreating into mysticism, he firmly denied the charge,
maintaining that he had always consistently advocated
a religion of harmony, which meant a balance between
meditation and activity.

That he had not cut himself off from the social life
of the world, and that he fully realized the practical value
of cultivating certain social contacts, was very evident.
The Viceroy, Lord Lytton, had missed the anniversary
lecture for 1877, and regretted not having heard the latest
developments in Keshub's ideas.[74] Keshub obliged him
by announcing a further lecture on the theme of madness
in the sanctified man, entitled 'Philosophy and Madness
in Religion'.[75] In this he set up a dichotomy consisting
of philosophy, which he equated with civilization, and
madness, or heavenly enthusiasm, equated with primitive
religion, and called for a harmonious eclectic reunion of
the two in one personality. It was obvious throughout
that he favoured the warm and poetic madness over cold,
languid, prosaic philosophy. The main message was his
usual one of harmony and eclecticism, although he did
draw a distinction between true, assimilated eclecticism

and superficial latitudinarianism. He also enlarged on his doctrine of *Adesh*, calling people to think of their actions not as based on individual choices but on divine commands—not "I ought not", but, from God, "Thou shalt not". The lecture ranged widely over everything from the Darwinian theory of evolution to the Hindu theory of transmigration, all of which he explained in terms of his own beliefs. The lecture ended on a political note, saying that Indians were bound to be loyal to the British Government, and to Queen Victoria, divinely appointed sovereign of India, otherwise they could be accused of ingratitude. He maintained that it was not a servile loyalty as it was based on a respectful exchange of different qualities—'philosophy', industry and science from England, and 'madness', meditation and spirituality from India.

Keshub had paid tribute to Britain and Queen Victoria earlier that year when he attended the Delhi Durbar at which Victoria was proclaimed Empress of India. He declined an official decoration offered to him on the occasion.[76] As he jokingly said to Sivanath Sastri once, he was already K.C.S.I. (Knight Commander of the Star of India, or Keshub Chunder Sen, I).[77] In another demonstration of loyalty, Keshub created the Albert Institute to perpetuate the memory of the visit of the Prince of Wales to India in 1870. The aim of the Institute was to promote literary and social intercourse. It included the Albert Hall, a venue for public meetings in the Bengali area of the city, and a good library. The total cost was 30,000 rupees, much of which was raised by public subscription, with citizens vying to prove their loyalty by the size of their donations. The Government also helped by giving a substantial grant.[78]

The new departures and innovations in the Brahmo creed were controversial. In religion, Keshub's 'progressive' opponents were conservative, preferring to stick by traditional Brahmoism and regarding Keshub's experiments as suspicious and irrational. A description of the *Sadhan Kanan* in the *Indian Mirror,* which Keshub had been worried about lest it be misunderstood, showed how little cause there really was for alarm over his activities : —

> Babu Keshub Chunder Sen and the disciples who live with him in the little garden (*Sadhan Kanan*) he has recently purchased, live in a perfectly primitive style. They all sit under the trees for their morning devotions which continue for seldom less than two hours and a half, squatting on grass mats, pieces of rough woolen stuff, and tiger-skins. Then they begin to cook their food which they finish eating by noonday time. Resting for half-an-hour, they engage in religious conversation which lasts for an hour. Then some of them do a little work, writing, reading, and otherwise employing themselves. In the afternoon they draw water, cut bamboos, make roads, and pave them, plant, remove, and water trees, construct their cabins, cleanse out various places, and are seen to work very diligently in the hot sun, some with pieces of wet cloth on their heads, some bare-headed. Working till six they rest for half an hour again, and then retire for solitary devotions. When the evening is advanced, say by half-past seven, they sing *Sankirtan* hymns, and issue out in a procession chanting through the jungle-skirted village lanes, and usually enter a poor man's hut, there singing and praying for the benefit of the household. . [79]

It is difficult to see what elements of this portrayal of such an active, disciplined and harmonious life people could have considered alarming or shocking. It was certainly not a return to the Hindu idea of asceticism. The move to communal religious living may have been too monastic for his English supporters, but it should not have disturbed the Brahmo community.

Another point of difference between Keshub and the new progressives was that most of them were involved in nationalist politics, whereas he was not—not only that, but the political views he espoused did not have much in common with theirs. Neither was he primarily concerned with social reform, which could always be construed as quasi-political. One of their most objectively valid grudges against him was against his autocracy. It was not a coincidence that Keshub was at the head, the President, of every single subsidiary com-

mittee or organization connected with the Brahmo
Samaj of India, even if he had declined to assume such
a title for the whole. He was supposed to have put the
congregation of the *mandir* on a constitutional basis in
1866, when he gave the congregation the power to elect
the Minister—but the effect of the proposal was virtually nullified when the charge of spiritual ministration
was then vested in him as Minister in perpetuity. The
*Samadarshi* group were dissatisfied with this and proposed
the formation or reorganization of the Pratinidhi Sabha
to share in the administration of the Samaj. Keshub
himself had founded such an organization in 1865, but
as there had been no meetings since then, it had died
out.[80] The Sabha made little headway. At the annual
meeting of the Brahmo Samaj of India in January
1877, three proposals were submitted for Keshub's consideration:—the repayment of debts, and appointment
of Trustees for the Mandir; drawing up of a census
of Brahmos; and the reorganization of the Pratinidhi
Sabha. The latter was finally constituted on 16 March
1877, with Keshub as Chairman, Ananda Mohan Bose as
Secretary, and Sivanath Sastri as Assistant Secretary.
Sastri said that Keshub stipulated that the Sabha would
only be an auxiliary body with no control over the
affairs of the Samaj. This was in the tradition of the
old Sabha, but Keshub must have known that it was not
what the new progressives wanted. They were trying
to establish at least some measure of democratic control,
a check to the judgements of Keshub alone.[81]   Another preoccupation of the progressives that was brought
up in the course of these meetings was the trusteeship
of the *mandir*. As it was built by public subscription,
they felt that the Brahmo public should have some say
in its administration. Keshub said that the debts of the
*mandir* stood in the way of a transfer of ownership,
though he agreed to appoint trustees after four months,
in which time he said the debts would have been paid.
His opponents were not satisfied with this postponement,
and offered to pay the debts themselves, but Keshub
was reluctant to agree.

Keshub had never had much tolerance for dissenters from his opinion, and his followers were even more
dogmatic. Neither Sivanath Sastri or Nagendra Nath
Chatterji completely fitted in to the *Bharat Ashram,* not
only because of their theoretical disagreements with
Keshub, whom they respected, but because of the
contempt with which they were treated by his
most loyal followers. Through lack of proper communication Keshub also became increasingly alienated from his opponents in the Samaj, whom he
cuttingly dismissed as "sceptics, secularists and unbe-
ievers".[82] Apart from their differences within the
Samaj, they objected to Keshub's wholehearted endorsement of the 'providential' character of British rule in
India. They, being in the crucial field of government
employment, felt the rancour of official discrimination
against Indians much more than Keshub did as a missionary who posed no threat to basic British policy and
was therefore received in the highest British circles.
The *Amrita Bazar Patrika* had made the point that
Keshub had been so well received in Britain because he
was a religious and not a political leader, and therefore
not so threatening.[83] The dissenters also believed in the
value of British rule, but they had numerous specific
grievances over its disregard for the opinions and achievements of the educated middle-classes. To rectify this situation Ananda Mohan Bose, Surendranath Banerjea and Sivanath Sastri founded the Indian Association to represent
the interests of the educated middle classes in July 1876.
Keshub did not participate, because his main interest
was in religion, and because he was more concerned with
change in the social sphere where he saw the British
as co-operative allies, a factor contributing to his firm
belief in the providential and sacred nature of British
rule which had always been a part of his thinking. He
had come closest to direct political involvement in England, when representing Indian demands to the British
Government, but he never presented himself as their
antagonist. There was only one isolated instance of
Keshub having taken part in political activity in this

formative period of fervent political excitement. He
was present at a protest meeting on 24 March 1877, on
the Government's decision to lower the age of Indian
Civil Service competitors from 21 to 19, a move designed
to exclude candidates from India. It was one of the
largest public demonstrations in Calcutta, and could
not have failed to attract his attention. Despite his
lack of political involvement, he was persuaded to move
the election of the President[84]—as his presence as a prominent religious figure meant political capital to those
organizing the meeting, who wanted to make the most
of his support.

As their aims and interests grew further apart, the
dissatisfaction of the *Samadarshi* group crystallized
Keshub no longer satisfied either their reforming zeal
or their devotional urges. They could not respond to
his religious development, so they set up a secret society
at the beginning of 1877, a little like the old Sangat Sabha
where members made vows to be consistently advanced in
social matters. They were never to encourage caste
or idolatry (which was a part of Brahmoism anyway
but they may have seen Keshub's use of Hindu names
of God and his homage to Jesus as eroding this), and
they were not to encourage marriage between men below
the age of 21 and girls below the age of 16—a very
stringent requirement which would not have been applicable to their generation, most of whom had already
been married at an earlier age. They also introduced
the subject of politics, vowing that "self-government
is the only form of political government *ordained by
God*" and that they would not work for a foreign government. The most prominent members of the group were
Sivanath Sastri, who did not actually take the vows until
he had left government service in 1878, and Bipin Chandra Pal, who was studying in Calcutta and beginning
to take an interest in public events. There were six
members originally, and nine by January 1878. Bipin
Chandra Pal felt that Sastri's kind of Brahmoism was
more in tune with the spirit of freedom and individualism
of the mid-nineteenth century than Keshub's. He described

their secret society as combining the religious and social
idealism of the Brahmo Samaj with the political idealism of Surendranath Banerjea. In the romantic strain
of early Bengali nationalism, they pledged to learn to
ride and shoot, and to preach the necessity of these
skills for the national cause.[85]

Apart from the consistency apparent in Keshub's
idea of trying to develop a 'future church' of religious
eclecticism and harmony, on most other questions his
position was ambiguous and vulnerable. He had helped
foster Indian national awareness and self-confidence, but
stepped back from involvement in the new nationalist
movement. Instead he became emphatic about the need
for loyalty to Britain. He could never have sanctioned
the secretive opposition to the Government typified by
societies like that of Sivanath Sastri and Bipin Chandra
Pal. He was a staunch supporter of British rule in
India, a position which, plainly stated, was beginning to
be unwise as it alienated him from the current of public
opinion and categorized him as a reactionary.

Personally he seemed confused. It was obvious that
despite Keshub's deep spirituality, he was a man of
the world. He was not socially retiring (although Protap Chunder Mozoomdar always maintained that he
was difficult to get to know intimately) and mixed in
high social circles. He was a friend of all the successive Governor-Generals of the time. However, he realized the snares this kind of social life presented, and
did not want himself or his followers to get caught up
in it, as it was inevitably a distraction from higher spirituality. He therefore initiated a programme of asceticism, but his own participation in it was only sporadic.
His own home was comfortable—his excuse being that
he could not impose disciplines on his family which they
had not chosen to undergo.[86] In the light of this it
seems unfair that he did impose such strictness on all
the inhabitants of the *Bharat Ashram* (and there were
102 of them altogether in 1874).[87] He did not share in
the poverty enjoined on the missionaries, but felt it to
be "instructive, suggestive, and sacred" to him.[88] He

was always conscious of his position as leader of the Brahmo Samaj, and the need to maintain appearances proper to that rank. Protap Chunder Mozoomdar felt that this was adequate justification for his having a large house, with many servants, and keeping a carriage. These would have seemed less incongruous if Keshub had admitted the need for them, but he was insistent on the need for lack of attachment to worldly goods, while keeping a firm grip on his own standing in the world. Keshub was unable to reconcile these two very different spheres, but neither could he give up either of them. In public speaking he favoured the role of the spiritual devotee, but in the practical decisions of life he assumed the role of the householder. His worldly nature would have fitted well into the pattern of the English clergyman, rooted firmly in society and with opportunities to rise to a higher rank, ecclesiastically and socially. Unfortunately for Keshub, Indian religious ideals were totally opposed to this, and there was no Indian equivalent to the English stereotype. His deeper spiritual nature rebelled against the idea of calm and steady comforts, and found satisfaction in emotional extremes, and for this he was drawn to the popular traditions of Hinduism in which great religious thinkers were those who had renounced all worldly cares and possessions. Again he seemed to be attempting the impossible, in trying to harmonize the roles of English clergyman and Hindu ascetic.

The conflict became a matter for public controversy when he purchased Lily Cottage, a large mansion with garden, tank and extensive lands adjoining, for 20,000 rupees as an independent residence. His joint family had complained of his continual flow of visitors,[89] and he felt that the rest of his family, still Hindus, were a hindrance to his religious development. The *Sadhan Kanan* was unsatisfactory for the requirements of his place in society. He intended to transfer the Brahmo community there to the area surrounding Lily Cottage (and sarcastic comments were made on the dimensions of Keshub's 'Cottage'), creating an atmosphere of comnunal suburban living. Protap Chunder Mozoomdar purchased Peace Cottage next door to Keshub, and others erected their own residences in the neighbourhood which was called the *Mangal Bari*.[90]

The ambiguity between personal and religious motives, and the hostility that had been building up against Keshub, was soon to explode destructively over the issue of the marriage of Keshub's daughter, generally known as the Cuch Behar marriage case.

## NOTES AND REFERENCES

1. J. C. Bagal, *Keshab* op. cit. pp. 46-47.

2. Keshub Chunder Sen, *Lectures* (1904) op. cit. pp. 274-298.

3. Gobind Chunder Dhur was a journalist, and sometimes wrote secular items for the *Indian Mirror*—Calcutta Literary Society, *Annual Report*, 1903.

4. P. K. Sen, *Biography* op. cit. Vol. II, p. 278. Taken from the Indian Reform Association Annual Report 1870-71, pp. 278-341.

5. Ibid. pp. 283, 350. For correspondence on the subject see pp. 383-391 from the I.R.A. Annual Report for 1872.

6. The clash was just as much her fault as his. She was just as strong-willed, and had very set ideas about India, based entirely on her English experience. She was shocked by Keshub's wife's 'gaudy' appearance, and annoyed at her lack of conversation, making no allowance for possible shyness. She was also shocked by the 'absence of clothing' of one of the teachers at Keshub's school. Beveridge, op. cit. pp. 89-90.

7. P. K. Sen, *Biography* op. cit., Vol. II, pp. 279-283.

8. Sasipada Benerji had had a similar idea earlier. He started a night school for workers, with a club and library in 1866 but Keshub's inspiration was more purely philanthropic than Banerji's, as one of the latter's intentions was to try and stop workers from striking. A. Banerji, op. cit. p. 71.

9. P. K. Sen, *Biography* op. cit., Vol. II, pp. 284-288. I.R.A. Annual Report. Appendix B, Opening of the Industrial School and Working Men's Institution, pp. 324-329. (Date given there should be 1870, not 1871.)

10. P. K. Sen, *Biography* op. cit. Vol. II, p. 325.

11. Ibid. I.R.A. Annual Report 1870-71, pp. 287-288.

12. P. K. Sen, *Biography* op. cit. Vol. II, p. 351. I.R.A. Report 1872.

13. Ibid. pp. 391-408. Those who replied to the circular included the old temperance advocate and teacher Peary Charan Sarkar, the old Brahmo and Derozian Shib Chunder Deb of Konnagar, the Rev. J. M. Thorburn of Lucknow, Rev. J. E. Payne, Dr Edmondstone Charles MD, Dr David B. Smith MD, Rai Rajendra Mullick Bahadur and Babu Nobeen Chunder Rai of Lahore—a good cross-section of respected Indians, missionaries and doctors.

14. P. C. Mozoomdar, *Life* op. cit. p. 155.

15. P. K. Sen, op. cit. Vol. II, pp. 290-292 (I.R.A. Report 1870-71)
    Most of these were short-lived. One of the more successfu
    cheap papers was the *Bharat Sramajibi* founded by Sasipada Baner
    ji in 1874, with a circulation of 15,000. A. Banerji, op. cit. pp
    78-79.

16. B. T. McCully, *English Education and the Origins of India
    Nationalism* (New York, 1940), p. 234.

17. His article on 'Men of Consequence' (P. S. Basu, op. cit. pp
    276-277) inciting the 'lower classes', or farmers and artisans, i
    hailed by Amiya Charan Banerji, in A. C. Gupta (ed.), *Studie
    in the Bengal Renaissance* op. cit. pp. 86-87, as showing Keshu
    to be a pioneer of socialism in India, differing from Marx onl
    in his Theism! This seems to be stretching the facts a grea
    deal. Some other articles from *Sulabh Samachar* are printed i
    J. Gupta, *Keshabchandra O Shekaler Shamaj* (Calcutta, 1949).

18. P. S. Basu, op. cit. p. 279.

19. P. S. Basu, op. cit. pp. 359-383. See the speeches made by th
    Bishop of Calcutta, Rev. Dr Murray Mitchell, Rev. K. M. Baner
    jea, Dwarka Nath Mitter, Protap Chunder Mozoomdar, Dr Mahen
    dra Lal Sircar, and Keshub at the first annual meeting of th
    I.R.A. on 13 April 1872.

20. P. K. Sen, Biography op. cit. Vol. II, pp. 60-61.

21. A. Seal, op. cit. p. 203.

22. S. Tattvabhushan, *The Philosophy of Brahmaism* (Madrass, 1909)
    p. 348.

23. P. C. Mozoomdar, *Life* op. cit. p. 158.

24. Rajnarain Bose, op. cit. pp. 203-206.

25. Quoted in S. Tattvabhushan, *Philosophy* op. cit. pp. 349-352.

26. P. K. Sen, *Biography* op. cit. Vol. II, pp. 295-323. The doctor
    were Dr Norman Chevers, Dr J. Fayrer, Dr J. Ewart, Dr S. G
    Chuckerbutty, Dr D. B. Smith, Dr T. E. Charles, Dr Chunde
    Coomar Dey, Dr Mahendra Lal Sircar, Babu Nobin Krishna Bose
    Tumeez Khan Bahadur, Atmaram Pandurang, and Dr A. W. White
    Professor of Midwifery at Grant Medical College, Bombay—a
    always, a cross-section of the community.

27. From Keshub's speech at the Town Hall, in Keshub Chunde
    Sen, *National Marriage Reform*, second ed. (Calcutta, 1951), p
    13.

28. S. Tattvabhushan, *Philosophy* op. cit. pp. 356-359. At the time o
    publication of this book (1909) the provision of divorce stil
    had not been used.

29 Bengal Social Association, *Transactions* Vol. V, 1871. 20 pages i
    the Education section.

30. In the ensuing discussion the Bishop of Calcutta maintaine
    that good secular education was impossible, as refinement anc
    morality came from religion.

31. He also quoted lines from Tennyson's *The Princess*:
    Woman's cause is man's; they rise or sink
    Together, dwarfed or goodlike, bond or free.

32. Drummound and Upton, op. cit. Vol. II. p. 4. Although Keshul
    gave Martineau that impression there is no other evidence to sup-
    port this.

33. Another speaker in the discussion, Dr Norman Chevers, pointed out that piety and refinement were not a great measure of advancement, as that was the common condition of women before their recent mid-nineteenth century enlightenment through education. He also said that, in education, Indian women were not too far behind the English.

Even in England, married women were far from being their husband's equal, though there was less of a cultural gap between the two than in the Indian middle-class situation. Miss Elizabeth Sharpe, a Theistic friend of Rajnarain Bose, wrote to him prior to her marriage in 1872 : —

> I am going to be married. This will change my life completely from what I thought it might have been. I shall never come to India now, which I thought I might possibly have been able to do, indeed I shall be able to do very little for your country, though I shall always care very much for her welfare, for I shall be so much occupied in my own home, and shall feel it my first duty, to spend all my best energies there. An English lady at the head of a household, has seldom much time or thought for objects beyond her home. . . . Rajnarain Bose, op. cit., pp. 188-189.

34. S. Sastri, *History* op. cit., Vol. I, pp. 256-257 and *Atmacharit* op. cit., pp. 113-114. They got Debendranath to conduct their first service—an incongrous alignment, as they were united only in opposition to Keshub. Their ideas on female emancipation would have been total anathema to Debendranath.

35. Keshub Chunder Sen, *Lectures* (1904) op. cit., pp. 299-320.

36. P. C. Mozoomdar, *Life* op. cit., p. 162.

37. Protap Chunder Mozoomdar put this very clearly :—"The Brahmo Somaj has no 'social ideal', apart from its religion. Faithfulness to that religion necessitates the removal of certain social evils, and conformity to certain social principles . . . .". *Theistic Quarterly Review,* I (March 1879), p. 27.

38. Keshub Chunder Sen, *Lectures* (1904) op. cit. p. 277. From his Bombay lecture 'Impressions of England and the English' after his return from England.

39. P. C. Mozoomdar, *Life* op. cit. p. 162.

40. Quoted in P. K. Sen, *Biography* op. cit. Vol. II, p. 63. From a translation of Bijoy Krishna Goswami's *Amar Jibaney Brahmo Samajer Pariksita Visaya* (Experiences of the Brahmo Samaj in my life).

41. S. Sastri, *History* op. cit. Vol. I, p. 252.

42. B. C. Pal, *Memories of My Life and Times* op. cit. Vol. I, p. 298.

43. S. Tattvabhushan, *Autobiography* op. cit. p. 41.

44. Lord Beveridge, op. cit. p. 90.

45. Keshub Chunder Sen, *Lectures* (1954) op. cit. pp. 148-161.

46. ibid. pp. 162-186.

47. ibid. p. 178.

48. ibid. pp. 187-201—'The Kingdom of Heaven'.

49. T. E. Slater, op. cit. p. 68. Taken from Brahmo Year Book, 1879.

50. S. Sastri, *Atmacharit* op. cit. pp. 125-126.

51. P. S. Basu, op. cit. p. 300.

52. P. S. Basu, op. cit. p. 456—Jeevan Veda, chapter VIII.

53. S. Sastri, *Atmacharit* op. cit. pp. 114-115.

54. This was closed and replaced by the *Banga Mahila Vidayalaya* in 1876, which finally combined with the Bethune School in 1877.

55.  Keshub Chunder Sen, *Lectures* (1954) op cit. pp. 202-238.

56.  G. C. Banerji, *Keshab Chandra and Ramakrishna* (Allahabad, 1931)
     p. 246 (recollections of Mahendra Nath Bose), pp. 214-215 (re-
     collections of Girish Chandra Sen), p. 224 (recollections of T. N.
     Sanyal.)

57.  There was a bitter controversy over the extent of Ramakrishna's
     influence on Keshub carried out by their respective followers.
     There is much evidence of this in G. C. Banerji, *Keshab* op.
     cit. and in Appendix 2 of R. Rolland, *Life of Ramakrishna*, fourth
     ed. (Almora, 1947).

58.  P. S. Basu, op. cit. p. 295.

59.  Sivanath Sastri went to see Ramakrishna after reading in the
     *Indian Mirror* (probably in the article quoted below) that Keshub
     was impressed with him. *Atmacharit* op. cit. p. 127.

60.  J. C. Bagal, *Keshub* op. cit. p. 65.

61.  Their fear of asceticism had been reinforced by some of the
     practices of the Anglo-Catholic revival, like J. H. Newman's mon-
     asticism and Hurrell Froude's literal mortification of the flesh
     through fasting.

62.  P. K. Sen, *Biography* op. cit. Vol. II, pp. 76-77 includes a letter
     from Keshub to S. D. Collect on this.

63.  P. S. Basu, cit. pp. 449-450—Jeevan Veda, chapter IV.

64.  P. K. Sen, *Biography* op. cit, Vol. II, I.R.A. Annual Report 1872,
     p. 352.

65.  J. E. Carpenter, op. cit. pp. 411-452, and P. K. Sen, *Biography*
     op. cit. Vol. II, pp. 411-425 (Appendix V).

66.  S. Sastri, *History* op. cit. Vol. I, p. 272. However, his report is
     exaggerated because of his bias against Keshub, as B. C. Pal
     (*Memories* op. cit. Vol. II, p. 60) said that Keshub was at his
     zenith in 1875.

67.  P. K. Sen, *Biography* op. cit. Vol. II, p. 54

68.  B. C. Pal, *Memories* op. cit. Vol. I, p. 302.

69.  P. S. Basu, op. cit. pp. 326-327.

70.  M. C. Parekh, op. cit. pp. 80-82.

71.  Keshub Chunder Sen, *Lectures* (1954) op. cit. pp. 239-270.

72.  Keshub Chunder Sen, *Lectures* (1954) op. cit. pp. 271-292.

73.  These three personalities also formed the subject of chapter
     XIII of the *Jeevan Veda*, 'The Triune Nature' in P. S. Basu, op. cit.
     pp. 470-473.

74.  P. S. Basu, op. cit. p. 334.

75.  Keshub Chunder Sen, *Lectures* (1954) op. cit. pp. 293-326.

76.  P. S. Basu, op. cit. p. 328.

77.  S. Sastri, *Atmacharit* op. cit. p. 107. J. C. Bagal, *Keshab* op. cit.
     p. 67 gives a different variant of this story.

78.  P. C. Mozoomdar, *Faith*, op. cit. p. 150.

79.  P. C. Mozoomdar, *Life*, op. cit. pp. 175-176.

80.  Although P. K. Sen maintained that it still existed officially,
     because meetings *were* held, despite the long lapses between
     them. *Biography* op. cit. Vol. II, pp. 165-166.

81.  This account of the constitutional movement is taken mainly
     from S. Sastri's *History* (op. cit. Vol. I, pp. 263-267), which is
     biased against Keshub. P. K. Sen (Biography op. cit. Vol. II, pp.
     166-171) attempted to refute his charges and defend Keshub,
     but even so it still seemed that Keshub was definitely reluctant
     to relinquish any of his powers.

82. S. Sastri, *Atmacharit* op. cit. p. 132.
83. J. C. Bagal, *Keshab* op. cit. p. 47.
84. S. N. Banerjea, op. cit. p. 44.
85. S. Sastri, *Atmacharit* op. cit. p. 142 and B. C. Pal, *Memories* op. cit. Vol. I, pp. 308-318.
86. P. C. Mozoomdar perceived this conflict between worldliness and asceticism, and attempted to explain it in his *Life* op. cit. pp. 189-193.
87. P. K. Sen, *Biography* op. cit. Vol. II, p. 166.
88. P. C. Mozoomdar, *Life* op. cit. p. 196.
89. P. C. Mozoomdar, *Life* op. cit. p. 187.
90. Above of Welfare.

# CHAPTER SEVEN

# THE CUCH BEHAR MARRIAGE CONTROVERSY (1878)

THE CUCH BEHAR marriage, between Keshub's daughter and Nripendra Narain, the Maharajah of Cuch Behar, was the most controversial event in the history of the Brahmo Samaj. It was the spark that led directly to the second split in the Brahmo Samaj and indirectly to the founding of two new and distinct schools of Brahmoism, that of the Sadharan Brahmo Samaj, and that of the Navavidhan, or New Dispensation. The major points of controversy were that the marriage contravened the minimum age prescription in Act III of 1872 (the Marriage Act passed through Keshub's efforts); and that it condoned idolatry and was not a pure Brahmo marriage. The marriage affair presents difficulties for analysis as the available documentation is mostly of a partisan character. The evidence on which this chapter is based consists in the series of letters and telegrams sent to Keshub by the British authorities, contemporary newspaper reports and eyewitness reports of those present at the marriage and letters from Keshub and other members of the Samaj.

The role of the British in the administration of Cuch Behar is an essential part of the background of the marriage. When the Maharajah acceded to the throne at the age of 10 months, the British Government saw a clear opportunity to extend its influence and intervene in the affairs of Cuch Behar. They removed the young Maharajah from the "evil and retrograde" traditions of the royal household run by the *Ranis*, at the age of five, and placed him in the Wards' Institute, Benares. They later sent him to Bankipur College, Patna, under an English tutor.[1] The British aimed to mould him into the model ruler of a modern state. To attain their object they intended to send him to England to finish his education. However, the ladies of the palace objected strongly. They

old Sir Richard Temple, the Lieutenant-Governor at
he time, that they feared it would further alienate him
rom his traditional surroundings.[2]  One way of ensur-
ng that this would not happen was to anchor his loya-
ties through marriage.  The British authorities[3] could
agree to this, but they differed from the *Ranis* in the
ype of girl they wanted him to marry.  They did not
vant him to marry, as he traditionally would have done,
a young girl of seven or eight who would submit meekly
to the regime run by the older *Ranis* and pull the Maharajah away from the modern British ways he had grown
used to.  Nor, in accordance with his modern image, did
hey want him to take more than one wife, although
polygamy was customary in Cuch Behar.  Thus they
wanted to find a suitable and educated girl for him to
marry. It is said that before settling on Keshub's daughter
they had already approached Durga Mohan Das, a prominent female emancipationist in the Brahmo Samaj, for
his daughter, but he had refused on principle because
he wanted her to marry a Brahmo, not Rajah.  It was
also rumoured that negotiations had been opened for
the daughter of an eminent Hindu gentleman in Madras.[4]
As both these rumours were used to discredit Keshub,
and as there was no documentary evidence of such negotiations given in either case, they can be dismissed as
not relevant to the final result, which was the decision
to approach Keshub for the hand of his daughter.[5]

Protap Chunder Mozoomdar first heard that the British Government had decided that Keshub's daughter
would be a suitable bride for the Maharajah in August
and September 1877.  He was in Bombay at the time,
and was informed through letters from Keshub and
others.[6]  Jadub Chunder Chuckerbutty was deputed to
be the agent for approaching Keshub, who was taken completely by surprise at the proposal. As he later said in
his own defence, he had not sought a marriage for his
daughter at all, even though she was over 13 and therefore getting beyond the marriageable age in orthodox
terms.  Because he had not initiated the idea, he regarded
it as coming from 'Providence'.  However, Keshub ini-

tially refused the match. He had many sound reason,
for doing so. The couple were both under the minimum
marriageable ages specified (14 for girls and 18 for boys
in Act III of 1872. There were clearly marked difference,
in their religious position and social status. The British
were reluctant to accept his refusal as final, as they had
determined that Sunity was the ideal partner for the
Maharajah. They pressed on, writing continually to Keshub
and bringing subtle pressure to bear on him by reminding him not of any pecuniary advantage to himself or
his family, but of the good that could be done for the
spread of Brahmoism in Cuch Behar and the challenge
to the old orthodoxy that this would present. According
to Keshub the arguments placed before him were on the
following lines : —

> Here is the Cooch Behar State, the den of ignorance
> and superstition, with a corrupt court given to dis-
> sipation, polygamy, intrigue and oppression. The
> young Rajah has been saved by the British Govern-
> ment acting as his guardian. The women of the Raj
> family have been mostly removed to Benares, and
> others will follow. The administration of the affairs
> of the State has greatly improved in all departments
> education, police, revenue, health etc. under the
> management of competent officers appointed by the
> British Government. The old palace will be pulled
> down shortly, and a new palace will be erected at a
> cost of about Rupees 8,000,000. Not a vestige will
> remain of the old regime and the ground will
> have been thoroughly cleared for political and social
> improvements when the young Rajah will be for-
> mally installed and begin to govern his immense
> territory. It is desirable, it is of the outmost im-
> portance, that he should have an accomplished wife. .

As and the time for the Maharajah's departure for
England drew near, the Government began to get impa-
tient. The Deputy Commissioner, Mr Dalton, wrote to
Keshub on 22 January 1878,[8] saying that the Lieutenant-
Governor had decided that the Rajah was to go to Eng-
land in March, and so should be married before then.
To overcome Keshub's repugnance at having his daugh-
ter marry before she turned 14, Dalton suggested that

it would not be a marriage in "the ordinary acceptance of the term", but a "solemn betrothal" only. In effect, the British authorities proposed a legal marriage which would not be consummated till the parties were of age. This was a compromise which would suit British purposes well, as it would have the outward appearance of a marriage, but it would also help to overcome Keshub's scruples about the couple being under what he had decided was the minimum marriageable age. Further compromises had to be made, however, if the *Ranis* were to agree to the marriage. One of their conditions was that Keshub should not give away the bride, because he had been to England. On this point, Dalton wrote to Keshub quite blatantly that "...I hope you will not arrest negotiations 'in limine' by refusing to accede to it". Keshub was made to feel that any attempt to stand up for his principles was a threat to the marriage, which he had already been persuaded to see as being of great benefit to the spread of Brahmoism and enlightenment in India. The letter also contained an ultimatum :—"Remember also, that if you care about this alliance, it is a question absolutely of now or never,...".

It was at this stage that Keshub testified that he heard the word of God assuring him that it was right to consent to this marriage. Once again in Keshub's career he proclaimed that his actions had been dictated by the voice of God, although looking at the objective reasons he had for reaching his decision it is clear that pressure from the British authorities was the earthly correlate of this Divine voice. In a letter to Frances Power Cobbe, which is the only available personal statement from Keshub at the time of the marriage, he said that he felt it his duty, as a public man, to consent to it.[9] He said that he did not think of the consequences—although as he saw the beneficial effects and was aware of the serious hazards involved, he must have decided that the former outweighed the latter, and in a sense come to a rational decision. He wanted the marriage to take place, for those reasons put to him by the British Government, but he abnegated his role in taking the decision by saying,

"I trusted, I hoped with all my heart that the Lord would do what was best for me, daughter and my country. Duty was mine ; future consequences lay in the hands of God." British persuasion, and Keshub's loyal response to it were the real factors influencing his decision. He told Miss Cobbe that

The British Government sought me and my daughter ; a Christian Government that knew me thoroughly to be a Brahmo leader, proposed the alliance, and the weighty interests of a State were pressed upon me with a view to induce me to accept the proposal and make the needful concessions..

Similarly, Keshub wrote to Max Müller at a later date that it was a political marriage:—"....A whole kingdom was to be reformed, and all my individual interests were absorbed in the vastness of God's saving economy, or in what people would call public good".[10] He believed in the desirability of the British plan to modernize Cuch Behar, and saw with them the necessity of an enlightened wife for the Maharajah—but it was to prove difficult for the Brahmo public, Keshub's followers, to see the marriage in the way that he did, in terms of a great sacrifice made for the good of the country.

The marriage was finally agreed to late in January 1878. Jadub Chunder Chuckerbutty was sent to Calcutta with instructions to get private assurances of Keshub's consent immediately, and then to make more detailed arrangements.[11] The Maharajah was also in Calcutta at this time waiting for an opportunity to see his bride. She had previously been interviewed by Mr Dalton. On that occasion she had been very nervous, as her father had told her that if they all agreed to the match, "perhaps some day you will marry a handsome young Maharajah".[12] Sunity and the Maharajah met several times during his stay in Calcutta, and on her account it was love at first sight for both of them.[13] This was another factor cementing the proposal. The obvious mutual attachment of the young couple meant that Keshub was even more deeply and personally involved in the affair, making any retraction a lot more difficult. He told Charles Voysey that the marriage was the result of a "natural and genuine attachment between the young people", which he did not feel he could overrule.[14]

From the time of Keshub's acquiescence and the meeting of the couple, the bargaining power passed entirely into the hands of the Cuch Behar Raj. The British wanted the marriage to take place above all. At first they had to persuade both Keshub and the *Ranis* of its desirability. Keshub proved the easier party to win over, so once he had commited himself the British put pressure on him to concede to more of the terms set down by the *Ranis*. Previously, in an effort to appear co-operative, they had even agreed that the marriage could take place under Act III of 1872.[15] That this had been suggested by Keshub is evidence that his first thoughts were in terms of marrying within the Act. Finally it was decided not to go through with this because it was politically unwise for the Maharajah to declare that he was not a Hindu—and as the British were more concerned with maintaining their control over the affairs of Cuch Behar than with upholding Brahmo principles, they persuaded Keshub to drop the idea, as, in any case, the Act did not apply to the independent state of Cuch Behar. The possibility of abiding by the Act was also ruled out by the *Ranis'* insistence that he marry before he went to England. Clearly Keshub did not see the Marriage Act as of paramount importance in itself, or he would have refused to continue negotiations at this point. Although Keshub had been the person most responsible for the passing of the Marriage Act, he denied all charges of inconsistency in agreeing to the marriage. He argued that precisely because he was most responsible for it, he also knew better than anyone else his reasons for getting it passed.[16] He had done so because he objected to the destructive physical and moral effects of early marriage. As this was to be a betrothal only, it could not be discussed in terms of a marriage. What he was hinting at was that it was the prospect of intercourse at that early age which was physically and mentally

abhorrent to him. He could thus claim that the marriage
was true to the spirit of the Act, if not the letter, as the
marriage was not consummated until after their real
Brahmo marriage in 1880, when Sunity was over 15, and
the Maharajah nearly 18. The delicacy of the debate
may have been responsible for much misunderstanding.
If Keshub had been able to declare plainly that the
marriage was not consummated, and that his main objection to early marriage was his repugnance to the idea of
intercourse before full maturity, people may have been
less ready to accuse him of deserting his principles,
although there would still have been some who felt that
he was admitting much more flexibility in his own interpretation than he would have given to others in a similar
position.

Protap Chunder Mozoomdar explained to the English
public that the Marriage Act was not the 'decalogue' of
the Samaj, and that "..When its objects are equally satisfied by departure from it as by conformity to it, to insist
upon technical conformity is to enforce a social and
moral slavery....".[17] It must be remembered that this
was not an early marriage by orthodox standards. A
much more flagrant endorsement of early marriage is
represented by cases in Bombay at that time where two
noted marriage reformers, President and Secretary of
the Ahmedabad Widow Re-Marriage Society, married
their sons to 'infant' girls.[18]

In fact, the bypassing of the Marriage Act was to
prove one of the major stumbling blocks in the way of
general acceptance of the marriage, and led to all kinds
of insinuations and allegations as to Keshub's motives
for agreeing to such a union. The Brahmo public was
beginning to get word of these developments, and major
consternation ensued when it was realized that the Maharajah was not a Brahmo, that he was not yet 16, and
that the bride was not yet 14, thus contravening the
Marriage Act. The opposition, led by those who had
been hostile to Keshub for some time past, the *Samadarshi*
group, used this as the main plank in their arguments
against Keshub. They said that they abhorred early

marriage, and were deaf to Keshub's protestations that he did too, only that this was an exceptional case. His arguments carried conviction, but as they were presented to Miss Cobbe and not to the Brahmos, it was inevitable that the Brahmo public should be shocked to see him taking such liberties with a law that he had gone to great pains to get passed. In a protest letter to Keshub, some Brahmo students (including Krishnakumar Mitra, Bipin Chandra Pal and Sitanath Tattvabhushan) argued that if he agreed to the marriage, they would all become more vulnerable to the importunities of their families.[19]

The *Raj Pandit* of Cuch Behar came to Calcutta for a week to settle the question of marriage rites with Gour Govinda Roy, the Brahmo minister who was to preside at the marriage. Conclusions they reached were that neither bride nor groom (who had written to Keshub assuring him that he was a Theist[20]), should take part in idolatrous ceremonies; that no images were to be present at the place of marriage; no mantras other than those in the printed programme were to be recited, nor were they to be omitted or modified.[21] Basically it was to follow the Hindu form of marriage minus the idolatrous portions, with some parts of the Brahmo marriage ceremony attached.

The first public mention of the marriage was in the *Indian Mirror* on 9 February 1878.[22] It hailed the marriage as progressive because it was an inter-caste marriage[23] between an enlightened, modern young couple, both educated along British lines—although even this writer made the qualification that "we only wish that the bridegroom and bride had been a little older than they now are". Once this marriage was made public, the correspondence columns of the Brahmo papers were filled with discussion of the forthcoming event. Most letters printed in the *Indian Mirror* naturally supported the marriage, while the papers set up by Keshub's opponents, the *Samalochak* and *Brahmo Public Opinion,* promoted the converse view.

On 14 February, 23 Brahmo protestors, including Durga Mohan Das, Ananda Mohan Bose, Dwarkanath Ganguli

and Shib Chunder Deb, published the first public protest against the marriage.[24] They said that other Brahmos
would follow Keshub's example in ignoring the Marriage
Act and be tempted by the "rank, wealth and position
of the groom", insinuating that these were the qualities
which had influenced Keshub, although leaving room for
him to differ by saying "whatever your reasons and
motives in this case". As one of the reasons for the
uproar created by the marriage was the idea that Keshub
had sold his principles, these claims deserve close
examination. These allegations took hold of the public
imagination, and were even designed to do so by some of
Keshub's long-term opponents, to discredit his reputation.
The marriage in fact created a pretext for a fullscale
agitation against Keshub, but whereas on previous issues
the protestors had been in a minority, now everyone's
faith in Keshub had been severely shaken. Sivanath
Sastri was particularly virulent in tossing around such
statements. An example of this was his assertion that
Lily Cottage was purchased by Keshub as a suitable venue
for showing his daughter to the Maharajah.[25] Some of
his enemies even wrote to the Government that Keshub
was appropriating funds from the Cuch Behar Treasury,
but not surprisingly when the police investigated they
found that the charges were without foundation.[26] Although Keshub was far from being a true ascetic, he
did not live a life of great extravagance and luxury. His
mode of living was not altered by the marriage. However, the temptations of rank and position may have
exerted more influence over him. Despite his profes-
sions of humility, Keshub had always been accepted as
a social equal by the higher ranks of English society and
the Indian educated elite. Even though personally he
may not have set much store by social distinctions, he
was well aware of the respect they commanded in the
community. It had always been his belief that he could
not impose his ideas of austerity on his family, and he
genuinely felt that this was the opportunity of a good
match for his daughter. She would be prosperous and
high ranking, and an agent for enlightenment and Brah-

moism in Cuch Behar as well. It is unlikely that he
would have consented to marriage with a Maharajah
merely for the sake of rank and position, but this was a
special case because the Maharajah was a modern, English-educated young man, who had avowed a faith in
Theistic principles[27], just the type of man he would
have chosen for his daughter to marry anyway. Keshub
was obviously very proud of his son-in-law. He gave
a reception at his house to introduce the Maharajah to
the elite of Calcutta,[28] a public expression of his approval of the marriage. Those present were leading representatives of the English and Indian communities, the latter
extending well beyond the Brahmo community to include
Rajah Jotindro Mohan Tagore, Sourendra Mohan Tagore,
Peary Chand Mitra, Abdul Latif Khan and Surendranath
Banerjea. It was clearly the Maharajah's British backing which was the decisive factor in his agreeing to the
match, but his satisfaction at this opportunity to enhance
his social status may have been a contributory factor.
In the short term, the marriage actually seemed to resolve many problems for Keshub. He had arranged a
suitable husband for his educated daughter, found an
opportunity to further encourage the spread of Brahmoism, and co-operated with the British to extend the benefits of their rule.

Keshub was soon made aware of the objections to
the marriage raised by the Brahmo community, but he
did not let their protests impinge on his actions at all.
He even admitted the objective validity of their com-
plaints, saying that if anyone else did what he was doing
he would also have felt bound to protest.[29] He refused
to disclose his reasons for the marriage. On the surface
his behaviour seemed calculated to shut out all doubt as
to the correctness of his actions, simply by ignoring all
protests against them. As he had done in the past, he
claimed controversially that the voice of God was not
amenable to argument, but it appeared that he was using
this as an excuse, and that in fact he was unable to
rationally justify the marriage to anyone other than
himself. His response to a delegation of Brahmos sent

to him on 2 February, before the official announcement,
to request further information on the rumoured marriage,
was a rare display of fiery anger.[30] He did not even
bother to read any of the protest letters. His reactions
revealed a real uncertainty about his plans. He was
aware of the force of public disapproval, aware of the
objective truth of their claims, but refused to justify his
own actions. Silence was one way of preserving his
dignity. He was also disinclined to argue as he knew
that the leaders of the protest movement disagreed with
him on many major issues, and were trying to oust him
from leadership, and thus were not to be expected to
sympathize with any of his reasons. Unfortunately, he
was also losing his reputation with the rank and file
of the Brahmo community, who were unable to compre-
hend his actions. Their loyalty was being tested to its
utmost.

The only public explanation of his motives that he
gave was not to his Brahmo followers at all, but, as
noted, to an English sympathizer Frances Power Cobbe.
He wrote a long and detailed letter to her, pouring out
his heart in such a way that suggested a release of emotion pent up over a long period. He was hurt at being
so misunderstood, and also resentful and indignant that
nobody believed in his integrity. He intended her to
publicize his letter in England as a vindication of his
actions. Years later he gave Max Müller a similar, but
less detailed, explanation.[31] He was evidently more concerned about his international reputation than about his
standing in his own community. He may have thought
that those far removed from the scene of the controversy
were more likely to listen to his reasons, and less likely
to emotionally prejudge him. They certainly judged
less harshly. Max Müller thought his mistake was that
he had been too kind and yielding a father.[32] He felt
that his friends in England were more loyal, and had
been touched by the assurances of support given to him
by many of them over this affair.[33] Most importantly,
he must have felt that his reasons for agreeing to the
marriage would not only be understood but also appre-

ciated and endorsed in England. These carried less
weight in India. In the formal statement issued to the
Brahmo public by P. C. Mozoomdar and Gour Govinda
Roy,[34] more stress was laid on the workings of Providence
than on the possibility of extending British enlightenment. As the nationalist movement was in its early
stages, such reasoning would not have furthered his cause.
Keshub's Anglicization may have also put him in a position where he did actually set more value on English
approval than that of his own countrymen. He saw
himself as a religious leader in India, not answerable to
questioning by his subordinates, while in England he
was explaining his position to a group of equal status
with himself.

Keshub's reaction to public criticism highlighted his
emotional personality. Though he believed that God
directed him to consent to the marriage, his subsequent
behaviour was not that of a devotee firmly following his
convictions, but of one who, while aware of having blun-
dered, was not prepared to admit it. He was accustomed
to being a universally esteemed leader, and was not
prepared to accept criticism from his subordinates. Despite his continual assertion of his own humility, when
hurt because his motives were misunderstood, he refused
to rectify the situation by giving an explanation, as
then his own underlying uncertainty about the rightness
of his choice would have been exposed. He wilfully
isolated himself from the Brahmo community by refusing to enter into any dialogue with them. He stubbornly
resisted this way of salvaging his reputation. An explanation by Keshub would certainly have calmed the
public agitation and alarm, and would have been enough
to satisfy some of his basically loyal but bewildered
followers, even though it would not have won over many
of the hard-core for whom the marriage case was just
one of many points of disagreement with him. Keshub
chose to make himself inaccessible—the only public statement that was issued came from his deputies, not from
him personally. Perhaps his reaction came from despair
that it was not worth trying to win back those who had

turned 'traitor', or perhaps from his persistent tendency
to self-dramatization, assuming the role of martyr and
persecuted hero, though this hypothesis is unlikely as
it proved to be an extremely damaging and painful 'pose'
to sustain. To react to criticism by withdrawal into
silence was a set response with Keshub. He had done
so on many past occasions, but at other times he had
been saved, as in the man-worship case, by the timely
intervention of others in his defence. This situation
was unique in that only he could exonerate himself.

Although numerous meetings were called to protest
against the marriage, there was only one meeting of
sympathizers, on 24 February.[35] Over 250 people signed
the congratulatory letter later presented to Keshub,
which was circulated at the meeting. Keshub's cause
was not helped much by this show of support owing
to the fact that most of those present were not from the
Brahmo community, and the most prominent person
addressing the meeting was the Editor of the *National
Paper* (organ of the Adi Brahmo Samaj), Nabogopal
Mitra. He was a member of the conservative Adi
Brahmo Samaj, and not one of Keshub's followers, so his
support gave the unfortunate impression that he was
welcoming Keshub into the conservative fold. He was
doubly unsuitable supporter in that he had been the
most vocal protestor against the 1872 Marriage Act. In
a meeting about the Act held in 1871, he had opposed
Keshub, maintaining that the Brahmo Samaj was a Hindu
movement, and that its marriages were valid according
to Hindu law.[36]

It is possible to conjecture that Keshub's eagerness
for the marriage to take place was because he saw in it
an opportunity to re-enter the Hindu fold. The growing
national consciousness of the time, and his close acquaintance with Ramakrishna, may have made this step attractive to him. It would have ended the long period of
comparative isolation, in the sense of being an outcast
from orthodox Hindu society, that he had suffered. This
hypothesis does not stand up to close examination.
Even if Keshub had his daughter married in a completely

orthodox way, it would not have resulted in his own readmission to caste society. One of the conditions laid down in the marriage proved this quite plainly. Keshub's brother Krishna Behari Sen gave away the bride, because Keshub was outcasted. Also, the marriage defied orthodoxy in a number of ways. It was non-idolatrous, at least in the officially approved ceremonial. It was itself a radical inter-caste marriage, Keshub's daughter being a Vaidya and the Maharajah being of a lower caste, the Sanchok or Rajbansi caste.[37] So in defying the caste rules of marriage, and in its form, it was not a real Hindu marriage. Nor was it, by Hindu standards, an early marriage. Even though Nabogopal Mitra's enthusiasm may have been due to his seeing the marriage as an endorsement of traditional values, in his speech he cited the approval given to the marriage by two Christians, Reverend Lafont, a Roman Catholic, and Reverend K. S. Macdonald, a Presbyterian.[38] On such evidence, it does not seem that Keshub's consent to the mariage denoted a desire to return to Hindu society. On the contrary, it exhibited a desire to extend the sphere of Western influence even further.

Keshub and his family went ahead with preparations to leave for Cuch Behar on 25 February. Preparations for the marriage did not run smoothly, thus increasing the alarm and outrage already rampant in the Brahmo community. Two days before the bridal party was due to leave Keshub received a telegram saying that the Brahmo part of the marriage ritual was unacceptable. He replied, protesting at this, to which he received a favourable reply agreeing to the conditions already laid down.[39] Hence, although Keshub did not go ahead merely because the train was booked, hoping to negotiate further when he arrived, as P. C. Mozoomdar (to the continual delight or disdain of all later biographers) had reported,[40] the situation was ominously precarious and indefinite. Protap said that Keshub went against his natural sagacity because he felt compelled to by God, but it was also already much too late for Keshub to withdraw from the situation without a total loss of face. He was committed

to the marriage because he had given his consent, becaus
it had been publicly declared, and because of the lov
that had grown up between his daughter and the young
Maharajah. Pulling out at such a late stage was not a
real possibility, and it is unlikely anyway that it would
have succeeded as a heroic gesture to win back those
who had lost their faith in him, as it would have cas
even greater doubt on his doctrine of *Adesh*, or the wil
of God, if it could so easily be reversed. Having trustee
in God and the good faith of the British so far, he continued to do so.

That it was the British rather than the Cuch Behar
authorities that were eager for the marriage to take place
became quite clear when the bridal party reached Cuch
Behar. They were given a very cold reception by the
palace. The British had to operate carefully, behind
the scenes, in Cuch Behar, so they did little to openly
intervene in the ensuing points of difference between the
two groups there. Once the stage had been set in Cuch
Behar, and all the players were present, the British
authorities hypocritically resumed their stance of religious neutrality and non-interference. They felt secure
in the knowledge that the bridal party, once there, would
not be likely to refuse to let the marriage take place.
However, they were inevitably drawn into the controversy, albeit unwillingly, when on 4 March the *Raj Pandit*
and other officials came to Keshub proposing major
changes in the marriage ritual. They, too, must have
intended to disarm Keshub when off his home territory,
but he was not as pliable as they had wished. According
to their new set of terms Keshub was not even allowed
to be present at the marriage, nor were any non-Brahmins
or ex-Brahmins allowed to officiate—thus ruling out
Gour Govinda Roy, a non-Brahmin. They wanted to
dispense with the public Brahmo Divine Service, and
the proclamation of marriage vows which was part of
the Brahmo reformed marriage rituals. They also wanted both the bride and groom to perform *Hom*.[41] The
marriage was supposed to take place on 6 March, leaving
little time for negotiations. Keshub's plight was pitiable.

Ie had never envisaged this depressing series of obstacles, ll calculated to make his actions and decisions look even vorse in the public eye. He was forced to take a stand efusing to agree to any of the new proposals, but he nust have felt desperate in the knowledge that he was oo commited to the marriage already to effectively ippose it. It was also said that he would have to pay he Cuch Behar Raj one and a half *lakhs* of rupees to reak it off.[42] He was powerless, but he did what he could, vhich was to call on the British Government to honour ts promises, trusting as always in their good faith. His rust was rewarded, as the Deputy Commissioner pro-luced a telegram from the Lieutenant-Governor decree-ng that the marriage was to be performed according to he rites as previously agreed on. In the short term they had saved Keshub from his predicament. The marriage vas sanctioned to take place without any further and greater compromises. Sunity did not attribute the turn in the tide of affairs merely to the British Government, out also to the strong ultimatum of her future husband, who asserted that if the marriage did not take place he would leave Cuch Behar for ever, for if he could not marry her he would marry no-one.[43] This may have given a fright to both the British and Cuch Behar au-thorities, all of whom had been regarding the Maharajah as a pawn in their political struggle.

Although they did save the situation then, the British did not act straightforwardly. The Lieutenant-Governor's telegram at first maintained a show of honour : —

> I consider that we are bound by terms of my tele-gram and letter—void of idolatrous mantras ; and I cannot say conscientiously that the 'Hom' is not in a manner idolatrous..

It then went on,

> In return for this concession I insist on everything in the marriage being purely Hindu, keeping of course to the original agreement of 'Ishwar' (God) for Bishtoo (Vishnu, Hindu Deity).[44]

It was an underhand shift of emphasis to assume that an instruction to abide by the original agreement was

in fact a concession. It was now clear that the British
hoped that the marriage would look as Hindu as possible
for the sake of their own future position in Cuch Behar
They had expressed this before, but not to Keshub himself. As Dalton wrote to Jadub Chunder Chuckerbutty

> Of course, my object is to avoid any unnecessary dis-
> play of Brahmoism. In marrying a Brahmo girl the
> Rajah makes a great concession to enlighted ideas,
> but it is most desirable that this connection should
> be softened as much as possible in the eyes of his
> relatives, at Cooch Behar and elsewhere, who are
> still wedded to the old superstitions, and who would
> look with horror upon any departure from the old
> Hindu formula.

> I wish therefore to dissuade Babu Keshub Chunder
> Sen from bringing with him any of those who might
> be called his followers, apart from such as are his
> immediate relatives. In fact, we cannot permit any
> Brahmo demonstration whatever, and those who
> come must bear in mind that a single speech in any
> way whatever relating to Theism versus Idolatry will
> will not be permitted.[45]

Dalton seems to have been an arbitrary despot in the
little realm of Cuch Behar.[46] He ruled that the novel
idea of bridesmaids was forbidden, and wanted the bride's
female entourage to be limited to immediate family and
one or two close friends. Even the Brahmo principle
of equality was undermined by the limitations imposed
on the male guests. Their social status was to be of the
level that they "are entitled to be admitted and given
a seat at the Lieutenant-Governor's Durbars". And,
going back on the inducements he had used to get Keshub
to look favourably on the marriage initially, Dalton said
complacently,

> It is possible that he may look upon this marriage
> as the inauguration of a new era in the history of
> social and religious progress. But in Cooch Behar,
> at all events, he must wait for the fructification of his
> work until the Rajah attains his majority.

Therefore the marriage did take place, but it was
not an occasion for rejoicing. The Cuch Behar party
fought a continual battle to retain Hindu usages, with

he British silently acquiescing through their policy of
non-interference. Sunity only narrowly averted being
an unwitting party to the Hindu ceremony of *prayaschit*,
or expiation. She was given a gold coin by a member
of the Cuch Behar family and told to give it to the
Brahmin priest, but her grandmother intervened so she
placed the coin on the floor instead.[47]  Unfavourable reports were sent back to Calcutta. In a detailed account,[48]
the correspondent of the *Indian Mirror* noted that, contrary to prior agreement, there were idolatrous objects
at the place of marriage, which although they were not
worshipped, were an open affront to Brahmo principles.
The ceremony itself was non-idolatrous. Brahmin priests
officiated, but the ceremony was presided over by Gour
Govinda Roy. The *Hom* ceremony was performed, in
defiance of the previous settlement, but as only the groom
was present it was incomplete. The Brahmo Divine
Service, conducted by Keshub, was marred by great uproar. The exchange of marriage vows took place privately in the inner apartments after the main ceremony,
not publicly as Keshub had wished.

> The principles of Brahmo marriage were barely
> preserved, but for all practical purposes the majority
> of our co-religionists present on the occasion were
> deeply dissatisfied. On the other hand the Ranees,
> and the representatives of the Hindu element in the
> Cooch Behar Raj, were equally dissatisfied. They
> felt that the essential requirements of a Hindu
> marriage had been set aside, and they were con-
> sequently distressed and angry...[49]

The concluding remark was that the essential principles
of Brahmo marriage had been maintained intact, and
that it was thus a valid Brahmo marriage.

Even so, both parties found the marriage unsatisfactory. Keshub felt deeply depressed, having already had
so many of his ideals quashed and rejected by the strong
Hindu conservatism of the Cuch Behar Raj. He was to
continue to be plagued by the issue of the marriage
ceremony, which was extremely awkward as being so
dissatisfied himself he was not in a good position to
defend it. Keshub's opponents reacted with heightened

indignation when they learnt of the compromises that
had been made. According to them Keshub had sold
his principles a second time, by condoning an idolatrous
marriage for his daughter. There was less substance in
this charge than in that of early marriage. Keshub had
opposed any deviation from prescribed ritual in so far
as he could. Every jarring thing that did happen was
arranged without consulting or informing him.

The Government did not help salvage Keshub's reputation for future biographers when, in the official
Administration Report of the Kuch Behar State,[50] it was
recorded that despite some concessions to Keshub it was
a Hindu marriage. The 'perfect orthodoxy' of the marriage
was proved by the Brahmins consenting to perform it,
although Keshub's defenders argued with equal conviction that so many rules had been broken that orthodoxy
could not possibly have been preserved. However, in
the Report on the Administration of Bengal, 1877-78,[51]
it was reiterated that

> Some difficulty was experienced in reconciling the
> Hindu and Brahmo ceremonial forms; for the Rajah
> is not a Brahmo, it was necessary to the legality of
> the marriage that the rites should be in accordance
> with the Hindu religion. The ordinary Hindu cere-
> mony was modified so as to meet the wishes of Babu
> Keshub Chunder Sen; but the fact that Brahmins
> consented to perform it shows that the marriage was
> recognized by the Hindus as orthodox...

Based on these reports, and on the obvious eagerness
of the British for the marriage to eventuate, a theory
has been formulated that this was part of a British plot
to ruin Keshub and discredit the Brahmo Samaj.[52] The
evidence for the conspiracy is very feeble, being based
firstly on an obscure book printed in 1872 which compared
the Brahmo Samaj to a live volcano, warning the Government that it was "spreading at such a rate as must inevitably prove speedily fatal to our present system of
Indian administration".[53] The Government supposedly
heeded this warning, despite the fact that Keshub was
at this time, and remained throughout his life, a close
friend of the highest British administrators, all of whom

gave active encouragement to his work and took great interest in his ideas and his movement. In England his views were respected, and his work admired. His only British opponents were certain of the missionaries, but they had little power to turn the Government against him. According to this 'conspiracy theory', the Government's first blow was to insert the pernicious clause "I am not a Hindu" in the 1872 Marriage Act. Their second blow was to arrest the growing power of the Brahmo Samaj by linking it with a feudal power—hence the Cuch Behar marriage. The assumption is that Keshub was the dupe of false propaganda from the British. While accepting that they did put a lot of pressure on Keshub to go through with the marriage, their failure to live up to their promises was because their primary object was to have this marriage performed to ensure the safe continuation of British influence in Cuch Behar.[54] They saw the Brahmo Samaj as an ally in carrying out the task of modernizing India, and there is no indication that they wanted to get rid of it.[55] Keshub's loyalty was public knowledge, and his consent to the marriage was a public endorsement of the benefits of British rule. Keshub's main opponents were more involved in political reform than he was, so it would not have been in the interests of the Government to precipitate a split in the Brahmo Samaj by which this group would gain prominence. Linking the Brahmo Samaj with the Cuch Behar Raj was not an attempt to discredit it, but to strengthen their own position there.

The bridal party returned to Calcutta on 18 March, and the Maharajah left for England that night.[56] Now that the marriage had taken place Keshub had no secure base to return to. He had to face his detractors. There was a series of unsatisfactory encounters between Keshub and his opponents, emotional and aggressive on their part, passive and aloof on his. They called a meeting to depose him, on the grounds that he had forfeited the confidence of the Brahmo community. Their decision was challenged on the grounds that they were unrepresentative of the Brahmo community, pointing to the fact that even Durga

13

Mohan Das was not a proper member because he had not paid his dues.[57] Amidst the chaos and after Keshub's supporters had left in disgust, the protestors managed to pass their resolution deposing Keshub from the position of *Acharya*.[58] Keshub was present at the meeting and although outwardly calm, the blow to his morale was crushing. He had virtually no one to turn to. Even his supporter did not wholeheartedly approve of his actions. His reaction was to turn inward, and heavenward, but not outward to the public. He would not try and regain sympathy by presenting the public with his reasons and appealing for understanding. He was asking a great deal from his followers—to give him their unqualified support.

This was the most serious crisis Keshub had had to face. The focus was on him, and at this point he was responsible for the fate of the Brahmo Samaj as a whole. He had done so much to mould it and hold it together that even though it may have been capable of an independent existence without him, he could not have assumed that its future was not bound up with his. It was also questionable whether he could exist without the Brahmo Samaj, as it had always been the channel for his views, and it was certainly the only body through which he could implement his far-reaching plans for the religious and social future of India. His dignity was put at a low ebb in the ensuing conflict. The protestors—not without some misgivings on the part of some of them[59]—had decided to break away and found their own organization. They engaged in physical violence in attempts to gain possession of the *mandir*, which were only quelled by Keshub calling the police. Unlike Keshub when he separated from Debendranath in 1865, this group of protestors had come under the influence of nationalist ideals of physical aggression and greater boldness, so their parting from Keshub was marked by extreme violence and bitterness. Despite a letter from P. C. Mozoomdar telling them that a real schism in the Brahmo Samaj was impossible because of their basic agreement on the cardinal doctrine of monotheism,[60] the protestors broke away and founded the constitutionally organized Sadharan Brahmo Samaj on 15 May 1878.[61]

The protestors who formed the Sadharan Brahmo Samaj did not include all those who objected to the marriage. Many had chosen to remain with Keshub, feeling that despite his drawbacks he was a more suitable leader than any of those opposing him. The leaders of the protest group—Ananda Mohan Bose, Sivanath Sastri, Dwarkanath Ganguli, Durga Mohan Das and Shib Chunder Deb—had used the Cuch Behar marriage as an opportunity to turn the tide of public opinion against Keshub, as they had had major disagreements with him for some time and wanted to diminish his power and leadership. They had already fought with him over such issues as the extent of women's emancipation, and the need for constitutionalism and representation in the Brahmo Samaj. Many of the most vehement protestors were motivated by personal animosity towards Keshub for various reasons. For instance, Sivanath Sastri had always resented Keshub's disapproval of his keeping two wives, Haranath Bose bore a grudge from the time of the *Bharat Ashram* libel case in 1874, and Jadunath Chakravarty had been barely reconciled to Keshub after his objections to man-worship in 1868. Bijoy Krishna Goswami had always maintained a stance of objective criticism rather than apostolic loyalty. Keshub was especially hurt by his desertion as he had been one of Keshub's closest disciples, and had studied the discipline of *bhakti* under him. The protestors were also fortunate in having the support of Shib Chunder Deb, an old Derozian who, being a veteran of the first split in which he had sided with Keshub, had proved his non-partisan integrity. The followers of the Sadharan Brahmo Samaj were made up of a sector of the middle-classes who had been more attracted to Keshub's philanthropic reform schemes than to his religious ideas, and so found it easy to break away from him. It also included a group of Young Brahmos attracted by nationalist ideals headed by Bipin Chandra Pal. Those who stayed with Keshub did so largely because they were bound by his charisma.

For instance, Sitanath Tattvabhushan left Keshub eventually, but could not do so at first because he felt bound to him by personal devotion.[62] They were attracted by his religious ideals and not disappointed that he was no longer as involved in pressing for social reform. Because of a common grudge against Keshub, the Adi Brahmo Samaj sided with the new organization.

The split had a disastrous effect on the prestige of the Brahmo Samaj in the community. At a time when it had gained momentum and formed a recognizably important sector of the educated community, its inability to maintain a united front, and the scandal that had been generated within it over the marriage, ruined its reputation and standing. It also disillusioned many of the peripheral followers of the Samaj, who needed to feel that they belonged to a strong and important body led by a confident, popular leader. These people drifted away, either back to the security of tradition or on to materialism and atheism.

Keshub himself was a completely broken man. The consequences of the marriage had been far worse than anything he had ever envisaged, and the benefits were hardly obvious.[63] His usual capabilities were completely undermined. His impulsive reactions were not calculated to deal effectively with the situation that had arisen. He had refrained from duty as Minister voluntarily for a period after the marriage, resuming on 28 April after his congregation persuaded him that they did want him. He craved for these demonstrations of faith and confidence in him. When they did not seem forthcoming, he fell into a state of extreme depression. He was ill with an unspecified disease early in July, but was reported to be better by the end of the month.[64] His health, affected by his mental state, remained shaky, and on 11 August it was reported that he had had a relapse. P. C. Mozoomdar said that he had delirium and brain fever, and the symptoms described in the newspaper report also suggest that he had had a kind of nervous breakdown. "Fever of a rather low type set upon him almost suddenly, and this was attended with increasing debility

and nervousness, so much so that his medical advisers—
Dr Charles among others—insisted upon an instant change
of climate....". With his family he took a river boat
on the Hughly. His condition improved slightly, physically and mentally, but then fell back. Nothing more
of this illness was reported, but by the end of September
he was evidently well enough to be back taking part of
the Divine Service and slowly returning to participation
in public affairs.[65] From October onward, broken only
by a recuperative holiday in Ranigunge in November
with his daughter the Maharani, Keshub began to resume
his place in the public eye. He presided over meetings
of the Indian Reform Association, and was on the Committee to form an Institution for Physical and Moral
Improvement of Indian Students.[66]

Unlike the first split with Debendranath, which was
ideological, this one was based mainly on objections to
the dominance of Keshub's personality, although ideological issues were also important. Keshub and Debendranath parted without any adverse reflections on the
capabilities of either, but the Sadharan Brahmo Samaj
group publicly deposed Keshub by a vote of no confidence.
In 1865 the conflict had been fought out with some reten-
tion of dignity, between two groups each headed by a
single leader. In this case the opposition was an organized group, and the attack was directed against Keshub
as an individual. It was in no way a generational conflict, nor was it easily classified into opposing ideologies.
The dichotomy between rationalism and mysticism is
hardly adequate to describe the complexities, especially
of Keshub's attitude. The protestors were united by a
distinct kind of enlightened rationalism, and their objection to Keshub was directed not only against his autocracy but against his confusion, or his imagination. His
ideas were continually developing and changing, following different directions, whereas they were consistent and
single-minded. Most of them had been attracted to the
Brahmo Samaj of India by Keshub, being impressed with
the power and stimulating enthusiasm of his personality,
but had eventually found it overwhelming because it

did not leave room for them to express their own views, or to leave their stamp on Brahmoism. Thus, although the separation came about because of the Cuch Behar marriage, it had deeper roots in a widespread alarm at the dominance of Keshub's personality.

Despite their recognition of the necessity to plough on, at the end of 1878 Keshub and his followers felt supremely discouraged. Many of the *mofussil* branches had declared their support for the Sadharan Brahmo Samaj. In Dacca, Banga Chandra Ray had been deposed as Minister simply for not joining the protest movement.[67] The Sadharan Brahmo Samaj was still small, with a membership of between 200 to 300 only, but its leaders were keen to put their own set of ideals into practice. They had a positive programme to initiate. Keshub's followers no longer had complete confidence in him as leader. It was still widely believed that Keshub had agreed to the Cuch Behar marriage out of a desire for wealth and status. The part played by the British in the affair, and that Keshub's agreement was primarily an indication of his endorsement of the benefits of British rule, was not generally realized, as he was also accused of wanting to revert to Hindu tradition. Keshub was thus faced with the task of restoring the influence and credibility of the Brahmo Samaj, a challenge to which he responded with the formulation of the doctrine of the New Dispensation.

## NOTES AND REFERENCES

1. Calcutta Literary Society, 26th *Annual Report*, 1902.

2. Sunity Devee, op. cit. pp. 45-46. The paper put out by the opponents of the marriage, the *Brahmo Public Opinion*, expressed sympathy with the *Ranis'* reluctance to allow the Maharajah to lose caste and thus cause their social degradation. This readiness to defend the orthodox viewpoint was uncharacteristic, and showed the determination to oppose Keshub even to the extent of siding with a faction to which it was ideologically opposed, like the *Ranis*. *Brahmo Public Opinion*. 4 April 1878, 'The Ranees of Kuch Behar and the Bengal Government'.

3. Those involved extended from the Lieutenant-Governor (Sir Richard Temple until January 1877, then Sir Ashley Eden), the Commissioner, Lord Ulick Browne, and the man on the spot, the Deputy Commissioner, Mr Godfrey Dalton.

4.  S. Sastri, *Atmacharit* op. cit. p. 143 said that the proposal went
    to D. M. Das first. The negotiations in South India were men-
    tioned in S. Sastri, *History* op. cit. Vol. I, Appendix G, p. 333. Also
    see the article 'Adjourned Protest Meeting' in *Indian Mirror,*
    2 March 1878.

5.  The Brahmo Missionary Conference told Max Muller that Keshub's
    opponents were bitter because Durga Mohan's daughter had
    been rejected in favour of Keshub's F. M. Muller, *Chips* op.
    cit. Vol. II, p. 97.

6.  P. C. Mozoomdar, *Life* op. cit. p. 204.

7.  B. Mozoomdar, *God-Man Keshub and Cooch Behar Marriage*
    (Calcutta, 1912) p. 8.

8.  P. K. Sen, *Biography* op. cit. Vol. II, Facsimile letter B, between
    pp. 184-185.

9.  B. Mozoomdar, *God-man Keshub* op. cit. pp. 7-9. The letter is
    dated 29 April 1878.

10. F. M. Muller, *Chips* op. cit. Vol. II, p. 114.   Letter dated 2
    May 1881.

11. Sunity Devee, op. cit. p. 52.

12. ibid. pp. 48-49.

13. ibid. pp. 54-55.

14. From a sermon preached by Voysey in London on 13 April
    1879, printed in the *Indian Mirror,* Sunday edition, 1   June
    1879.

15. B. Mozoomdar, *God-Man Keshub* op. cit. p. 10.

16. B. Mozoomdar, *God-Man Keshub* op. cit. pp. 12-13. Keshub's
    defenders, in their public statement, partially undermined his
    avowals by stating that the Act was really directed against
    consummation of marriage before puberty—and Sunity
    Devee had already fulfilled this condition. As Keshub's cri-
    tics were quick to point out, if this was merely a betrothal,
    there was no point in mentioning that the bride had reached
    puberty. *Brahmo Public Opinion* 23 May 1878, in an extract
    from the *Bengal Times.*

17. *Brahmo Public Opinion* 18 July 1878, in an extract from
    the *Inquirer,* 8 June 1878. The letter is dated 2 May.

18. *Indian Mirror* 23 September 1881.

19. B. C. Pal, *Memories* op. cit. Vol. I, p. 338.

20. P. K. Sen, *Biography* op. cit.   Vol. II, Facsimile letter C
    between pp. 188-189.

21. ibid. p. 189.

22. *Indian Mirror,* 9 February 1878.

23. In a meeting about the Brahmo Marriage Bill in 1871 Keshub
    had stressed that its radicalism lay in the provision for inter-
    caste marriage. Keshub Chunder Sen, *National* op. cit. p. 12.

24. *Indian Mirror,* 14 February 1878. See also S. Sastri, *History*
    op. cit. Vol. I, pp. 330-335, at the end of which is a full
    list of signatories.

25. S. Sastri, *History* op. cit. Vol. I, p. 274.

26. P. C. Mozoomdar, *Life* op. cit. p. 212. See also F. M. Muller,
    *Chips* op. cit. Vol. II, p. 93. Letter from Keshub dated 22
    December 1880.

27. P. K. Sen, *Biography* op. cit. Vol. II, Facsimile letter C, between pp. 188-189. While some refused to believe the Maha rajah's avowal, maintaining that he was a Hindu, others use it as an indictment of his character, showing his lack of firmness *Brahmo Public Opinion* 9 May 1878.

28. *Indian Mirror*, 21 February 1878.

29. P. C. Mozoomdar, *Life* op. cit. p. 205.

30. S. Sastri, *History* op. cit. Vol. I, p. 276.

31. F. M. Muller, *Chips* op. cit. Vol. II, pp. 93-94, 113-114. Letters of 22 December, 1880 and 2 May 1881.

32. Mrs Muller, *Life* op. cit. Vol. II, p. 59.

33. A notable exception was S. D. Collet, who sided with the protestors.

34. S. Sastri, *History* op. cit. Vol. I, pp. 336-351.

35. *Indian Mirror*, 26 February 1878.

36. Keshub Chunder Sen, *National* op. cit. pp. 7-10. Nabogopal Mitra was also an ardent Hindu nationalist organizer of the annual Hindu Mela.

37. *Indian Mirror*, Sunday edition, 28 April 1878.

38. The support given by these two was later qualified and thus considerably weakened. Next day Nabogopal Mitra wrote to the *Indian Mirror* (27 February) saying that he had only heard of Father Lafont's approval indirectly, through another source. Rev. K. S. Macdonald wrote in to say that though this marriage would be beneficial, his real sympathy was with the protestors as he was against early marriage. (*Indian Mirror*, Sunday edition, 3 March).

39. P. K. Sen, *Biography* op. cit. Vol. II, p. 195.

40. P. C. Mozoomdar, *Life* op. cit. pp. 207-208.

41. P. K. Sen, *Biography* op. cit. Vol. II, pp. 197-198.

42. Count Goblet d'Alviella, *L'Evolution Religieuse Contemporaine chez les anglais, less americains et les hindus* (Paris, 1884), p. 335.

43. Sunity Devee, op. cit. p. 65.

44. P. K. Sen, *Biography* op. cit. p. 201.

45. Letter quoted in Sunity Devee, op. cit. pp. 58-59.

46. An article on the Maharajah's Installation in the *Liberal and New Dispensation* of 18 November 1883 criticized Dalton's European arrogance, saying that he took as his motto 'L' Etat, c'est moi'. P. C. Mozoomdar also wrote to Max Muller that Keshub did not disclose more about the marriage because it would have exposed the conduct of high officials in the Bengal Government. F. M. Muller, *Chips* op. cit. Vol. II, p. 150. Letter of 14 February 1881.

47. Sunity Devee, op. cit. p. 63.

48. *Indian Mirror*, Sunday edition, 17 March 1878.

49. loc. cit.

50. *Indian Mirror*, Sunday edition, 22 December 1878. Report signed by Dalton. The same document, printed in F. M. Muller, *Chips* op. cit. Vol. II, pp. 99-101, uses the spelling Cutch Behar throughout.

51. *Indian Mirror,* Sunday edition, 22 December 1878.  This report was not signed, but was presumably also by Dalton.

52. A. C. Gupta op. cit. Article on 'The Brahmo Samaj' by Jogananda Das, pp. 494-498.

53. Robert H. Elliot, *Concerning John's Indian Affairs.*

54. There were rumours that the Government had been thinking of annexing the state of Cuch Behar, but they decided against it.  *Liberal and New Dispensation,* 18 November 1883.

55. Sir Richard Temple, in an article in the *Fortnightly Review* discussed in the *Liberal and New Dispensation* 4 February 1883, said that Brahmoism posed no danger to British rule, although its political force should be "borne in mind" by Anglo-Indian statesmen. He showed no knowledge of any conspiracy to undercut that force, as it was not seen as a current problem.

56. *Indian Mirror,* 19 March 1878.

57. ibid. Sunday edition, 23 March 1878.

58. S. Sastri, *Atmacharit* op. cit. p. 148.

59. S. Sastri, *Atmacharit* op. cit. p. 144 gave an account of the agony gone through by Ananda Mohan Bose before arriving at the decision to found a separate Samaj.

60. *Indian Mirror,* 15 March 1878.

61. ibid. Sunday edition, 19 March 1878.

62. K. Mitra, op. cit. p. 134.

63. Ultimately Keshub and the British proved right, and the marriage did further 'progress' in Cuch Behar. A Brahmo Samaj, and schools and colleges were established by the Maharani. She was very Westernized, in close contact with England and British royalty. Queen Victoria was godmother to one of her sons. Lady Dufferin commented that the Maharani must have been very intelligent, as "she has so quickly and completely got into European ways . . "—Lady Dufferin, *Our Viceregal Life in India* (2 vols, London, 1889), Vol. I. p. 62.

64. *Indian Mirror,* Sunday edition, 14 July and 21 July 1878.

65. ibid. Sunday edition, 29 September 1878.

66. ibid. 27 October 1878 and 29 October 1878.

67. *Indian Mirror,* Sunday edition, 31 March 1878 and also *Yearly Theistic Record,* 1880-1881.

# CHAPTER EIGHT

# ECLECTICISM OR CHAOS :
# THE NEW DISPENSATION (1879-1884)

KESHUB CHUNDER SEN'S anniversary lecture for 1879, on 'Am I an Inspired Prophet ?'[1], indicated that he had at least partially recovered has confidence, broken by the blows of the previous year. Because of the marriage controversy, the lecture attracted even greater crowds than usual. His audience was expectant, eager to see how he was going to clear himself, and on what new basis he was going to establish his branch of the Brahmo Samaj. The audience included the most prominent of the Christian missionaries, including Rev. K. S. Macdonald and Rev. Dall, the Muslim leader Syed Ahmed, the political leader Surendranath Banerjea, and the least vindictive of his adversaries, Ananda Mohan Bose.[2] Keshub soon deflated the hopes of those who wanted him to clarify the events of the past year, insisting that he was

> ...simply going to draw my inner self out of myself, in order that you may see and understand it. I am not going to justify my conduct, nor to defend my recent movements and actions. Judgement belongeth to the Lord. It is not possible for you to convict nor acquit me.[3]

Nor did he present anything very new. He declared that he was not a prophet because he was not holy, not worthy even to touch the shoes of the worlds least prophet. Such marked emphasis on his fallibility and such exaggerated humility could have been one way of engaging public sympathy for his past actions and of averting further opprobrium, as it would have been pointless to continue to blame one who had declared openly that he was a vile sinner.[4] Nonetheless he did admit to being a singular man. When young, Providence had brought him into the presence of John the Baptist, who taught

m "Repent ye, for the kingdom of heaven is at hand";
Jesus, who told him "Take no thought for the morrow";
d lastly Paul, whose message was "Let them that have
ives be as though they had none". Significantly, his
rly religious experience was based firmly on Biblical
urces. Given that these early experiences pointed him
wards an ascetic life, he attempted to justify his present
ppearance of prosperity by the ingenuous explanation
at it was a gift of God which he could not refuse :—

> Perhaps my appearance is that of one of the weal-
> thiest and richest men in the world. My true self
> must not be identified with outward appearances,
> which are only the result of shifting circumstances.
> Whatever the Lord gives to me I am bound to accept.
> Be it riches or penury, I must submit to all the ordi-
> nances and dispensations of God ...[5]

is famed eloquence was also seen by him as God-given,
s it only came to him when God chose to speak through
im, at which times he was "all fire", while at other times
e was speechless. The 'secular' explanation of this
henomenon seemed to be that as he excelled at public
peaking on all occasions, he must have felt confident
hen performing, or pontificating, for an audience, and
hat the role which was most congenial to him was that
f the public figure. His message was not to be given to
nyone personally—he wanted to inspire mankind. His
rand ambitions inhibited him from expending much
ffort on personal relationships, but he responded to the
hallenge of a crowd, which held out the possibility of
nfluencing large numbers of people. The main point of
is lecture confirmed this impression. He said that his
nission, which he had devoted his life to fulfilling, was
he union of East and West. He set out his own idea
f himself and the way he envisaged such a union so
learly that it is worth quoting at length :—

> All science is religion, and all religion is science.
> There is as much science in prayer as in the loco-
> motive engine, as much science in inspiration as in
> the microscope and the telegraph wire, and the latest
> inventions of science. Thus pantheism and mysti-
> cism, science and positivism, are with me. Pantheism

and mysticism are things of Asia, while positivism and all the sciences of the day belong to Europe. M Church is an Asiatic Church. I am in my very bone and blood, in the very constitution of my soul, essen tially an Asiatic. As an Asiatic, I would encourag and vindicate devotion to the extent of mystic com munion. But here you will probably say there is n harmonious development. It is all prayer and con templation, and no work. I say there *is* harmony If I am mystical, am I not practical too ? I an practical as an Englishman. If I am Asiatic in devo tion, I am a European in practical energy. My creec is not dreamy sentimentalism, not quietism, no imagination. Energy, yes, energy—I have that i a very great measure in my character and in m Church. It is the vigour and energy of the English man and the American. My Church is a vast Euro pean Church, full of resolution, heroism, strength and vivacity. My Church has in it all the elements o European practical life. It encourages education social reformation, the improvement of women, th promotion of cheap journalism, the advancement o science, and material prosperity. Like a mighty river, the stream of national devotion comes into my Church from the Vedas and the Upanishads, the pantheistic books and mystic scriptures of ancien India. None can, none would, resist this torrent But in my Church warm devotion and practical en thusiasm are commingled. Can I forget that I have received an essentially Western training ? I canno indulge in dreams. I must work....[6]

Keshub was very aware of having been moulded by Western influences, but exaggerated the Hindu influence on him. He knew very little about the Vedas or the Upanishads, and his main relation to tradition was through Vaishnavism, not the Brahmanical tradition. However, in an age of rediscovering past glories, it was more accep table and effective to appeal to ancient Indian scriptures than to popular folk tradition.

This lecture, and that delivered a few months later on 'India Asks: who is Christ ?',[7] were almost equal in impact to those he had given twelve years previously on 'Jesus Christ: Europe and Asia' and 'Great Men', and were also very similar in theme. What he had to say in 1879 differed very little in essence. Although there

ad been many changes in the Brahmo Samaj as an orga-
ization, Keshub's relation to Christ and Christianity, and
is aim of harmonizing East and West, remained at the
ore of his thinking. Keshub was prompted to air his
iews on Christ publicly once again, after long years of
ilence, in answer to queries about his feeling for Christ
rom an Anglican monk, Father Luke Rivington. Riving-
on was in Calcutta for a period in 1879, and made him-
elf very popular with Keshub and educated Indians by
is openness and enthusiasm. He kept his own Chris-
ianity unobtrusively in the background and admitted
he divine inspiration of portions of the Hindu scriptures.[8]
Ie delighted them by coming forward to meet them on
heir own ground. On one occasion he joined Keshub and
he Brahmos in eating "a truly Native dinner in native
tyle",[9] sitting on the floor with them, showing a lack of
he over-refined concept of their own dignity common to
ost Europeans in India. Rivington thus provided en-
ouragement for Keshub to pursue his plan of bringing
ogether East and West, giving positive proof, through
is actions and attitudes, that it was not an impossibility.

Keshub explained in the lecture that he had chosen
he topic because as India had been conquered by Christ
rather than just Britain) and was imbibing the spirit of
hristian civilization, India should be informed about the
eal character of Christ. He answered his own rhetorical
uestion by claiming that the real Christ was an Asiatic.
he germ of this view had been the main point of his
ecture in 1866, but as well as expanding on it, Keshub
ow also embarked on a controversial discussion of the
uestion of Christ's divinity. On this point his ideas
id show a development. Formerly he had seen Christ
s a great man, but now he saw him as one with God and
ith man, partaking of the divine nature. He quoted
xtensively from the New Testament, but deduced rather
puriously that the idea of Christ expressed therein was
ssentially Hindu. Jesus fitted into his idea of Indian
eligion because he saw his absorption in God as pan-
heism, a key concept of Vedantic Hinduism. As was
requently the case, in discussing the Hindu aspect Keshub

relied on vague generalization with no supporting r
ferences from the Hindu scriptures. His argume
extended to Asia as a whole, and was not intended as
display of nationalism. Unlike Rajnarain Bose in h
lecture on 'Hindu Dharmer Shreshthata'[10] he did not fe
that Hinduism on its own was sufficient. He called (
India to accept Christ as a fellow Asiatic whose doctrin
were basically Hindu, because he thought Christ w
better than anything offered in Hinduism. For instanc
he said that Christ was a true Yogi, but he did not sha
the defects of pride and mysticism of the Hindu asceti
Keshub had chosen Christ as his master, but did not s/
him as being necessarily attached to the Christian religio
Keshub's Christ was flexible and adaptable, and h
feeling for Christ was intensely personal and emotiona
The intensity of his feeling for Christ was one of th
main reasons for his never becoming a Christian, as I
could better express these feelings through Hindu dev
tionalism than through the accepted Christian worshi

Predictably the lecture on Christ aroused a stror
response, which was mainly antagonistic. The patter
of reaction was similar to that following his previous le
ture on Christ. There was a volley of answering lecture
from Christians and Theists: two lectures by Fath
Rivington on 'An Answer to India's Question—who
Christ ?';[11] a sermon at St John's Cathedral, Calcutta, t
Archdeacon Baly, who expressed the hope that Brahm
would realize that Christianity was not compatible wit
traditional Hindu thought;[12] a pamphlet on 'Who
Christ ? Can India rest satisfied with Babu Keshu
Chunder Sen's answer to this question ?' by Rev. W. I
Blackett of the Divinity School, Krishnagar;[13] and anothe
sermon by Charles Voysey in London condemnin
Keshub's excessive veneration for Christ and launchin
a general tirade against the divinity and person of Chris
He called on Brahmos to have nothing to do with Chri
tianity, a religion that was essentially idolatrous.
Keshub's lecture was also reviewed extensively in jou
nals and papers throughout India, giving wide publicit
to his views and proving that his lectures were still abl

to provoke a great deal of response, although it came mostly from the Christian community. His opinions still seemed to matter to Christians in England and India, even if they were not so influential among his own community. In fact, his elevation of Christ alienated many of his countrymen, and was especially resented by those in the Brahmo Samaj who did not share his beliefs.

Keshub seemed determined to prove, by a burst of public activity, that the marriage affair had not been a major setback to his plans for the religious future of India. He still studiously ignored his opponents, though he often lamented their treachery in the columns of the Sunday edition of the *Indian Mirror*. He spent his energies devising new ways of regaining stability, unity and public attention. This eventuated in the New Dispensation in 1880, but prior to that he went ahead with various small schemes designed to contribute to these ends.

He started the Arya Nari Samaj, for Brahmo women, in May 1879. As well as being sincerely concerned with improving the position of Indian women, this also showed his opponents that he was not neglecting the social activities of the Brahmo Samaj, which had been one of the charges levelled against him. Even so, they may not have approved of his project, which was very conventional, with the unprepossessing aims of preserving health by baths, good diet, pure air, neat clothes, and sleep ; of acquiring knowledge by studying natural sciences, biographies of good women, sermons, ethics, history, literature and arithmetic, and of cultivating the spirit by prayer, congregational worship, meditation, good company and conversation. The highest domestic duty was to be the service of one's husband, in support of which Keshub quoted that handy poem depicting the Victorian man's idea of a woman's proper place and duties, Tennyson's 'The Princess'.[15] As Keshub's lack of enthusiasm for the higher education of women only seemed to be criticized by his opponents in the Sadharan Brahmo Samaj and not by any Englishmen, his views must have been quite acceptable to the average Victorian. Keshub saw himself as a 'patron' of women. He instituted for them a series of *bratas*, or relationships, to follow as examples, ranging from those typified by Maitreyi, Savitri, Draupadi and Lilavati on the Hindu side, to Nightingale and Victoria from England.[16] The Lilavati *brata*, supposedly catering for women seeking knowledge and scholarship, showed the low level at which Keshub estimated women's capabilities, as in it she was to learn seven striking phenomena in nature illustrative of God's wisdom, seven important historical facts, seven wonders of the world and seven Sanskrit texts on the duties of women.[17] His aim was clearly to inculcate morality and discipline rather than the pursuit of knowledge for its own sake.

Keshub continued to encourage the Band of Hope, he attended meetings of the Bengal Social Science Association and the Utterparah Hitakari Sabha, and gave an address to the Bethune Society on 'Materialism and Idealism'.[18] His attendance at these middle-class gatherings was motivated not only by his interest in their proceedings alone, but by a desire to show the rest of society, and especially his opponents, that he had not by any means been 'ruined' by the schism.

Clearly Keshub felt a strong need to establish that he was, still, a prominent public figure. Having demonstrated this among the middle-classes, mainly through his Town Hall lectures, he set out to prove it amongst a wider audience through a missionary expedition.[19] The distinguishing feature of this expedition was its aggressive militancy, the whole tour being conceived of in military metaphors. His model was the British Salvation Army, yet another indication of Keshub's affinity with religious developments in England, as the Salvation Army was only founded there in the previous year, 1878.[20] The campaign began in Calcutta, with Keshub addressing about 700 students in College Square—a 'warm-up' exercise for the work that was to come. They arrived at Chinsurah on 1 November, armed with flags, a bugle and the normal *sankirtan* instruments. Next day Keshub lectured at the local Hari Sabha—a Hindu organization—on Chaitanya, judiciously selecting a subject likely to be appreciated by his audience, who showed their appreciation by shouting *"Hari Hari bole"*. The Hindus joined the Brahmos in *sankirtan*. One man got so caught up in the devotional atmosphere that he prostrated himself and rolled in the dust, a common sign of effusive devotion among Hindus, but beyond the limits of Brahmo devotionalism, highlighting how 'respectable' Keshub and the Brahmos were in comparison to real devotees in the Hindu tradition. The party of Keshub and eight missionaries continued to travel north, giving the usual series of lectures, processions and services in each place. Taking no thought for the morrow, as was their motto, they sometimes ran out of funds, but were rescued by donations or by the sale of Brahmo publications.

The Devotional column of the Sunday edition of the *Indian Mirror* declared the object of the expedition to be "to establish the reign of the Mother in this land".[21] The concept of God as Mother was the main repository for Keshub's attempts to unite Hinduism and Christianity. Whereas his view of Christ had formed part of his beliefs throughout, he seemed to use the doctrine of the Motherhood of God as an emotional catch-cry, calculated to excite 'automatic' devotional sentiments in the hearts of his hearers. He knew that it was a doctrine frowned on by the rationalists of the Sadharan Brahmo Samaj, and liked to prove that he did not abide by their cold standards of judgement.

Despite Keshub's attempts to popularize his religious views, the essential foreignness of his campaign was obvious in its systematic missionary structure. The ambivalence of his position, in trying to self-consciously create a national form of religion which would satisfy everyone, was well illustrated by his stay at Mozufferpore. Keshub was intent on moving a 'warlike charge' to arouse the 'inert mass'. He began by giving a Bengali address to a mixed (local and Bengali) audience, concluding with a few token words in Hindi. This was followed by a colourful singing procession complete with flags, bugles and torches. The next day Keshub called on Bishop Johnson,

14

Bishop of Calcutta, who was also there on a passing
visit. There was a Brahmo Sunday service at the house
of a wealthy Bengali *zamindar*. The following day
Keshub gave a public lecture to a European and Indian
audience on 'India and India's God', about the Providential basis of British rule in India. The climax of his visit
was an open-air demonstration attended by people of a
wide range of social strata. Keshub stood on a platform
surrounded by his 'preaching army', and addressed the
crowds for ten minutes in English, ten minutes in Bengali,
and forty minutes in Hindi. The subject he chose was
non-controversial—on Theism and communion with God—
but it succeeded in firing all Mozufferpore with the spirit
of devotion, encouraged by a *kirtan* immediately after
Keshub's talk. A similar pattern was repeated in Gaya
and Bankipore, although the latter was more varied
because it included a visit to the *ashram* of a Sikh *Mohunt*
and being received as the guests of a Native Prince. The
expedition included 36 lectures and sermons, 16 open-air
meetings, 24 *nagar kirtans,* and was estimated to have
been heard by about 10,000 people.[22] The *Statesman*
carpingly remarked that there was no record of any
actual converts,[23] but Keshub replied that its object
was not to convert but to "excite and animate the
public mind". Keshub was satisfied that the expedition
had proved the Brahmo Samaj to be still a living, growing
power in the land. He wound up the campaign with a
'Proclamation from India's Mother' to all her soldiers,
binding them to help fulfil the designs of Providence by
absolute loyalty to Queen Victoria and the British Government, and by fighting sectarianism and all false systems
of worship. Keshub's synthetic approach knew no bounds,
even using the Hindu idea of the Mother to justify British
rule. It showed how he tended to gather all his interests
together under the one heading, without any attempt to
relate the different elements to each other. He relied
on establishing loose connections between ideas, as this
example shows:—

The influence of the earthly mother at home and
of the queen mother at the head of the Government

will raise the hearts of my Indian children to the
Supreme Mother, and I will gather them in the
Kingdom of Heaven and give them peace and sal-
vation.

Keshub's staunch loyalty to Britain held its own rewards,
as he was among those Indians invited to the annual
public Levee at Government House, although none of his
opponents were.[24]

During the 1880 anniversary festivities Keshub announced to the world his doctrine of the *Nava Bidhan,*
or New Dispensation.[25]   Although his anniversary lecture
that year, 'God-Vision in the Nineteenth Century' made
no mention of it, Keshub had alluded to this idea as far
back as 1875.[26]   It differed from the Brahmo Samaj in
that it was to represent a higher stage of spirituality.
The Brahmo Samaj was an earthly body which could be
understood by all as 'a fact of history', but the New Dispensation could only be perceived by the devout believer.[27]
The beliefs of the New Dispensation did not differ from
those of the Brahmo Samaj, and the creed of the New
Dispensation was made up of familiar precepts :--

One God, one Scripture, one Church.
Eternal Progress of the Soul.
Communion of Prophets and Saints.
Fatherhood and Motherhood of God ; Brotherhood of
man
and Sisterhood of woman.
Harmony of knowledge and Holiness, Love and
Work, Yoga
and Asceticism in their highest development.
Loyalty to Sovereign.[28]

The change in name served to dissociate him from
the Sadharan Brahmo Samaj.  He sensed the need for
a revival to boost the morale and reputation of his
church, which had fallen because of the marriage, and
changing its name was an effective way of arousing enthusiasm and interest as it had the novelty and excitement of a new discovery.  There was also an element of
pure egoism in the formation of the New Dispensation.
It was a way of focusing public attention once again on

Keshub and on his religious views. At last he had a
church that was entirely of his own making, of which
he was once again the undisputed leader. There was no
room in it for opposition, as the Dispensation was to be
kept pure, 'undefiled' by criticism and unbelief. In an
article on 'Hints to Young Men' Keshub recommended
that they be "full of faith and the spirit of teachable-
ness".[29] He was not looking for enquiring minds but
for receptive ones among his followers. Indirectly the
split had given him greater freedom than before because
he no longer had the responsibility of trying to satisfy
those whose opinions differed from his.

Lengthy explanations were given as to why this was
a *new* Dispensation, but in fact there was nothing in it
that had not formed a part of Keshub's thought in the
past, apart from a greater tendency to experimentation.
The New Dispensation was, above all, eclectic, proclaiming the unity of *all* religions although in practice its aim
was to unite East and West, Hinduism and Christianity.
Rajnarain Bose archly referred to it as 'religious coque-
try', being all things to all men.[30] During the last four
years of Keshub's lifetime in which he was experimenting
with the New Dispensation there was little actual development in his ideas, only what seemed like random experiment broadly related to the general principle of
eclecticism and religious harmony. Paradoxically, although it was supposed to be more spiritual than the
Brahmo Samaj, the New Dispensation appeared to be a
religion formed by a scientific spirit of trial and error.

Keshub set out the theory behind his New Dispensation in his anniversary lecture for 1881, on 'We the
Apostles of the New Dispensation'.[31] He defined its
basic belief as "the harmony of all scriptures and prophets and dispensations", "the science which binds and
explains and harmonizes all religions"—"It gives to history a meaning, to the action of Providence a consistency,
to quarelling churches a common bond, and to successive
dispensations a continuity". He put it on a level with
the Jewish, Christian and Vaishnava dispensations, but
regardless of this analogy he did not proclaim that he

was the prophet of the New Dispensation, although he acknowledged that he was the central figure in it. To ward off criticism, he claimed that his community would not tolerate egotism, and that he was hidden among his brother apostles and the Church, but his declaration was unconvincing in the face of his obvious strong leadership and direction. He isolated the main features of the New Dispensation as its synthetical nature, "a whole host of churches resolved into a scientific unity", and its subjectivity, in that the outward Deity had to be translated into each person's subjective consciousness. The address was characteristically Biblical in its rhetoric, and showed once again his persistent concern with applying the spirit of Christ in India, for the union of East and West :—

> And we command Europe to enter into the heart of Asia, and Asia to enter into the mind of Europe, and they obey us, and we instantly realize within ourselves an European Asia and an Asiatic Europe, a comingling of oriental and occidental ideas and principles. We say to the West, Roll back to the East. We summon ancient India to come into modern India with all her rishis and saints, her asceticism and communion and simplicity of character, and behold a transfiguration ! The educated modern Hindu cast in Vedic mould ! How by yoga once nation becomes another ! How Asia eats the flesh and drinks the blood of Europe ! How the Hindu absorbs the Christian ; how the Christian assimilates the Hindu ![32]

Keshub recognized a range of prophets and precursors of the New Dispensation, and felt that their teachings should be made alive for every generation. With this aim, he established the *Sadhusamagama*, or 'Pilgrimages to the Prophets', during 1880.[33] He explained that these 'pilgrimages' were a practical application of the New Dispensation idea of subjectivity. Apart from the theoretical justification they were also a lively and attractive form of devotion, giving Keshub full opportunity to exercise his sense of theatricality. He disapproved of theatre for its own sake, although from his public lectures it was obvious that he was imbued with a feeling

for dramatic performance. He could only indulge his
love of theatre when he felt it was attached to a moral
purpose. Each pilgrimage was akin to a historical
pageant. Keshub verbally created vivid scenes of distant lands to form a total atmosphere for the devotees.
The first pilgrimage was to Moses, set on Mount Sinai,
with the congregation taking on the role of the Israel-
ites. The pilgrimage to Socrates, next in the series,
was less confused and more immediate. Keshub opened
the session with an almost hypnotic attempt to create
Athens as a living reality :—

> This is not Calcutta, this is the city of Athens ; this
> is not Bharatvarsha, but the Commonwealth of
> Greece. Twenty-two hundred years ago the great-
> souled Socrates was born in the city of Athens, in
> Greece. After the lapse of twenty-two hundred
> years we are assembled here within the blazing fire of
> the holy spirit.[34]

He drew moral parallels between Athens and Calcutta,
both "immersed in the conceit of intellectualism and
the pleasures of the flesh". Although the pilgrimage to
Moses had been greeted with derision, this one was not,
because of the respect that the rationalists had for
Socrates.[35] Keshub was characteristically eclectic in his
selection of prophets. The series continued with Sakya,
the *Rishis,* Christ, Mohammed, Chaitanya, Scientists
(Galileo, Newton, Keplar, Faraday and Sushruta) and
Men of Genius (Emerson, Dean Stanley and Carlyle).
The pilgrimage to Christ was predictably the most elaborate. It involved seven days of preparatory services,
during which the life of Christ was conveyed by Keshub
with great vividness and immediacy. Thest qualities can
be seen in the following extract from the beginning of
the 'journey' to Christ :—

> Here we are at last, within the gates of the city
> of Israel. Hurry, brother pilgrims, hurry. We are
> but a handful. What a change in the scenery. The
> hills, the homesteads, the stalls and the market place
> all look strange. It is not Hindusthan, it is the land
> of Israel, and for the time we are all Israelites. Lord,
> where is the new-born son of man for whom, guided

by the star of hope, we have pilgrimmed so far ?
Where is the child who is said to give eyes to the
blind, heal the sick, and who is building up a new
kingdom ? We have come to see and hear him. Grant
Thou our petition. Since we are here let us not
like strangers sit apart in a corner but join the festive
throng. Whose is the face that throws a halo over
the mother's bosom ? The smiling child in the bosom
of its smiling mother, and brooding over them both
the benignant face of the Divine Mother....[36]

Less time was devoted to Chaitanya, although this was
one of the most enthusiastic pilgrimages because it
struck a chord of greater familiarity than those to
foreign lands. Because it embodied the spirit of *bhakti*,
it also afforded the greatest release of inhibition. Vaishnava devotionalism provided an outlet for the tension of
identity present in Keshub and his Western-educated
followers :—

Every place had turned into a Nuddea today. The
barrier of four hundred years has vanished. O
Chaitanya, come to us, English educated Indians, and
dance your way into our heart ?[37]

The idea of 'pilgrimages' was looked on by many as an
eccentricity. Christians accused Keshub of pantheism,
and derided the practice. Keshub's defence was that his
critics were too literal-minded to understand, "they mis-
construed poetry and then ridiculed it as fact".[38]
Keshub's ideas of great men and prophets were closely
linked with the idea of some of the Freethinking
churches, and incongruously, his avowed enemies the
Positivists. The English Positivists under Frederic
Harrison organized large pilgrimages to the tombs or
houses of great historical figures like Chaucer, Bunyan,
Shakespeare and Darwin to foster reverence and gratitude. The 13 months of the Positivist calendar were
named after great men of Western civilization from
Moses and Aristotle to Shakespeare and Dante.[39] Moncure Conway, a major Freethinker, wrote approvingly to
Keshub when he heard of the practice of pilgrimages,[40]
as the walls of his own South Place Chapel were deco-

rated with the names of great men like Socrates, Jesus, Buddha, Mohammed and Theodore Parker.[41] On the international scene, Keshub's was not an isolated voice in the call for eclecticism.

Another theatrical ideas of Keshub's was regarded with similar disfavour by his critics. This was the *Nava Brindaban Natak,* a moral drama about the New Dispensation. The plot was melodramatic and sentimental (and five hours long), about the conversion of a sinner and his final entrance to the kingdom of heaven.[42] The play was a success with its audiences. One reason may have been that as they were barred by the strictness of Brahmo morality from going to the theatre, a dramatic performance of any kind was a rare and enjoyable event in their lives. The *Nava Brindaban Natak* was written not only to preach the New Dispensation, but also to show the potential of a reformed theatre. It represented "the ideal of dramatic morality", written by a pure minded devotee (Trailokyanath Sanyal) and performed by a pious set of actors.[43] Keshub was able to gratify his own dramatic urge by taking the part of a juggler whose role showed the eclecticism of the New Dispensation.[44]

The introduction of ritual in the New Dispensation was the main point of departure from the former practices of the Brahmo Samaj. Brahmos had been used to feeling that ritual bore with it the taint of 'Romanism', which for them was equated with decadence. In the introduction of ritual Keshub was endeavouring to use his sense of visual, theatrical effect to arouse the interest and devotional fervour of his followers. He was experimenting with ritual. He tried to endow traditional symbols with a new meaning. He conceded that a concrete symbol could be an effective devotional aid, in representing something greater than itself, but did not seem fully aware of the danger of the symbol becoming an end in itself—a return to the dreaded idolatry.

Among the Hindu rituals taken up and purged of their idolatrous meaning was the *Hom* ceremony. Keshub lit an elaborate fire, which he then addressed as

he spirit of Agni, not only a physical force but the
force which had the power to burn up sin and temptation.[45] He purified the meaning of the *Durga Puja*
festival, by proscribing the actual idol-worship that took
place and explaining the true Durga as a representation
of the concept of God as Mother.[46] Keshub also gave an
Indian form to the Christian rituals of Baptism and Holy
Communion. For the former Keshub and a band of
devotees went to the bathing *ghat* of the tank near Lily
Cottage Sanctuary, where Keshub sat on a tigerskin and
addressed Varuna, the water of life. After this invocation Keshub anointed himself with flower-oil and thrice
immersed himself in the water, as a tribute to the concepts of the Trinity and *Sacchidananda*.[47] For the latter,
Keshub and the other apostles sat on the floor around
a silver plate of rice and a small goblet of water, surrounded by flowers. Keshub asked for God's blessing on
the rice and water (after reading the description of the
Last Supper in Luke XXII), and they were then con-
sumed.[48]

In his absorption of such disparate rituals and symbols from different traditions Keshub exhibited an im-
patience to force a synthesis. He made a conscious
attempt to incorporate different religions, through use of
their rituals, forgetting that these rituals were powerful
and effective in their own traditional setting not only
because of the excitement and visual attraction they
displayed but also because of the sanctity that had been
conferred on them by being part of a long tradition. He
failed to see that tradition was something which had to
evolve, and which could not be randomly borrowed and
used and still retain its effect. Brahmoism had begun to
build up its own traditions, but these did not satisfy
Keshub's urge for novelty. He did not see the contradic-
tion inherent in trying to present tradition and novelty
at once. His use of ritual was unspontaneous and self-
conscious.

Keshub was accused by many of drifting back to
Hinduism through the New Dispensation, because of his
attempt to include Hindu rituals and concepts under its

banner. Keshub had been interested in Hinduism for
many years before this, and had overcome his early re-
pulsion at Hindu idolatry to see that Hinduism could not
be overlooked or rejected. As a Theist he rejected the
idol, or image, but not the spirit behind it. He explained
that every Hindu idol represented different aspects of
the one God, and the use of a multiplicity of names and
images was simply a way of ensuring that one's percep-
tions be continually refreshed by the stimulation of
novelty. Such experimental 'use' of Hindu symbolism
to further his religious ideals should hardly have been
grounds for accusing him of having become a Hindu. He
continued to see himself as fighting the immorality of
idolatry when it did not rise beyond the level of image-
worship.[50] Although he preached asceticism and *yoga*,
he gave those terms quite different meanings from those
commonly understood in the Hindu tradition. Keshub
preached a sermon on 'The Selfish Ascetic and the Philanthropic Ascetic', in which the traditional world-
renouncer was condemned as selfish whereas the philanthropic ascetic who tried to "serve the world and make
it happy" was held up as a model.[50] Keshub's *Yoga* did
not involve any mystic trances or states, nor even any
"laborious and artificial processes of concentration". His
*Yogi* observed an easy posture, with an easy mind, and
rejoiced in God-consciousness.[51]

Keshub was shaping Hindu thought and custom to
fit in with his own eclectic, theistic beliefs, on the one
hand, and also trying to make the New Dispensation
appealing to Hindus. His adaptation of Hinduism differed
so much in meaning from the original that it would
probably not have been recognizable to orthodox Hindus.
The common people responded enthusiastically to his use
of Vaishnava practices, but would not have been aware
of the ideas he was trying to convey. The *nagar kirtans*
were always popular, with many non-Brahmos joining
the procession and giving expression to their devotional
feelings. The adoption of Hindu forms gave the Brahmos
a wider basis for communication with Hindus, but they
did not attract Hindus as converts because they could

already find satisfaction in these forms within Hinduism. Hindu families sometimes called for the services of the kirtan singers, but only because they could appreciate the forms of their expression without having to pay particular attention to their underlying philosophy.[52]

Keshub was accused of pantheism and mysticism, but the New Dispensation was anti-idolatrous and denied the supernatural in the sense of the occult world.[53] The ridicule of Keshub as a mystic was based on very superficial grounds, mainly the adoption of certain Hindu forms of ritual and devotion. When Keshub preached a sermon on seeing God as a life-giving force in rice, it was said sarcastically that the next step would be the divinity of *Dal* and *Maccher Jhol*.[54] These accusations overlooked the fact that Keshub was, throughout his life, not only a spiritual leader and devotee, but also an English-educated man of the world. His language and thoughts always bore the mark of the Bengali educated middle-class society in which he grew up. A look at the language of Keshub's *Jeevan Veda* demonstrates that his spirituality was interconnected with his worldliness. One chapter is headed, 'The Marvellous Calculus'. In another chapter he used a commercial simile :

> When in God's Happy Fair (i.e., religious life) I first opened my stall, it was made the rule that nothing was to be bought or sold on credit. As were my assets and resources, in the same measure should purchases be made and things sold against cash price —such was my custom from the outset...[55]

At times Keshub's universalist rhetoric was so sweeping and vague as to perhaps create an impression of mysticism, but in fact his lectures and sermons all build up a cumulative picture of a man firmly rooted in the society of the second half of the nineteenth century. His religious eclecticism was typical of a current of thought in contemporary Europe and America. Apart from his own religious experience, his faith was based on sources typified by the texts set for study at the Brahmo Theological School. These were Max Müller's *Introduction to*

*the Science of Religion;* Monier Williams' *Hinduism;*
Rhys David's *Buddhism;* Life and Teachings of Christ
from the New Testament; Cousin's *History of Philosophy;* Butler's *Imitation of Christ* and Jeremy Taylor's
*Holy Living and Dying.*[56] Keshub's students relied on
English commentaries even for the study of Hinduism
and Buddhism, and they were made familiar with the
New Testament but not with any Hindu Scriptures, even
though they were available in English translation.
Keshub did nonetheless come to recognize the importance of a proper disciplined study of the Vedas, and he
founded a Vedic School in Calcutta, the *Veda Vidayalaya,* in 1883, where instruction was given by a *pandit*
from Nuddea. Keshub exhorted the students to study
the Vedas as they were "the root of their national life
and literature and theology".[57] Keshub had shown little
interest in the Vedas when he was in the Brahmo Samaj
under Debendranath, and his late interest may have been
in response to the tide of feeling of national pride in the
past glories of the Aryan race that was beginning to
form part of the ideological background of the educated
Indian. He could never be fully absorbed in Vedic studies himself, however. The Supreme Being of the Rig
Veda was too deistic for Keshub, whose emotional ties
were with the Vaishnava sect and its devotional practices.

Many who claimed that Keshub had become a Hindu
were interested in using this as proof of Ramakrishna's
influence over him. Viewing their relationship more
objectively, it appeared that it was similar to that of
Keshub and Debendranath, in that they recognized each
other's innate spirituality and delighted in each other's
company but differed widely in all external points of
comparison. There was a large cultural gap between
them which was bridged only by the emotional bond,
but which meant that Keshub could never have accepted
Ramakrishna as his *guru* in the traditional Hindu sense.[58]
The most easily perceptible differences were in their
education and background. As Protap Chunder Mozoomdar put it, and it applied equally to Keshub,

What is there in common between him and me ? I a Europeanized, civilized, self-centred, semi-sceptical, so-called educated reasoner, and he a poor, illiterate, shrunken, unpolished, diseased, half-dressed, half-idolatrous friendless Hindu devotee ? Why should I sit long hours to attend to him, I who have listened to Desraili and Fawcett, Stanley and Max Müller, and a whole host of European scholars and divines, I who am an ardent disciple and follower of Christ, a friend and admirer of liberal-minded Christian missionaries and preachers, a devoted adherent and worker of the rationalistic Brahmo Samaj,—why should I be spellbound to hear him ?...[60]

Religiously they shared a belief in eclecticism, although Ramakrishna's eclecticism was not a consciously held article of faith like Keshub's. Ramakrishna's eclecticism was of the kind that spontaneously perceived God in all things, whereas Keshub was wedded to the idea of an institution, with an organizational structure headed by himself, in which eclecticism and synthesis were guiding principles. Ramakrishna was renowned for his horror of the twin evils of 'woman and gold', which stood in direct contrast to Keshub's approach to both. Keshub's way of showing his disapproval of worldliness was evident in sermons like 'Address to the Rupee', in which he first berated its "false shining surface" with its powers of temptation, and then lauded it for its ability to promote charity and philanthropy.[61] Keshub had a positively articulated objection to Ramakrishna's views, as in one of his sermons he said that

Some think that to touch money or to behold the face of a woman is rank sin ; that this world is the veritable hell, and the "burning ghat" a paradise... It is to lay the axe at the root of this mistaken opinion that the New Dispensation is born.[62]

Ramakrishna was also said to have influenced Keshub's use of Bengali.[63] Keshub's message became more accessible by the use of more colloquial, colourful language. Even so, he was always much more self-conscious and inhibited than Ramakrishna, whose language was earthy and direct to the point where Keshub felt bound to reform his vulgarity. The following remark of Ramakrishna to Keshub's mother was typical of his style of speaking :—

> Look here, mother, later on the whole world will dance with even your entrails, for it is your womb that held this son...[64]

This remark could never have been attributed to Keshub, and highlights Keshub's puritanical morality which was not shared by Ramakrishna. Keshub's puritanism was that of the typical Victorian, prudish and self-righteous. He was an upright temperance advocate (he supported the Blue Ribbon Temperance Union started in Calcutta in 1882 as well as the Band of Hope), with a stern hostility to gambling, prostitution, and opium smoking, which also ruled out the minor pleasures of social drinking, playing cards and going to the theatre. Ramakrishna was not concerned that his followers included men who drank and smoked. He was also unperturbed about 'decency' in dress, whereas the New Dispensation was advertising for suggestions for a "decent but not costly" design for the reformed Hindu woman's dress.[65] Ramakrishna had absolutely no interest in the reform of society. He was a true mystic, but was shrewd enough to perceive that Keshub was not. He objected to Keshub and the Brahmos trying to lead a spiritual life while living in the world with their wives. He often alluded to Keshub's desire for "name and fame", and his comment on the 1878 schism was that it was like a manager dismissing good actors because they took a share of the profits.[66] Keshub's interest in Ramakrishna had the unintentional result of producing a figurehead, or an ideal symbol for the growing Hindu revivalist movement of which he was not a part.

The imbalance attendant on seeing Keshub as having returned to Hinduism is obvious when one sees how his interest in Christianity was also heightened over the period of the New Dispensation. Keshub entered into dialogue with a wide circle of Christians to a greater extent than ever before. He was friendly with the Roman Catholic Father Lafont, and the Anglican monk

Luke Rivington. He got to know members of the Oxford Mission, who had gone to Calcutta partly in response to the interest in Christianity represented by Keshub and the Brahmos.[67] He championed the cause of the Salvation Army when it was being persecuted by Bombay police in 1882. These Christians, of widely varying denominations, were at one in their willingness to reach out to Indians as social equals. The wife of the Salvation Army leader in India, Major Tucker, wore a long white Rampore *chudder* in the street processions, and one of the members of the Oxford Mission often wore a *dhoti* instead of trousers.[68] Both Rivington and the Oxford Mission shared 'Native style' meals with the Brahmos. Keshub was still no closer to fitting into any existing Christian sect, because of his aversion to sectarianism and because he was too independent, and also because his relationship to Christ was of a Hindu devotional character. He had managed to synthesize and reconcile the two traditions within himself by transforming them into something new, which barred him from ever identifying exclusively with either. His idea of a church, however, was based solidly on the Christian model. His manner of preaching relied heavily on an Evangelical style of Biblical rhetoric. He wanted a structured congregational institution, with laymen and missionaries. The Mission Department of the New Dispensation was a tightly run organization, with a central office in Calcutta which provided directives to missionaries stationed and travelling all over India. All missionaries came together annually for a conference to give reports of their progress. Their upkeep was paid for out of Samaj funds and from donations.[69] In 1882 there were 15 missionaries, each with his alloted sphere of work.[70] Many of Keshub's reformed life-cycle ceremonies, especially those of marriage and initiation, were very similar to the coresponding rites in Christianity (initiation being based on Confirmation). The *Nava Samhita*, a guide to daily living written by Keshub in 1883, embodied Christian ethics and a Victorian sense of order,[71] shown in the following examples :—

*The House.*

2. For next to godliness is cleanliness, and every ma
who loveth our God is commanded to keep his spirit
clean and his body clean and his house clean, makin
each a fit tabernacle for the Lord.

14. And the bed shall be clean, and the clothes in th
wardrobe shall be well arranged, and the books in th
library, and all articles of furniture, and all crocker
and all earthen, metal and glass plates and vesse
and all cooking utensils shall be tastefully arrange
each in its proper place.

*Business.*

3. For punctuality is the soul of success, and its viol
tion is condemnable in the sight of God being a wi
ful violation of the rule of veracity.[72]

One of Keshub's main aims was to establish th
spirit of Christ in India. He saw the Christian missior
aries as helping him fulfil this aim, not as rivals. O
the occasion of the Bishops' Conference in Calcutta i
1883 Keshub wrote to Bishop Johnson suggesting in
provements in the Christian method of propagation. F
urged the Bishop to make all Christians in India set
good example by regular church attendance; to try i
reconcile the different sects; to pay respect to India
religion and to have greater sympathy with the "nativ
of the soil". Bishop Johnson replied that he would
his best, but that there were difficulties in overcomir
the barriers that existed.[73] Keshub was actually a muc
more effective agent for the spread of Christianity tha
the missionaries, because being an Indian he was n
alien and met with less resistance. The Brahmo Sam
and New Dispensation under Keshub were channels f
the propagation of Christian ideas in India.

As he had reformulated and incorporated Hinc
polytheism into his Theism, so did he manage to inco
porate the Christian Trinity. In his lecture 'That Ma
vellous Mystery—the Trinity'[74] he equated it with th
*Sacchidananda* of Hinduism, in that three manifest
tions of divinity were represented, not three persor
His eclecticism had come full circle, including and i
corporating, explaining and legitimizing, doctrines whi

had formerly been rejected as incompatible with pure
Theism.

The way he viewed Britain was closely linked to
his relation to Christianity. For him, British rule was
Providential because it had brought the spirit of Christianity to India. Loyalty to Britain was part of the
creed of the New Dispensation, a duty and a necessity.
He was grateful for the religious spirit and values introduced by the British, and hence it followed that "our
politics is our religion, and our allegiance to Thee and
Thy daughter Victoria is one thing".[75] He was proud of
his own country and wished to build up its self-respect,
but he was much more emotional, fervent and insistent on
the need for loyalty to England than he was about Indian
nationalism. In a nationalist era, this may have been
because he had never, personally, felt oppressed by the
British. As a Brahmo leader he had never come into conflict with the Government. Outside the official administra-
tive system he had attained heights of responsibility and
authority that were not possible for those working
directly for the British. He was aware that the New
Dispensation was "historically the result of England's
rule in the East, religiously the effect of Western thought
upon the Indian mind...."[76] and therefore was desirous
for these influences to continue as a part of British rule.

As religious universality became an increasingly
important part of his thinking, he began to look beyond
the familiar spheres of India and Britain to make his
voice heard. He had a small following of Universalists
and Freethinkers in America, and had received letters
of support from as far afield as Sweden and Norway.
In Wales, a New Dispensation Circulating Library was
started. It did not have any works by Keshub, but its
aim was to include them in its stock.[77] Keshub addressed himself to the world at large in a New Year's Epistle
in January 1883, which he sent to newspapers all over
India and also Europe, America, Australia, China and
Japan, requesting them to print it. It proclaimed the
existence of the New Dispensation and called for an
end to discord and for the establishment of peace, har-

mony and unity.[78] Most Indian papers obligingly printed
it, but it is doubtful whether it had the impact Keshub
intended. The *Statesman* commented that it read like
a parody, the *Indo-European Correspondence* took it as
a sign that Keshub had passed from spiritual pride to
spiritual madness, the *Indian Churchman* regarded it
with cynical satire, and the *Indian Daily News* felt that
it was an old and imitative message, to abstract to be
effective.[79] Keshub was systematically trying to enter
the international religious community. He wrote to ask
Max Müller for the names of liberal Christians in
Europe who could help secure readers for the *New
Dispensation* there,[80] and also asked Müller to publicize
the New Dispensation himself among leading clergy and
laymen of the Broad Church party.

Keshub was unable to devote his full energies to
publicizing and developing the New Dispensation as he
was plagued by ill health, mainly the result of strain
and tension, a condition of 'nervous debility'. Coinci-
dentally he showed a fascination with madness, writing
articles in the *New Dispensation* about his experiences
as a *pagal* or madman. His interest was not totally new,
but it may have been an indication of his need for release
which was not available to him in his position of public
responsibility. The missionary community of the New
Dispensation were totally dependent on him, and complained and criticized when their needs—material and
spiritual—were not immediately provided for.[81] The
discrepancy between worldliness and asceticism in
Keshub's life remained unresolved. His asceticism was,
judged by Hindu standards, mere dalliance. He maintained a comfortable standard of living—many of the
foreign missionaries who visited him commented on the
European style and size of his house—while satisfying his
conscience by such means as taking the Vow of Poverty
on himself for a period of 30 days only. During this
time he shaved his head and pledged to live exclusively
on alms.[82] He legitimized the life of the man of the
world (which needed some justification in the face of
challenge from the ascetic ideal of Ramakrishna) by

establishing the Vow of Self-surrender, for 'lay ascetics' who were engaged in secular work but devoted all their earnings to the New Dispensation, through the institution of the Bidhan Deposit Bank.

Despite his growing international reputation, Keshub presented a rather sad figure during these last years of his life. He seemed to be weighted down by responsibilities, under the strain of which his health gave way. He had been discredited in his own lifetime, and must have been aware that he was no longer the influential social leader that he had once been. His hopes were centred around his doctrine of the New Dispensation, but even that was threatened by internal discord among the missionaries.

His last public lecture, in January 1883, was on 'Asia's Message to Europe'.[83] The 'message' was the familiar one of synthesis between East and West. He did not set out, like Vivekananda did, to tell the West about the East, but called on both to come together in harmony and brotherly love. He used the word 'Christian' to mean the set of values that he believed in, not a religion belonging exclusively to the West:—

> Can there be any form of goodness or goodliness which is not Christian ? I do firmly believe that whatsoever is true and good and beautiful is of Christ.[84]

Such an avowal showed the force of the reverse of his topic—Europe's message to Asia, as although Keshub saw Christ as an Asiatic, his knowledge of him came from England and not from the Middle East. The lecture was attended by about 2,000 people, Europeans and Indians. Rev. Dall explained that such interest was shown as the result of a general impression that Keshub had gone into his dotage, and an ensuing curiosity to hear what he still had to say. Dall's consensus was that the lecture showed the "inevitable intellectual failure of arrested development", eloquent as always but basically "the same old song".[85]

For the greater part of 1883 Keshub's activity was reduced by sickness. His last public act was the consecration of the new Sanctuary at Lily Cottage.[86] His

eclecticism was with him till the end. When there was
wrangling among his friends over methods of treatment,
his suggestion was that doctor, *kabiraj* and *hakim* should
work together to cure him.[87]   On his sickbed he received
visits from Debendranath, Ramakrishna and the Bishop
of Calcutta.[88]   On his death he was supposed to have
cried out 'Mother', 'Mother of Buddha', and to have asked
for a hymn about Christ's sufferings in Gethsemane.[89]
After prolonged suffering he eventually died of diabetes
on 8 January 1884.   His body was cremated on 13 January
according to the reformed rites of his own *Nava Samhita*.
The Memorial Meeting in the Town Hall was attended
by over 2,000 people from the Muslim, Hindu, Brahmo
and Christian communities,[90] overlooking their differences
to unite in mourning the loss of a man whom Max Müller
described as India's "greatest son".[91]

## NOTES AND REFERENCES

1. Keshub Chunder Sen, *Lectures* (1954) op. cit. pp. 327-350.

2. *Indian Mirror*, Sunday edition, 26 January 1879.

3. Keshub Chunder Sen, *Lectures* (1954) op. cit. p. 328.

4. Charles Voysey, in a London sermon, termed this "morbid self-reproach", displaying signs of a "weak and shaken mind". Text of Voysey's sermon given in *Indian Mirror*, Sunday edition, 1 June 1879.

5. Keshub Chunder Sen, *Lectures* (1954) op. cit. p. 337.

6. Keshub Chunder Sen, *Lectures* (1954) op. cit. pp. 344-346.

7. ibid. pp. 351-377.   Delivered on 9 April 1879.

8. *Indian Mirror*, Sunday edition 27 April 1879, from an article in the *Statesman*.

9. *Indian Mirror*, Sunday edition 20 April 1879.

10. The Superiority of Hinduism. A lecture given by Rajnarain Bose in 1871.

11. *Indian Mirror*, 18 April 1879.

12. *Indian Mirror*, Sunday edition 20 April 1879. He took as his text Matthew XVI, 15-16 "He saith unto them, but whom say ye that I am? And Simon Peter answered and said, Thou art the Christ, the Son of the Living God". The full text of his sermon was published in the *Indian Mirror*, Sunday edition of 4 May and 11 May 1879.

13. Advertisement for this was in the *Indian Mirror* 28 April 1879.

14. *Indian Mirror*, Sunday edition, 18 May 1879.

15. *Indian Mirror*, Sunday edition 18 May 1879.

16. *Indian Mirror*, 8 June 1879.

17. ibid. 6 July 1879.

ibid. 20 December 1879.

19. Reports of the expedition are from the *Indian Mirror* from 31 October to 14 December 1879.

20. The Salvation Army and its structure were first mentioned in the *Indian Mirror*, Sunday edition, 21 September 1879, with the remark "Why does not the Brahmo Samaj operate a similar movement in the metropolis ?".

21. *Indian Mirror*, Sunday edition 9 November 1879.

22. *Indian Mirror*, Sunday edition 14 December 1879.

23. Article from the *Statesman* quoted in the *Indian Mirror*, Sunday edition, 30 November 1879.

24. *Indian Mirror*, Sunday edition, 28 December 1879.

25. P. C. Mozoomdar, *Life* op. cit. p. 253.

26. Lecture on 'God-Vision . . .' in Keshub Chunder Sen, *Lectures* (1954) op. cit. pp. 378-415. He had mentioned it in 1875 in 'Behold the Light of Heaven in India'., pp. 202-238.

27. *New Dispensation*, 6 August 1882, 'Is there any difference'— "The Brahmo Somaj is plain and patent to all. Even the world's scoffers and rationalists recognize it as a little deistic school set up by men. But God's New Dispensation none can see or believe but those to whom heaven's light has come".

28. *New Dispensation*, 24 March 1881.

29. *Indian Mirror*, Sunday edition 4 January 1880.

30. From his letter to S.D. Collect in the *Yearly Theistic Record* 1880-1881, p. 15. However, he qualified the harshness of his judgement in a letter to the *Liberal and New Dispensation*, saying that he did recognize some merit in the New Dispensation. (27 August 1882).

31. Keshub Chunder Sen, *Lectures in India* (1954) op. cit. pp. 416-454.

32. Keshub Chunder Sen, *Lectures* (1954) op. cit., p. 448.

33. All pilgrimages were published in Keshub Chunder Sen, *Sadhusamagama* (Calcutta, 1956), translated by J. K. Koar.

34. Keshub Chunder Sen, *Sadhusamagama* op. cit., p. 11.

35. *Sunday Mirror*, 28 March 1880.

36. Keshub Chunder Sen, *Sadhusamagama* op. cit. pp. 35-36.

37. Keshub Chunder Sen, *Sadhusamagama* op. cit. p. 63.

38. Keshub Chunder Sen, *Lectures* (1954) op. cit. p. 422.

39. W. S. Smith, op. cit. pp. 85, 98.

40. P. C. Mozoomdar, *Life* op. cit. p. 251.

41. W. S. Smith, op. cit. pp. 121-122.

42. 'The New Dispensation on the Stage', *New Dispensation*, 10 September 1882.

43. *Liberal and New Dispensation*, 17 September 1882.

44. *New Dispensation*, 1 April 1883 and 15 April 1883.

45. *New Dispensation*, 9 June 1881. See also 16 June issue for 'True Meaning of the Fire Ceremony'.

46. ibid. 22 October 1882.

47.  ibid.  16 June 1881.

48.  ibid.  24 March 1881.

49.  *New Dispensation*, 7 October 1881 and 23 August 1881.

50.  ibid.  26 May 1881.

51.  *New Dispensation*, 22 July 1881.

52.  An old Hindu lady 'of high family' expressed a wish to hear the *kirtan* hymns of the New Dispensation on her deathbed, so that she could hear the name of God in a soothing manner. *New Dispensation*, 9 June 1881.

53.  This distinguished it from the increasingly popular doctrine of Theosophy.  ibid.  22 July 1881.

54.  Lentils and fish curry. The *Bengal Magazine*, VIII, December 1879.

55.  *Jeevan Veda* in P.S. Basu, op| cit. p. 462.

57.  *Liberal and New Dispensation*, 1 January 1882.

58.  *New Dispensation*, 7 January 1883. See also 24 December 1882. The school met for two hours, three times a week.

59.  Despite what Ramakrishna's followers said in R. Rolland, op. cit. Note II.

60.  *Theistic Quarterly Review*, III, October 1879.

61.  *New Dispensation*, 5 November 1882.

62.  From 'God as Lakshmi', sermon preached on 18 July, *Sunday Mirror*, 1 August 1880.

63.  (T. N. Sanyal) op. cit. p. 150.

64.  G. C. Banerji, *Keshub and Ramakrishna* op. cit. p. 51. From a life of Keshub's mother by J. L. Khastigir.

65.  *New Dispensation*, 31 March 1881.

66.  (Mahendranath Gupta), *Gospel of Sri Ramakrishna*, second ed. (Madras, 1947) pp. 124, 348.

67.  F. Lillingston, op. cit. p. 2 and *Indian Mirror*, Sunday edition, 21 September 1879.

68.  *New Dispensation*, 24 December 1882 and 14 April 1881.

69.  ibid.  25 April 1883. It cost 22 rupees a month for Keshub's upkeep, covering the cost of food, clothing, skimmed milk and medicine.

70.  ibid.  29 January 1882.

71.  R. Rolland, op. cit. p. 136 said that the *Nava Samhita* showed Keshub's "innate need of unitarian discipline", which could merge into spiritual imperialism.

72.  Keshub Chunder Sen, *The New Samhita*, New edition (Calcutta, 1915) pp. 5, 7-8, 24.

73.  *New Dispensation*, 11 February 1883 and 1 April 1883.

74.  Keshub Chunder Sen, *Lectures* (1904) op. cit. pp. 1-48.

75.  *New Dispensation*, 7 July 1881.

76.  *New Dispensation*, 24 March 1881, 'Our Politics'.

77.  ibid.  27 May 1883. To begin with they only had 250 copies each of three books.

78.  ibid.  7 January 1883.

79. *New Dispensation,* 14 January 1883.

80. F. M. Muller, *Chips* op. cit. Vol. II, p. 117. Letter dated 16 May 1881.

81. See article 'What we should not expect from the Minister' in *New Dispensation,* 18 March 1883.

82. P. C. Mozoomdar, *Life* op. cit. pp. 256-257.

83. Keshub Chunder Sen, *Lectures* (1904) pp. 49-119.

84. ibid. p. 85.

85. *Liberal and New Dispensation,* 4 February 1883.

86. P. C. Mozoomdar, *Life* op. cit. p. 315.

87. *Liberal and New Dispensation,* 20 January 1884.

88. S. Sastri, *History* op. cit. Vol. II, p. 93.

89. P. C. Mozoomdar, *Life* op. cit. p. 319, J. N. Farquhar, op. cit. P. 68 ; and R. Roolland, op. cit. p. 137.

90. *Liberal and New Dispensation,* 3 February 1884. W. W. Hunter presided over the meeting. Those present included Sir Jotindra Mohan Tagore, Raja Sourindra Mohan Tagore, Abdul Latif Khan, Kristo Das Pal, Pandit Mahesh Chundra Nyaratna, Rajendra Lal Mitra, Father Lafont, Manockji Rustomjee, Mahendra Lal Sircar, Rev. K. M. Banerji, Bankim Chandra Chatterjee and S. Banerjea.

91. Mrs F. M. Muller, *Life* op. cit. Vol. II, p. 153.

# CONCLUSION

ALTHOUGH, in later years, he had little contact with the major currents of thought and activity among Indians, Keshub was in many ways a pioneer of those movements. He had contributed to nationalism by making Indians aware of themselves as one nation, and by his successes abroad and at home which made them feel proud and self-reliant. He had introduced the key figure of the Hindu revival to the Indian public, but he could never have identified with Hinduism or India to the exclusion of all else. Keshub's outlook was too broad, and his independence too great, for him to be involved in any form of nationalism. His loyalty to Britain also precluded him from taking part.

At the time of Keshub's death, educated Indians were looking to the past, and to traditional Hinduism, for solutions to their present dilemmas. Keshub's New Dispensation was a religion of the future, representing change and universality, not stability and Hinduism. In the main arena where others welcomed change—in politics—Keshub resisted it. The New Dispensation was essentially an alien doctrine, despite its attempts to appeal to and satisfy a wide range of people by drawing on an extended stock of different traditions. The New Dispensation was also an alien movement because joining it required a conscious rejection of parts of Hinduism. As the New Dispensation had to be grafted on to existing systems of belief, it is not surprising that the championing of Hinduism attendant on the Hindu revival was much more readily taken up.

The generation after Keshub attempted to mould his doctrines according to the new nationalist ideals. This met with little success, because too much distortion of fact was necessary to see him as "the Hindu of Hindus", as a Vedantic monist, or as "an exponent of the Hindu social consciousness".[1] Because of inconsistencies and imperfections in his career and character which

proved difficult to overlook, Keshub was never able to
fit into the Indian tradition of Great Men. Only his
followers saw him as such, so he has been studiously
overlooked as a historical figure.

Unlike many others of his generation, Keshub, in the
New Dispensation, had managed to resolve within himself
many of the conflicts of allegiance that beset the English-
educated middle-class. The New Dispensation seemed
to provide a solution of the Hindu-Christian, Indian-
English conflict for its members, but the Sadharan Brahmo
Samaj, despite its strong sense of Indian nationalism,
offered little spiritual satisfaction to its members. Sivanath Sastri was very conscious that the insistence on constitutionalism of the Sadharan Brahmo Samaj had meant
that they almost ceased to function as a religious body,
because they had no charismatic leader.

Keshub typified the rootlessness of his generation.
He sensed this tension in those around him and moulded
the New Dispensation to meet their needs. Unfortunately, satisfaction of spiritual needs entailed commitment to Keshub himself which many were unwilling
to accept. A significant number of men who joined the
Brahmo Samaj because it seemed to be the logical religion for the educated, middle-class, Indian and who
later parted with Keshub because of the marriage controversy and became part of the Sadharan Brahmo Samaj,
found the latter alien and drifted away from it to find
solace in the security of traditional Hinduism.

Two leading figures in the Sadharan Brahmo Samaj,
Umesh Chandra Datta and Kalinath Datta, joined the
*karta bhaja* sect of Vaishnavas[2] which was supposed to
worship its *guru*. They remained in the Samaj, but
Bijoy Krishna Goswami, who also became a *karta bhaja*,
was asked to leave the Sadharan Brahmo Samaj because
it was felt that he was dabbling too much with idolatry by
having images of Radha and Krishna in his room.[3] Bijoy
Krishna Goswami was in turn taken up as the guru of
Bipin Chandra Pal, in 1895.[4] Bipin Chandra realized
that the Sadharan Brahmo Samaj did not provide any
spiritual warmth, so he looked for this quality in tradi-

tional Vaishnavism. Sivnarain Agnihotri, of the Punjab Brahmo Samaj which sided with the Sadharan Brahmo Samaj at the time of the split, also left it to set himself up as a *guru* in the Hindu style in his own new sect, the Dev Samaj.[5] Ramkumar Vidyaratna, one of the main protestors over the Cuch Behar marriage and a missionary of the Sadharan Brahmo Samaj, left it to become a Hindu ascetic and *guru*.[6] One of the most famous cases is that of Narendranath Dutt, or Vivekananda, who left the Sadharan Brahmo Samaj to become a disciple of Ramakrishna and eventually utilised the public, institutional methods of the Samaj in the revival of Hinduism.

The New Dispensation fell apart after Keshub's death because his personality had been so important to the smooth functioning of the institution, and because he had been the guiding inspiration behind it. It also failed because of the formidable task Keshub had set for it. Eclecticism was superficially easy, but it covered a mass of potential discord between seemingly opposed factors like science and religion, Christianity and Hinduism, asceticism and worldliness, which only gained cohesion from the force of Keshub's personality.

Keshub, in his time, achieved great things for India. He gave impetus to intellectual and social activity, and prevented society from becoming stagnant or complacent. He made a significant contribution in the fields of journalism, education, social reform, religious reform and national awareness. The ultimate failure of his movement is no reflection on the merits of what he did achieve.

### NOTES AND REFERENCES

1. He was seen as such by B. C. Pal (1893 address on 'The Greatest Hindu Reformer of the Age'), Dhirendra N. Chowdhury, and Pratul Chandra Som respectively. G. C. Banerji, *Keshub as Seen by his Opponents* op. cit. pp. 30, 73, 97.

2. B. C. Pal, *Memories* op. cit. Vol. II, 137.

3. B. C. Pal, *Saint* op. cit. pp. 54-77.

4. B. C. Pal, *Memories* op. cit. Vol. II, pp. 198-207.

5. S. Sastri, *History* op. cit. Vol. II, p. 403, and J. N. Farquhar, op. cit. pp. 173-177.

6. S. Sastri, History op. cit. Vol. II, p. 195.

# BIBLIOGRAPHY

## Primary Sources

*Newspapers and Periodicals*:

*Bengal Magazine* (Calcutta) 1879.
*Brahmo Public Opinion* (Calcutta) 1878-1879.
*Illustrated London News* (London) 1870.
*Indian Charivari* 1880.
*Indian Mirror* (Calcutta) 1878-1884.
*Indian Mirror, Sunday edition* (Calcutta) January 1878—March 1880.
*Liberal and New Dispensation* (Calcutta) 1882-1884.
*New Dispensation* (Calcutta) 1881-1883.
*Pall Mall Budget* (London) 1870.
*Punch* (London) 1870.
*Saturday Review* (London) 1870.
*Sunday Mirror* (Calcutta) March 1880—December 1881.
*Theistic Quarterly Review* (Calcutta) 1879-1881.
*The Times* (London) 1870.
*Yearly Theistic Record* (Dacca) 1880-1881.

*Reports*:

Bengal Social Science Association, *Transactions* 1869-1871 Calcutta.
Bethune Society, *Proceedings and Transactions* 1859-1869 Calcutta, 1870.
Calcutta Literary Society, *Annual Reports* 1901-1902 Calcutta.

*Works by Keshub Chunder Sen*:

(a) Bengali

*Jibanbed* Eighth edition, Calcutta, 1954. (First published 1883)
*Maharshi Devendranath and Brahmananda Keshub Chandra—Two Documents Reprinted* Calcutta, 1935. Bengali, with English translation by J. K. Koar.

(b) English

*The Bible of Life* Calcutta, 1928. (A translation of *Jibanbed*, by V. Rai)
*Brahmagitopanishat*: *Discourses on Yoga and Bhakti* Calcutta, 1956. (translated by J. K. Koar).
*The Brahmo Somaj*: *Discourses and Writings* Calcutta, 1904.
*The Brahmo Somaj—Lectures and Tracts* London, 1870. (Edited by S. D. Collet)
*Divine Worship* Calcutta, no date. (Pamphlet)
*Faith and Culture of the New Dispensation* Howrah, 1930. A selection from his writings in the *New Dispensation*.
*Keshub Chunder Sen's English Visit* London, 1871. (Edited by S. D. Collet).
*Keshub Chunder Sen in England*: *Diary, Sermons, Addresses and Epistles* Third edition, revised and enlarged. Calcutta, 1938. First published in England (see above) in 1871. First published in India in two volumes, in 1881 and 1882.
*Lectures delivered in the Brahmo School* Five weekly lectures delivered between 22 February 1873 and 22 March 1873. Ranchi, no date.
*Lectures in India* London, 1904.
*Lectures in India* Fourth edition, Calcutta, 1954. This contains a different selection of lectures from the 1904 edition.
*Maghotsava*: *Discourses Heralding One World-Community* Calcutta, 1959. (Translated by J. K. Koar)

*National Marriage Reform. A full report of the Town Hall Meeting on the Brahmo Marriage Bill with an address on National Marriage Reform* Second edition, Calcutta, 1951.

*The New Dispensation* Second edition, two volumes, Calcutta, 1915 and 1916. A reprinting of articles by Keshub in the *New Dispensation* between March 1881 and November 1883.

*The New Samhita* Calcutta, 1915.

*Regenerating Faith* Calcutta, 1968. (pamphlet)

*Sadhusamagama : Discourses on Pilgrimage to Prophets* Calcutta, 1956. (Translated by J. K. Koar)

*The Theist's Prayer Book* Third edition, Calcutta, 1870. (First published 1861)

*The Voice of Keshub* Second series, Calcutta, 1970. (Compiled by Harendra Chandra Deva)

*Contemporary Works :*

(a) *Bengali*

Bose, Rajnarain *Atmacharit* Third edition, Calcutta, 1952. (First published 1909)

Mitra, Krishnakumar *Atmacharit* Second edition, Calcutta, 1974. (First published 1936)

Roy, Gour Gobinda *Acharya Keshabchandra* Centenary edition, vol. I, Calcutta, 1938.

(Sanyal, Trailokyanath) *Keshab-charit* Third edition, Calcutta, 1931. (First published 1884) Sanyal uses the pseudonym Chiranjib Sharma.

Sastri, Sivanath *Atmacharit* New edition, Calcutta, 1952.

Tagore, Debendranath *Jiban-charit* Second edition, Calcutta, 1911. With appendices edited by Priyanath Sastri.

(b) English

Banerjea, S. N. *A Nation in Making—being the Reminiscences of Fifty Years in Public Life* Madras, 1925.

Banerjee, H. C. *Brahmo Theism in India* Calcutta, 1869.

Bradley-Birt, F. B. *Twelve Men of Bengal in the Nineteenth Century* Calcutta, 1910.

Buckland, C. E. *Bengal under the Lieutenant-Governors* Two volumes, Calcutta, 1902.

*Dictionary of Indian Biography* New edition, New York, 1968. (First published 1906)

Carpenter, J. E. *The Life and Work of Mary Carpenter* London, 1879.

Carpenter, M. *Six Months in India* London, 1868.

Chunder, B. *Raja Digambar Mitra, C.S.I. His Life and Career* Two volumes, Calcutta, 1893 (volume I) and 1907 (volume II).

Cobbe, F. P. *Life of Frances Power Cobbe by herself* Two volumes, London, 1894.

Collet, S. D. 'Indian Theism, and its Relation to Christianity', in *Contemporary Review,* XIII (1870).

Cowell, G. *Life and Letters of Edward Byles Cowell* London, 1904.

*The Credentials of Conscience. A few reasons for the popularity of 'Ecce Homo' : and a few words about Christianity* Anonymous, London, 1868.

Das, H. *Life and Letters of Toru Dutt* Oxford, 1921.

Day, L. B. *Recollections of Alexander Duff* London, 1879.

Drummond, J. and Upton, C. B. *The Life and Letters of James Martineau* Two volumes, London, 1902.

Duff, A. *A Description of the Durga and Kali Festivals, celebrated in Calcutta, at an expense of Three Millions of Dollars* New York, 1846.

Dufferin and Ava, Marchioness of *Our Viceregal Life in India—Selections from my Journal* 1884-1888 London, 1889.

Edwards, T. *Henry Derozio, the Eurasian Poet, Teacher and Journalist* Calcutta, 1884.

Fremantle, W. H. 'The Brahmo Somaj and the Religious Future of India', in *Contemporary Review*, XV (1870).

Gangooly, J. C. *Life and Religion of the Hindoos, with a sketch of my life and experience* London, 1860.

Ghose, L. *The Modern History of the Indian Chiefs, Rajas, Zamindars* Two parts, Calcutta, 1879 (I) and 1881 (ii).

Ghose, M. N. *The Life of Grish Chunder Ghose: The founder and first editor of "The Hindoo Patriot' and 'The Bengalee' by one who knew him* Calcutta, 1911.

(Gupta, M. N.) *The Gospel of Sri Ramakrishna* Second edition, Madras, 1947. (Translated by Swami Nikhilananda. First published in Bengali in five volumes between 1897 and 1932) Gupta uses the pseudonym 'M'.

*Kristo Das Pal: In Memoriam* Calcutta, 1884.

Leonard, G. S. *A History of the Brahma Samaj, from its rise to the present day* Calcutta, 1879.

Long, J. *Selected Papers* Calcutta, 1968. A collection of papers presented by Long between 1846 and 1868.

Macpherson, G. *Life of Lal Behari Day—convert, pastor, professor and author* Edinburgh, 1900.

Maunder, S. *The Biographical Treasury; a Dictionary of Universal Biography* Thirteenth edition, London, 1866.

Mitra, S. C. *Isvar Chandra Vidyasagar: A Story of his Life and Work* Calcutta, 1902.

Mozoomdar, P. C. *The Faith and Progress of the Brahmo Somaj* Second edition, Calcutta, 1934. (First published 1882)
*Keshub Chunder Sen and His Times* Calcutta, 1917. This forms the introduction to his *Life and Teachings*. . . .(see below)
*Lectures in America and other papers* New edition, Calcutta, 1955.
*The Life and Teachings of Keshub Chunder Sen* Third edition, Calcutta, 1931. (First published 1887)
*The Oriental Christ* Second edition, Calcutta, 1933. (First published in Boston, 1883)
*The Spirit of God* New edition, Calcutta, 1918. (First published in Boston, 1898)

Muller, F. M. *Auld Lang Syne* Second series—My Indian Friends. London, 1899.
*Biographical Essays* London, 1884.
*Chips from a German Workshop* Volume II, New edition, London, 1895. This was a reprint of *Biographical Essays* (see above).
*Chips from a German Workshop* Volume IV, Essays chiefly on the Science of Language. London, 1875.

Muller, Mrs F. M. (ed.) *The Life and Letters of the right honourable Friedrich Max Muller* Two volumes, London, 1902.

Murdoch, J. (ed.) *Indian Year Book for 1861* Madras, 1862. *Indian Year Book for 1862* Madras, 1863.

Oman, J. C. *The Brahmans, Theists and Muslims of India* Second edition, London, 1907.

Pal, B. C. *The Brahmo Samaj and the battle for Swaraj* New edition, Calcutta, 1945.
*Memories of My Life and Times* Two volumes, Calcutta, 1932.
*Saint Bijaykrishna Goswami* New edition, Calcutta, 1964.

Roy, G. G. *Keshub's Religion of Inspiration* Bombay, no date. (Translated by J. K. Koar)

Sastri, S. *History of the Brahmo Samaj* Two volumes, Calcutta, 1912
*Men I have Seen* Calcutta, 1919.
*A History of the Renaissance in Bengal—Ramtanu Lahiri:
Brahman and Reformer* (Edited by R. Lethbridge, translated by
S. K. Lahiri) New edition, Calcutta, 1972. (First published in
1904)
*Theistic Church in India* A collection of lectures delivered in
1906, 1907 and 1910. Calcutta, 1966.
(Seeley, J. R.) *Ecce Homo: a survey of the Life and Work of
Jesus Christ* Eighth edition, London 1867.
Sen, N. *A Needed Disclaimer* Calcutta, 1909. (Pamphlet)
Sengupta, N. C. *Selections from the Writings of Hurrish Chunder
Mookerjee* compiled from *The Hindoo Patriot* Calcutta, 1910.
Skrine, F. H. *An Indian Journalist, being the Life, Letters, and
Correspondence of Dr Sambhu C. Mookerjee, late editor of
'Reis and Rayyet'*, Calcutta, 1895.
Slater, T. S. *Keshab Chandra Sen and the Brahma Samaj: being
a brief review of Indian Theism from 1830 to 1884 together with
selections from Mr Sen's works* Madras, 1884.
Sunity Devee, Maharani of Cooch Behar *The Autobiography of an
Indian Princess* London, 1921.
Tagore, D. *The Autobiography of Maharshi Devendranath Tagore*
London, 1914. (Translated by S. Tagore and Indira Devi)
Tagore, R. *Reminiscences* Seventeenth edition, London, 1971. (First
published in 1917)
Tattvabhushan, S. *Autobiography* Calcutta, no date.
*The Philosophy of Brahmaism Expounded with reference to its
History* Lectures delivered before the Theological Society,
Calcutta, in 1906-1907. Madras, 1909.
University of Calcutta *Convocation Addresses* 1880-1898 Calcutta,
1914.
Williams, M. M. *Religious Thought and Life in India* London, 1883.
Young, E. *The Poetical Works of Edward Young* New edition,
London, 1866.
Zetland, Marquess of *On Keshub Chunder Sen* Allahabad, 1938.
(Pamphlet reprinting section of his *The Heart of Aryavarta*).

(c)  French

d'Alviella, le comte Goblet *L'Evolution Religieuse Contemporaine
chez les anglais, les americains et les hindous* Paris, 1884.

## Secondary Sources

(a)  Bengali

Bagal, Jogeshchandra *Keshabchandra Sen* Calcutta, 1958. No. 97
in the *Sahitya Sadhak Charitmala* series.
*Ramkamal Sen* Second edition, Calcutta, 1955. No. 72 in the
*Sahitya Sadhak Charitmala* series.
Gupta, Jogendranath *Keshabchandra o Shekaler Shamaj* Calcutta,
1949.

(b)  English

Banerji, A. *An Indian Pathfinder* New edition, Calcutta, 1971.
Banerji, G. C. *Keshub as Seen by his Opponents* Allahabad, 1930.
*Keshab Chandra and Ramakrishna* Allahabad, 1931.
Basu, P. S. *Life and Works of Brahmananda Keshav* Second
edition, Calcutta, 1940.
Basu, P. S. *Life and Works of Brahmananda Keshav* Second edition,
Calcutta, 1940.

Beveridge, Lord *India Called Them* London, 1947.

Bose, N. S. *The Indian Awakening and Bengal* Calcutta, 1960.

Chadwick, O. *The Victorian Church* Third edition, two volumes, London, 1971.

Chaudhuri, N. C. *The Autobiography of an Unknown Indian* London, 1951.

Das, H. *'The Early Indian Visitors to England'* in the *Calcutta Review*, Series III, XIII (1924).

De, S. K. *Bengali Literature in the Nineteenth Century* (1757-1857) Second edition, Calcutta, 1962.

Dutt, S. N. *The Life of Benoyendra Nath Sen* Calcutta, 1928.

Farquhar, J. N. *Modern Religious Movements in India* London, 1924.

Gupta, A. C. (ed.) *Studies in the Bengal Renaissance* Bengal, 1958.

Heasman, K. *Evangelicals in Action. An Appraisal of their Social Work in the Victorian Era* London, 1962.

Heimsath, C. H. *Indian Nationalism and Hindu Social Reform* Princeton, 1964.

Kincaid, C. A. *Teachers of India* Oxford, 1927.

Kopf, D. 'The Brahmo Domestication of Unitarianism : Protap Chandra Mazumdar and the Spread of the Bengal Renaissance in South Asia' in *West Bengal and Bangladesh : Perspectives from 1972* Michigan, 1973. (Edited by B. Thomas and S. Lavan) *South Asia Series*, Occasional Paper No. 21.
*British Orientalism and the Bengal Renaissance : The Dynamics of Indian Modernization, 1773-1835* Berkeley, 1969.

Kripalani, S. *'An Unfinished Autobiography'* in the *Illustrated Weekly of India*, XCVI (1975), No. 1.

Lillingston, F. *The Brahmo Samaj and the Arya Samaj in their bearing upon Christianity—A Study in Indian Theism* London, 1901.

Lipski, A. 'Bipinchandra Pal and Reform Hinduism' in *History of Religions*, XI (1971), No. 2.

Macnicol, N. *The Living Religions of the Indian People* London, 1934.

Majumdar, B. *History of Indian Social and Political Ideals from Rammohun to Dayananda* Calcutta, 1967.

Majumdar, R. C. *British Paramountcy and Indian Renaissance* Bombay, 1963.
*Glimpses of Bengal in the Nineteenth Century* Calcutta, 1960.
*History of the Freedom Movement in India* Three volumes, Calcutta, 1962.

McCully, B. T. *English Education and the Origins of Indian Nationalism* New York, 1940.

Morrison, J. *New Ideas in India during the Nineteenth Century : a study of Social, Political, and Religious Developments* Edinburgh, 1906.

Mozoomdar, B. *God-Man Keshub and Cooch Behar Marriage* Calcutta, 1912.
*Mahayogi Keshub and Europe* Calcutta, no date. (Pamphlet)

Natarajan, S. *A Century of Social Reform in India* Second edition, Bombay, 1962.

Niyogi, N. *The Apostles and Missionaries of the Navavidhan* Calcutta, 1923.

Parekh, M. C. *Brahmarshi Keshub Chunder Sen* Rajkot, 1926.

Poddar, A. *Renaissance in Bengal : Quests and Confrontations 1800-1860* Simla, 1970.

Price, P. 'Charles Dall as a backdrop to the Brahmo Samaj of India 1855-1866' in *West Bengal and Bangladesh : Perspectives* from 1972 Michigan, 1973. (Edited by B. Thomas and S. Lavan) South Asia Series, Occasional Paper No. 21.

Ray, B. V. Keshub Chunder Sen. An attempt at understanding him Calcutta, 1938. (Pamphlet)

Rolland, R. Life of Ramakrishna Fourth edition, Almora, 1947 (First published 1929)
Life of Vivekananda and the Universal Gospel Fifth edition Calcutta, 1960.

Sarkar, H. Sivanath Sastri Calcutta, 1929.

Seal, A. The Emergence of Indian Nationalism. Competition and Collaboration in the Later Nineteenth Century Cambridge, 1971

Sen, P. K. Biography of a New Faith Two volumes, Calcutta, 1950 (I) and 1954 (II).
Keshub Chunder Sen Calcutta 1938. Earlier version of his Biography (see above).
Keshub Chunder Sen and the Cooch Behar Betrothal, 1878 Calcutta, 1933. This was reprinted as part of his Biography (see above).

Sen, P. L. 'Keshub Chunder Sen—A Study' in East and West, 1902 The Man of the New Dispensation Calcutta, 1974. (Pamphlet)

Sinha, P. Nineteenth Century Bengal: Aspects of Social History. A study in some new pressures on society and in the relation between tradition and change. Calcutta, 1965.

Smith, W. S. The London Heretics 1870-1914 London, 1967.

Wilbur, E. M. A History of Unitarianism : In Transylvania, England and America Second edition, Boston, 1969.

Younghusband, F. E. The Gleam London, 1923.

Unpublished thesis

Piette, O. L. Responses of Brahmo Samaj to Western Cultural Advances, 1855-1880 : An Episode in India's Intellectual History Ph. D. thesis Syracuse University, 1974.

# INDEX

WITHDRAWN
FROM
COLLECTION

FORDHAM
UNIVERSITY
LIBRARIES